Growth and Finance of the Firm

Growth and Finance of the Firm

Models of firm behavior tested on data from Swedish industrial firms

Göran Eriksson

Published for
The Industrial Institute for Economic and Social Research
by

Almqvist & Wiksell International
Stockholm – Sweden

A Halsted Press Book
John Wiley & Sons
New York – London – Sydney – Toronto

ISBN 91-22-00106-9
First published in Sweden by Almqvist & Wiksell International

Published in the U.S.A., Canada, Latin America and The United Kingdom
by Halsted Press, a Division of John Wiley & Sons, Inc., New York
ISBN 0-470-99230-1
Library of Congress Catalog Card No.: HG4212.E7513 658.1'5'09484 77-26840

Printed in Sweden by
Almqvist & Wiksell, Uppsala 1978

Contents

Figures

Tables

Preface

Financial conditions, investment behavior and growth of the firm have been a central area of inquiry at the Industrial Institute for Economic and Social Research (IUI) for a long time. This publication "Growth and Finance of the Firm" contains a systematic theoretical inquiry into this topic. The analysis starts from that branch of recent literature in which the mutual dependence of financial and investment decisions are emphasized.

A capital value maximizing firm with well specified conditions of production and financing constitutes the core of the theoretical part of the book. The main purpose is to demonstrate the optimization process behind production, investment and financing decisions at the firm level and to show how these three decisions are interrelated. An attempt is also made to determine the optimal values of the firm's decision variables with goal functions including the rate of return, the rate of growth and the capital value and also to study how these solutions are influenced by changes in exogenous factors such as input prices, the corporate income tax rate, financial parameters, etc.

In another section of the book assumptions made and theoretical results arrived at are tested empirically at the firm level. The data used are the survey statistics of the Swedish Engineering Employers' Association and annual reports of manufacturing companies quoted on the Stockholm Stock Exchange. One empirical conclusion is that the rate of return is negatively influenced by the rate of growth. This result suggests the existence of costs associated with raising the rate of growth. These empirical tests also support the well known hypothesis that the interest rate and stockholders' required rate of return rise with the leverage ratio and decrease with the pay-out ratio.

The book is written by Dr Göran Eriksson. A Swedish language version of it was submitted as his doctoral thesis at the University of Stockholm. We wish to thank Professor Hans Brems at the University of Illinois for several valuable suggestions that have improved the English version of the book in many important respects. Earlier versions of the manuscript have been discussed in seminars at the IUI and at the Stockholm University. Professor Lars Werin's interest and knowledge have contributed greatly to this book. Thanks also go to Professor Börje Kragh, Dr Claes-Henric Siven and Dr Alex Markowski for valuable comments. Mr William Melton has translated the book into English and the translation has partly been financed by "Statens Råd för Samhällsforskning".

Stockholm in November 1977

Gunnar Eliasson

The Industrial Institute for Economic and Social Research, Stockholm

CHAPTER 1

Introduction

1.1. Background and purpose

In recent decades several studies have been published dealing with the diversification and growth of firms (e.g. Penrose [1959], Marris [1964], and Gould [1968]). A significant factor contributing to the growth of firms despite limitations imposed in existing markets is their ability to affect the demand for their products. A firm not only determines price and quantity for every product it supplies but also, given exogenous relationships between price and demand for the products, it can increase the quantity sold at a given price through sales stimulating measures and can expand by devoting resources to the development, production, and marketing of completely new products.

However, the creative and administrative capacity of the firm's management is not unlimited. The greater the number of ideas for new products or sales stimulating measures which the firm tries to put into operation at the same time, the less is the management capacity available to any one of them. A higher rate of growth can therefore be expected to result in reduced efficiency and a lower rate of return on total invested capital. It has also been claimed that the possibilities for growth are limited by increasing costs of finance (see Gordon [1962] and Lerner & Carleton [1964]). On the other hand, there are those who maintain that costs of finance are independent of the firm's debt and dividend policies (Modigliani & Miller [1958]).

One purpose of this study is to analyze the factors which determine the extent to which a higher rate of growth lowers the rate of return on total capital. We also examine how an expansion of operations financed with outside capital and with retained earnings influences the rate of interest on borrowing and the rate of return demanded by stockholders.

The firm's actual financing depends of course on its objectives. To realize its objectives, the firm must make three different kinds of economic decisions. First, the firm must determine the scale of production, its product mix, and the required quantity of factors of production. Second, the firm must decide how much money to invest in different types of assets. Third, it must decide how these investments will be financed.

Despite the high degree of interdependence of production, investment, and financial decisions, only two investigators (Vickers [1968] and Turnovsky

[1970]) have attempted to analytically integrate these decisions in a complete model of the firm. With these two exceptions, theories in which different activities of the firm are treated simultaneously have only dealt with the relation between either production and investment decisions or investment and financial decisions.

A second purpose therefore, is to state the criteria according to which decisions concerning production, investment, and finance are made, assuming that the firm seeks to maximize the welfare of its owners. We shall also point out the interdependence between these three types of decisions within the firm.

While the optimization process itself has been analyzed thoroughly in earlier theoretical studies of investment and finance, not very much attention has been paid to the question of how optimal decisions are affected by changes in the firm's external environment. Among the few researchers who have recently studied the effects of exogenous factors on firm decisions are Solow [1970], Stiglitz [1973], and King [1974]. However, the main concern of these authors has been to ascertain the effect on the firm's behavior of changes in tax laws.

The third purpose of this study is to show how factors outside the firm affect its behavior. We will derive relationships which show how its factor mix, leverage rate and dividend policy, are influenced by exogenous changes in the rate of interest on borrowing, stockholders' required rate of return, the company's income tax liabilities, etc. We also seek to determine the effects of these external influences on the firm's profitability, rate of growth and capital value.

Our analysis is restricted to the individual firm. Macroeconomic aspects, such as the question of how firms in different markets interact are outside the scope of this study, as are special phenomena such as the birth, mergers, and the death of firms.

1.2. An outline of the study

Chapter 2 starts with a short presentation of some general phenomena which are of importance in formulating a theory of the firm. The dynamic steady state model of the firm which we employ in this study is then presented. The firm is assumed to maximize the present value of the owners' future dividends. We also assume that its production conditions are described by a neoclassical production function with labor and capital as input factors, and that the external market conditions are described by given price functions for the firm's input factors and production volume.

Certain assumptions may be empirically tested. In *chapter 3* we test the hypothesis that an increase in adjustment costs follows upon a higher rate of growth of the firm. In *chapter 4* we test the hypotheses that the interest rate on borrowing increases with a higher leverage ratio and that the stockholders' required rate of return declines with a higher payout ratio.

In presenting the theoretical analysis of the behavior of the firm, *chapter 5* deals, first, with the criteria according to which the firm determines its production, investment and financial decisions. Then the optimal values of the decision and of the firm's other endogenous variables are derived as functions of the exogenous factors in the model. These functions show how the firm according to our model reacts to changes in its environment.

Chapter 6 is devoted to the empirical testing of some of the theoretical results. For example, we test the marginal conditions for borrowing and dividend policy. We also test the relation between the rate of return on equity, the required rate of return of stockholders and the interest rate on borrowed capital which follow from the marginal conditions. In *chapter 7* the model is generalized to ascertain to what extent the earlier theoretical results are modified with the introduction more of general assumptions.

In order to make the book more readable, some sections of a more technical nature, such as mathematical derivations, econometric calculations, etc., have been presented in *appendices A–F*.

CHAPTER 2

The size, profitability, growth, and value of the firm

Why do firms grow? What are the forces that make firms attempt continuously to expand their operations? Is it likely that economies of scale and expectations that profitability increases with size are the main causes of growth? Or does growth simply depend on the favorable effect on profitability of growth itself? If large firms can attain a higher return on their capital than small firms what are the obstacles which prevent small firms from growing at a very rapid rate in order to realize the advantages of large scale?

In what follows we shall present the firm's objectives and the important relationships that exist between the size, profitability, growth, and value of the firm. These will constitute the basis of a theoretical analysis of the behavior of the firm and provide answers to the questions posed above.

2.1. Elements of a dynamic theory of the firm

Consider a multiproduct firm which uses different factors of production, and operates plants in many locations. It is assumed to grow by diversifying and dispersing production geographically through the establishment of new plants.

The *internal conditions of production* of the firm are defined by a production function which relates the output of the firm's various products to the required factors of production. The explanatory variables in this production function are labor, capital, the distribution of production among the different plants, and the growth rate of the firm (expressed as the rate of growth of its capital resources).

The *external conditions of production* are stated by the exogenous demand functions of products and the supply functions of factors of production facing the firm. We also assume that the firm borrows money which it invests in production. In addition, it is assumed that financial capital is obtained by the retention of earnings and the issuing of new shares.

Below, we shall discuss in greater detail some of the characteristics of the firm's internal and external conditions.

2.1.1. The internal conditions of production

Size

The firm's productivity usually increases with size due to the indivisibilities of labor and capital inputs. These resources cannot be divided into an infinite number of parts without the productive capacity of the whole being reduced. Examples of this kind of indivisibility are the greater relative production capacity of larger capital equipment, and the fact that certain tasks in a firm are most effectively performed by persons with specific training and professional experience. Moreover, deliveries of goods and payment flows to and from a firm are to a greater or lower degree independent of each other in time; consequently, the greater the size of the firm, the smaller are the reserves of liquid assets and goods as a proportion of sales, required to obtain a certain minimum protection against unforeseen production stoppages and occasional inability to meet payments.

However, there are factors which can cause the overall productivity of the firm to decline as size increases. One such factor is the limited capacity of its management to plan and organize operations. Difficulties in communication and coordination within the group of people constituting the firm's management would mean that increasing the size of the group would lower the efficiency of management service. Nor is it possible to increase managerial capacity and yet maintain efficiency by hiring such services from the outside, since management's organizational ability is to a great extent tied to experience gained from earlier activity in the firm.

While decentralization of decision-making can make possible successive increase in the size of the firm, the problem is that such decentralization often makes the coordination of different firm activities more difficult. Moreover, the firm can be forced to diversify production because of negatively sloped demand functions for its products so that economies of scale in the production of particular products and in large plants cannot be fully exploited.

It therefore seems likely that the advantages gained from cost decreases per unit of output that can be achieved through expansion diminish rather quickly once the firm has passed a certain critical point. Empirical support for this hypothesis has been obtained from studies which show that the total unit cost for firms and plants declines quickly as size increases within the smallest size classes and then flattens out and changes insignificantly in the larger size classes (Bain [1956]). Furthermore, several studies suggest that returns to scale for inputs of labor and capital are, in general, constant (Douglas [1948], Niitamo [1958], Aukrust & Bjerke [1959], and Solow [1960]).

Growth

There is reason to believe that the firm's efficiency depends much more on growth than it does on size. As the firm's operations expand, new tasks must be performed, new personnel must be hired and trained, investment projects must be planned, etc. Consequently resources must be reshuffled within the firm. Moreover, the new tasks which are associated with growth are often of a non-routine character, so that they cannot easily be delegated to lower staff members and in fact can only be performed by top management (Penrose [1959], Eisner & Strotz [1963] and Gould [1968]).

The faster the firm grows, the more capacity must management devote to planning and organizing the expansion itself. As the rate of growth increases sooner or later a limit will be reached beyond which the efficiency of the overall firm declines.

2.1.2. The external conditions of production

Size

Limited markets for the products of the firm impose a restriction on its size since prices decline as supplies of the products increase. Likewise, limited markets for the firm's input factors, i.e., rising factor prices as the demand for the factors increases, can be a barrier to expansion.

However, in the long run these restrictions seem less binding. The firm bypasses them by introducing new products and dispersing manufacturing to new regions. Every firm should therefore be capable of expanding almost without limit, if it could only adjust structurally to its changed size. In addition, the limited market on both the product and factor sides offers the firm potential advantages through a monopolistic price policy.

The net effect of these factors on the profitability of the firm can scarcely be determined on theoretical grounds, and earlier empirical studies have provided only ambiguous results. Some studies have shown that profitability is positively correlated with size, but that the positive relationship becomes weaker with larger size and finally disappears for the largest firms (Stekler [1964], Hall & Weiss [1967]). Other empirical studies indicate that there is no influence or even a negative influence of size on profitability if one takes into consideration the total numbers of firms of different size (Singh & Whittington [1968]).[1]

Growth

More than anything else limited markets could potentially restrict the growth of the firm. If the firm grows faster than the exogenously given demand and supply in the markets in which it sells and in the markets in which it buys, respectively, it must continually devote resources to stimulating sales (ad-

---

[1] Note that changes of profitability which follow from changed size can also be caused by increasing returns to scale.

vertising and other sales promoting measures), to research and to development of new products, and to geographic dispersion of production.[1]

Since both the number of profitable new products and the market for any one of them should be limited, as well as the possibilities of quickly shifting production to new regions, diminishing returns will set in when the firm expands at a rate which is higher than the rate of growth of the markets for its products or factor inputs.[2] The financial aspect provides another obstacle to growth. Specifically, faster expansion requires an increased inflow of money to the firm, that can only be obtained through retention of earnings, borrowing or issuing of new shares.

First, retained earnings during a given period can never exceed profits. Second, a higher leverage ratio would increase the risk that the firm will be incapable of amortizing the borrowed funds and paying the interest should its profitability temporarily deteriorate. This increasing risk for the lenders ought to lead to an increase in their required rate of interest and since the increased financial risk must also concern the shareholders, an increased required yield would be expected by them. Third, there is reason to believe that shareholders' risktaking and thus their required rate of return is an increasing function of the extent to which the firm's operations are financed through issue of shares. In chapter 4 the theoretical justification for these hypotheses is given.

2.1.3. Some functional relationships and identities

Against the background of what has been said in the preceding section concerning the firm's internal and external conditions of production and how these affect its possibilities of growth, some important relationships between various real and financial variables will now be given. These relationships are shown in figure 1 together with an indication of how they are expected to affect each other. We assume that the firm's decision variables are fixed.[3]

It is clear from sections 1 and 2 in the figure that the firm's production during period t (Q_t) is determined by its size (S_t), various institutional factors (X_t), the factor inputs (f_t) and the mix of products to be produced (d_t). The

[1] While the market limitation does not in general seem to set a definite upper limit to the size which any firm can attain through possibilities for improving its products, of diversifying the range of products, etc., these dynamic adjustments would not seem to preclude the existence of a limit to the firm's maximum rate of growth.

[2] One way of avoiding the above mentioned external obstacles to growth is external expansion—i.e. acquisition of other firms. In this way a firm should be able to grow much more quickly. However, in this study we will not analyze this kind of external growth. One reason for this is the great problem of satisfactorily defining the external expansion of firms. See e.g. Rydén [1972].

[3] We relax this assumption in chapter 5, since the discussion there proceeds under the assumption that a given objective steers the firm's behavior, so that one consequently can state how the (optimal) values of the control variables are determined.

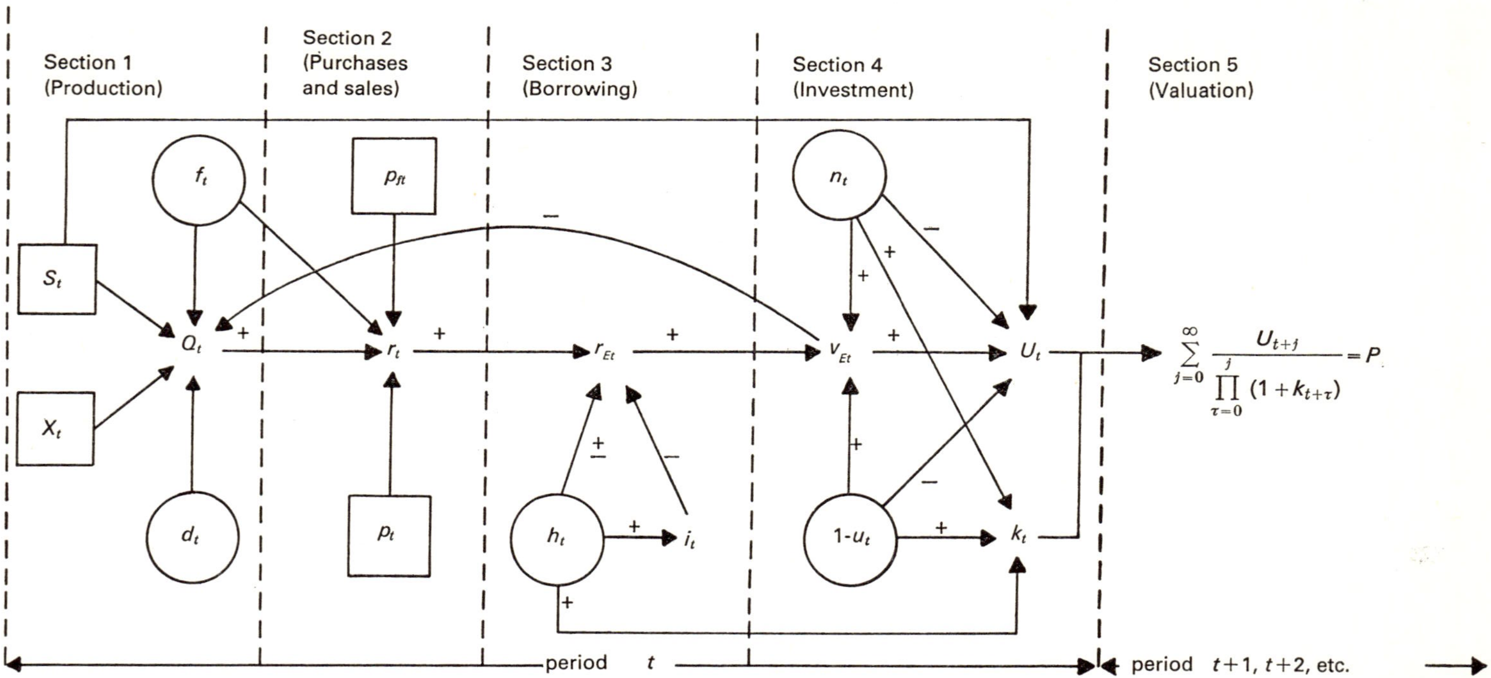

Figure 1. *Flow chart of relations between certain central firm variables*

Note: The exogenous variables are enclosed in rectangles and the firm's control variables in circles. If the planning horizon extends beyond a single period, *t* size S_t is endogenous because S_t for a given period is predetermined from earlier periods. The arrows connecting the variables indicate the direction of causation between them, given the values of the control variables and the exogenous variables. Relationships which can be expected to be positive first positive and then negative, and negative, are denoted by $+$, $\pm$ and $-$, respectively.

rate of return on total capital (r_t) is in turn a function of the amount of production, the amounts of factor inputs and the product and factor prices (p_t and p_{ft}).

In section 3 we show that the increased risk caused by a higher reliance on borrowed capital (higher leverage ratio h_t) means that the interest rate (i_t) is affected positively by h_t. Moreover, it follows that given the rate of return on the firm's total capital, the rate of return on equity capital (r_{Et}) is determined by h_t. This follows from the identity $r_{Et} = (1 + h_t)r_t - h_t i_t$.[1] If profitability on total capital r_t exceeds the interest rate i_t when the firm has no debt, then a small increase in h_t will increase r_{Et}. The increase in the rate of return on equity is an expression of the "leverage" effect due to borrowing.

In section 4 it is illustrated that given an unchanged rate of return on equity, its rate of growth, v_{Et}, is a positive function of the retention ratio $(1 - u_t)$ and of the new issue ratio n_t. The latter is defined as the ratio of capital acquired through share issues during period t and the amount of equity capital existing at the beginning of the period. The growth rate is expressed by the identity $v_{Et} = (1 - u_t)r_{Et} + n_t$. As noted above, the rate at which shareholders discount their dividends, k_t, is expected to rise as the retention ratio $(1 - u_t)$, the leverage ratio h_t or the new issue ratio n_t is increased.

Moreover, dividends U_t are affected positively by the pay-out ratio u_t, the rate of return on equity r_{Et} and the size of the firm as measured by equity K_{Et}.[2] The effect of K_{Et} on U_t is illustrated by an arrow going from S_t to U_t, where it is assumed that K_{Et} stands in a given relation to S_t. Given this assumption, we can also show with an arrow from v_{Et} back to Q_t in section 1 the existence of the influence mentioned above, that the growth of the whole firm has on its total productivity.

The identities and functions that have been illustrated in the figure and discussed up to this point all refer to the same time period t. This is not the case, however, for the share valuation formula which is stated in section 5. According to this, the firm's share value at the beginning of period t (P_t) is equal to the discounted sum of all future dividends where each future period's dividend U_{t+j} is discounted by the cumulated interest factor $\prod_{\tau=0}^{j} (1 + k_{t+\tau})$.

Note that the process of the firm's growth has not been shown in the figure. At the beginning of the next period $(t+1)$ the firm's equity capital changes from K_{Et} to $K_{E(t+1)}$; i.e., it grows by the amount of $v_{Et}K_{Et}$. On the basis of this larger capital stock, the same relationships are obtained for the period $(t+1)$ as were illustrated above for period t. Given the values of the control variables f_{t+1}, d_{t+1}, h_{t+1}, u_{t+1}, and n_{t+1} dividends U_{t+1} and the capital stock $K_{E(t+2)}$ are accordingly generated. The same procedure is repeated during period $(t+2)$ in order to obtain U_{t+2} and $K_{E(t+3)}$, etc.

---

[1] The derivation of this identity is given in appendix A, p. 127.

[2] This follows from the identity $U_t = u_t r_{Et} K_{Et}$.

2.1.4. The objectives of the firm

There are basically two competing theories concerning the objectives of the firm: the behavioral and the neoclassical. According to the behavioral theory, firms attempt to achieve power, prestige, status, high incomes for the firm's management, financial independence, etc. These objectives can be associated with the firm's size or its rate of growth. A simplified and often used formulation of the firm's objective is maximization of its rate of growth subject to certain side conditions, e.g., that the firm's profit level or its solvency should not be less than given minimum values (Galbraith [1952]).

The behavioral objectives are assumed to coincide with management's wishes and should therefore apply especially in firms with widely spread ownership and minimal owner influence (Marris [1964]). Another reason for such goals is uncertainty concerning the future. One way to reduce the risk of erroneous decisions under such circumstances is to resort to simple rules of thumb, for example, trying to achieve certain given targets for profitability, solvency, the pay-out ratio, etc. (Baumol [1959]).

Briefly, the neoclassical goals are commonly believed to be synonymous with maximizing the welfare of the firm's owners which is regarded as taking place through the maximization of the present value of all future dividends of the firm—i.e., its market value of shares. An important prerequisite is that the owners directly or indirectly should have a significant influence over decisionmaking which is made within the firms. This should be the case in smaller firms with only a few owners as well as in larger firms with ownership distributed very unevenly.

Of course growth maximization would lead to an unreasonably high rate of capital investment if no constraints were imposed on the firms' access to internal and external finance. Profit maximization—without complementary secondary objectives—would also lead to excessively large investments. In the long run, the firm can always increase future profits by increasing retained earnings. The highest present value of future profits is obviously obtained when the pay-out ratio in each period is equal to zero.

Neither growth maximization nor profit maximization distinguish between funds which are distributed to increase the owners' private wealth and those which are retained in the firm. Moreover, growth maximization actually implies that the firms' utility functions lack any time preference. Profits and dividends are not assigned lower weights if they occur in the distant future. In fact, maximization of a firm's share value will be achieved only in a situation where consideration is given not only to time preference but also to the fact that only profits distributed as dividends increase the incomes of owners.

2.2. A growth model of the firm

In this section we present a model of a growing firm which is the basis for our empirical and theoretical analysis. We start from a number of simplifying assumptions and then define the variables and state the relationships between them. Some of the assumptions will be modified in chapter 7, where we present a more generalized version of the model.

2.2.1. The assumptions

(a) *Production and prices*

We assume that the firm engages only in production and does not invest in interest yielding investment instruments. There is no production for inventories, so that the amount of goods sold is always equal to the amount produced. Production is expressed in a homogeneous volume measure, and only two homogeneous factors of production are used in the process of production: labor ($\hat{L}_t$) and capital ($\hat{K}_t$).[1]

The production function has the usual neoclassical properties—i.e., the volume of production $\hat{F}_t$ is an increasing (at a decreasing rate) function of $\hat{L}_t$ or $\hat{K}_t$. We have pointed out that it does not seem unreasonable to assume constant returns to scale with respect to these two inputs. We have also given reason for the volume of production being affected negatively by the growth rate of the firm. To simplify the model, let us furthermore assume that labor is a perfectly variable factor and that only the growth rate of real capital $\hat{v}_{Kt}$ has the effect of reducing productivity.[2]

Thus we have the following production function:

$$\hat{F}_t = F(\hat{L}_t, \hat{K}_t, \hat{v}_{Kt}), \tag{2: 1}$$

where $\partial\hat{F}/\partial\hat{L} > 0$, $\partial^2\hat{F}/\partial\hat{L}^2 < 0$, $\partial\hat{F}/\partial\hat{K} > 0$, $\partial^2\hat{F}/\partial\hat{K}^2 < 0$, and $\partial\hat{F}/\partial\hat{v}_K < 0$.

Perfect competition is assumed so that the firm can affect neither the product price (p_t) nor the prices of labor and capital (p_{1t} and p_{2t}). In addition it is assumed that prices are time-invariant.

(b) *Financing*

Funds for investment are obtained only by borrowing and retaining profits. No new issues of shares occur. As a consequence of the expected increase in the risk to lenders implied by an increased relative indebtedness of the firm (see chapter 4, pp. 48 ff.) we presume that the rate of interest on borrowed capital i_t is affected positively by the debt-equity ratio h_t. It means that

$$i_t = i(h_t), \tag{2: 2}$$

where $\partial i/\partial h > 0$.

The rate by which future dividend income is discounted—i.e., share-

---

[1] The symbol ^ indicates a real (non-monetary) magnitude.

[2] Similar assumptions have been made by, among others, Gould [1968] and Treadway [1967].

holders' required rate of return k_t is a decreasing function of the pay-out ratio u_t, where this function declines at a diminishing rate. The justification for this hypothesis is given in chapter 4, p. 56. Thus we have

$$k_t = k(u_t), \tag{2: 3}$$

where $\partial k/\partial u < 0$ and $\partial^2 k/\partial u^2 > 0$.

(c) *Other assumptions*

The firm is supposed to expand over time at a constant rate. This implies time-invariant financial ratios, while all non-ratio variables grow exponentially. With this assumption of a balanced and constant rate of growth, it is possible to study long-run variable relationships without regard to the significant mathematical complications to which a dynamization of the relationships otherwise leads.

Strictly speaking, a constant rate of growth hardly exists in reality. On the other hand, there is reason to believe that a modified form of such expansion, with short-run fluctuations around given trend values, describes rather well how firms expand. Sample surveys and empirical studies have shown that various financial ratios, in firms' plans as well as in the observed time series, are on the whole constant over longer time periods (Dean [1951], Downie [1958], Lintner [1964] and Marris [1964]).

The firm's planning period is conceived to be infinitely long and to be comprised of an unlimited number of shorter subperiods. The relations between variables which exist at the beginning of the planning period are expected to hold true indefinitly. Furthermore, its expansion is assumed to take place continuously.

Given our preceding discussion, the firm's objective is assumed to be the maximization of the value of its shares. If dividends are expected to be distributed to the owners during an unlimited space of time, this value, given steady state and balanced growth, is determined by[1]

$$P_0 = uV_{E0}/(k-v), \tag{2: 4}$$

where P_0 is the present value of future dividends at time $t=0$[2] and V_{E0} is return on equity. Note that this type of growth implies $u_t = u_{t+j} = u$, $k_t = k_{t+j} = k$ and $v_t = v_{t+j} = v$.

[1] The derivation of this formula for share value is given in appendix A, pp. 126 f.

[2] In order that P_0 takes only positive and finite values, it is required that $k > v$. Otherwise, the discounted dividends will not converge with increasing t. Naturally, during shorter periods a situation can be imagined in which the rate of growth of dividends (v) is greater than the rate of discount (k). If on occasion $k < v$, the rate of return on equity would be very high, and would stimulate the firm to increase investment so that the rate of return would fall, finally restoring $k > v$. Another reason for why k can scarcely be less than v for longer periods is that when v increases, e.g., as a result of a reduced dividend percentage and/or an increased debt ratio, k should increase. See Gordon [1962].

2.2.2. The equation system

In addition to functions (2: 1)–(2: 4)[1] the model consists of a number of other identities. Presented below is the equation system in its entirety formulated for period t.

Production and prices

$$K_t = K_{Ft} + \bar{K}_{Et}{}^{2} \qquad (2:5)$$

$$\hat{K}_t = K_t/p_2 \qquad (2:6)$$

$$\hat{L}_t = \hat{l}\hat{K}_t \qquad (2:7)$$

$$\hat{F}_t = F(\hat{L}_t, \hat{K}_t, \hat{v}_K) \qquad (2:8)$$

$$r = p\hat{F}_t/p_2\hat{K}_t - p_1\hat{L}_t/p_2\hat{K}_t - a \qquad (2:9)$$

Finance and investment

$$K_{Ft} = h\bar{K}_{Et} \qquad (2:10)$$

$$i = i(h) \qquad (2:11)$$

$$r_E = (1-t_V)\{r + h(r-i)\} \qquad (2:12)$$

$$U_t = uV_{Et} = ur_E\bar{K}_{Et} \qquad (2:13)$$

$$\hat{v}_E = (1-u)r_E \qquad (2:14)$$

$$v = v_K = v_E = \hat{v}_K = \hat{v}_E \qquad (2:15)$$

$$k = k(u) \qquad (2:16)$$

Objective function

$$P_t = ur_E\bar{K}_{Et}(k-v)^{-1}. \qquad (2:17)$$

(2: 5), (2: 6), and (2: 7) define capital K_t, the real capital $\hat{K}_t$, and the labor input $\hat{L}_t$. Note that K_{Ft} is debt capital, $\bar{K}_{Et}$ is equity capital, p_2 is the price of capital, and $\hat{l}$ is the labor intensity. The total rate of return r in equation (2: 9) is obtained through the profit identity $V_t = p\hat{F}_t - p_1\hat{L}_t - p_2a\hat{K}_t$ being divided by $p_2\hat{K}_t$ where a is the percentage depreciation, and $p_2a\hat{K}_t$ states the cost per period, in terms of real capital used up in the production process. The debt equity ratio h is defined by (2: 10) and (2: 12) is the identity for the rate of return on equity capital (r_E). Note that r_E is defined net of the profit tax. This identity is derived in appendix A, p. 127.

The pay-out ratio u is defined by (2: 13), where U_t is dividends, and V_{Et} is profit on equity. According to (2: 14) the rate of growth of the volume of equity capital ($\hat{v}_E$) is equal to the retention rate $(1-u)$ multiplied by the rate of return on equity. We recall the assumption that no financing takes place through new issue. Since we have also assumed balanced and constant growth and unchanged prices, all real and monetary non-ratio variables will grow at the same rate (v) as indicated in (2: 15).

2.2.3. The structure of the model

The variables p, p_1, p_2, a and t_V are assumed to be exogenously given. During the initial period $t=0$, equity capital $\bar{K}_{E0}$ is of a magnitude pre-determined

[1] Equations (2: 8), (2: 11), (2: 16) and (2: 17) are these functions.

[2] $^{-}$ above K_{Et} indicates that this variable is predetermined.

from earlier periods. On the other hand, equity is naturally an endogenous variable during all succeeding periods. $\hat{l}$, h and u are assumed to be decision variables which the firm adjusts so as to maximize its share value. Other variables, such as K_{Ft}, K_t, $\hat{K}_t$, $\hat{L}_t$, etc. are endogenous. For given values of the decision variables, the model gives a unique set of values for the endogenous variables.

If one abstracts from internal growth costs—i.e., drops the growth rate ($\hat{v}_K$) as an explanatory variable in (2: 8)—then all the equations will form a recursive system for given values of $\hat{l}$, h and u. Since $\overline{K}_{Et}$ is predetermined it follows that the factor inputs $\hat{L}_t$ and $\hat{K}_t$ are obtained from (2: 5)–(2: 7) and (2: 10). Once $\hat{L}_t$ and $\hat{K}_t$ are determined, the volume of production ($\hat{F}_t$) and the total rate of return (r) are obtained from (2: 8) and (2: 9), which in turn, with the help of equations (2: 11) and (2: 12), give the interest rate on borrowed capital (i), the rate of return on equity (r_E), and so forth. In the presence of the growth costs this recursivity in the model ceases due to the fact that a two-way causal relationship is established between the growth rate of real capital ($\hat{v}_K$) and the volume of production ($\hat{F}_t$) within the subsystem (2: 8)–(2: 15).

It may be of interest to note the limitations in our model regarding its analysis of the firm's economic activities as compared to the model sketched in figure 1. The following relationships in figure 1 are not found in the system (2: 5)–(2: 17):

1) The influence from institutional factors (X_t) on the volume of production (Q_t).

2) The influence of the leverage ratio (h) and the new issue ratio (n) on the rate of discount (k).

3) The influence of the new issue ratio on both the growth of equity capital (v_E) and dividends (U_t).

It should be noted that in the equation system (2: 5)–(2: 17) we have included only those variables that are utilized in our theoretical analysis. For the sake of completeness, identity relationships for a number of financial variables which have been neglected here, such as depreciation, gross saving, gross investment, etc., are summarized in appendix A, p. 127.

2.3. Earlier studies

In this section we summarize some of the theories which have influenced our analysis. These can be divided into two groups: theories which for the most part arise from neoclassical assumptions and treat firms' investment and production activities, and theories which are principally concerned with the investment and financial activities within firms.

2.3.1. Theories of investment and production

In traditional capital theory it is assumed that each firm borrows funds at a rate of interest determined exogenously, and that it invests until the yield on the last invested dollar in each investment project is equal to the given interest rate plus the rate of depreciation for the project concerned. Even if this description gives a highly simplified picture of reality, it nevertheless states the main principle according to which the profit maximizing firm, in perfect markets, carries out its investments and acquires capital for them.

A similar marginalistic conception underlies the theories in which changes in the optimal capital stock are assumed to be one of the main determinants of investment. A central theme in these theories is that firms strive to achieve a desired (optimal) capital stock which is determined through profit maximization given expectations of future product demand, factor prices, etc. The difference at every point in time between the desired capital stock (K_t^*) and the actual capital stock (K_t), together with the speed (μ) at which the firms try to close the gap between these two, determine in each period the level of investment (I_t). Net investment can then be explained by the simple relationship $I_t = \mu(K_t^* - K_{t-1})$.[1]

Among the models of this type is that of Jorgenson & Siebert [1968]. Under the assumption that the firm maximizes the present value of future net revenue (which is shown to be equivalent to maximization of profit on equity in each period), the authors come to the conclusion that the optimal capital stock is proportional to the ratio of the value of output to the cost of capital services. This cost is determined in turn by the price of investment goods, the rate of return and the rate of depreciation.

Jorgenson & Siebert also assume that depreciation is a geometrically declining function over time of the acquisition value of investments, which implies that depreciation is a constant proportion of the capital stock. In their model, production decisions influence investment through changes in the volume of production. However, they do not present a thorough analysis of the role of production decisions for the capital accumulation process.

A study which specifically takes up the problem of the interdependence between production and investment decisions under neoclassical conditions is that undertaken by Smith [1966]. Taking as a point of departure a given production function and given price functions for finished products and input factors, an optimal intertemporal production and investment program that maximizes the discounted present value of the firm's future net earnings is

---

[1] If the adjustment of actual to desired capital stock takes place during a single period, i.e., $\mu = 1$, and the size of the desired capital stock is determined by only current period sales, the capital adjustment process is simplified. If it is further assumed that a proportional relationship exists between the desired capital stock and sales, the net investment is a proportional positive linear function of the change of sales, i.e., the pure form of the accelerator theory holds for determination of investment.

derived. Smith's optimization analysis also takes into account the optimal economic life of various investment goods given their prices and scrap values, and the rate of interest with which future earnings are discounted.

The above mentioned investment theories do not explicitly consider the fact that changes in the firm's capital stock create internal adjustment costs. These costs affect the factors which in turn determine the optimal capital stock (K^*), sales, profitability, etc. Once costs of adjustment have been specified, it is possible to justify the use of distributed lags in analyzing investment behavior. In other words, the adjustment cost function indicates that costs of growth restrict the size of the reaction coefficient (μ). See, for examples, Eisner & Strotz [1963].

Integrated models of production and investment, in which particular attention is given to costs of adjustment following from capital accumulation (internal growth costs) have been presented by Gould [1968], Lucas [1967] and Treadway [1969]. Like Smith, they assume that the firm has perfect knowledge of the future and that its objective is the maximization of the firm's market value. In order to simplify the analysis, they assume that the stock and the flow of capital are independent of each other in the production process. Thus, an independent function for adjustment costs is constructed in which the volume of investment is an explanatory variable. These costs plus the direct expenditures for the purchase of investment goods constitute the firm's total investment costs. In our model we integrate adjustment costs in the production process by allowing the growth rate of real capital to appear as an explanatory variable in the production function.

Finally, the work of Modigliani & Miller [1958] has greatly influenced theoretical development in this field. An important contribution is their attempt to explain the connections between borrowing, investment and the yield on shares in the context of how firms, lenders and shareholders mutually influence one another's behavior through the market mechanism. According to Modigliani & Miller, a central precondition is that the market value of the firm's total assets in perfect markets is determined only by the future earnings of the firm—i.e., that this market value and the capital costs are independent of the firm's financial policy.

2.3.2. Theories of investment and finance

Neoclassical theories in which investment and financial decisions are assumed to be separate abstract from the existence of imperfect financial markets. On the other hand, this is taken into consideration by some authors who emphasize that an increased accumulation of capital through borrowing and share issues results in increasing capital costs. According to them firms assign a markedly lower cut-off rate to investments financed internally than to those financed externally; from which it follows that the flow of profits becomes the factor which, in the first instance, influences investments (Kalecki [1937], Duesenberry [1958], and Meyer & Glauber [1964]).

Once increasing external financial costs are taken account of, dividend policy becomes important. The relevant objective then is to maximize the present value of future dividends. More recently a large number of studies have appeared in which the firm is assumed to have this objective and in which, in particular, the significance of internal finance for investment and growth is focussed upon. Here we may mention the studies of Gordon [1962, 1964], Lintner [1963, 1964], Lerner & Carleton [1964] and Bennet, Graham & Tran Van Hoa [1969].

Important control variables in the models dealing with the present value of dividends are the pay-out ratio and the leverage ratios. It is assumed, as in the present study, that firms grow exponentially over time, that the interest and discount rates are positively related to the leverage ratio and that discount rate is a negative function of the pay-out ratio. Under these assumptions the optimal values are derived of the two financial variables which are then used in the determination of the firm's optimal investment.

In these models firms' investment and financing decisions are integrated. In addition, the models would seem to constitute an important refinement of neoclassical investment theories, since they show clearly the double role which profitability plays, both for the inflow of finance for investments and for the inclination to carry them out. Also, the fact that the models give explicit attention to the significance for investment decisions of increased indebtedness and reduced dividends leading to rising financing costs would seem to be an essential contribution.

In all of these studies, however, production activities have been left out of the analysis. The consequence of this is that the mutual dependence between production activities on the one hand and investment and financing activities on the other can never be clarified. This problem is taken up for theoretical treatment by Vickers [1968] and Turnovsky [1970]. However, their analyses are in terms of comparative statics, so that a number of interesting questions related to the process of growth cannot be analyzed.

2.3.3. The models of Gordon, Marris, and Vickers

The theoretical analysis in this book has been influenced particularly by the three investigations of Gordon [1962], Marris [1964], and Vickers [1968]. Hence we shall present a somewhat more detailed account of these studies below.

(a) *Gordon's theory*

Gordon assumes a balanced steady state expansion of the firm just as we do. He further assumes that the interest rate (i) is positively related on the debt-equity ratio (h), while the discount rate is negatively related to the pay-out ratio (u). Gordon's basic model can be summarized as follows.

$$r_E = (1+h)r - ih \qquad (2{:}\ 18)$$

$$v = v_E = (1-u)r_E \qquad (2{:}\ 19)$$

$$i = i(h) \qquad (2{:}\ 20)$$

$$k = k(u) \qquad (2{:}\ 21)$$

$$P_t = ur_E\overline{K}_{Et}(k-v)^{-1} \qquad (2{:}\ 22)$$

$\partial i/\partial h > 0$ and $\partial k/\partial u < 0$.

Equations (2: 18)–(2: 22) correspond to equations (2: 11)–(2: 12) and (2: 14)–(2: 17) given above. Our model differs from Gordon's principally in that we take into consideration the firm's production activities, and thereby the influence on the rate of return, growth and capital value, of changes in the production volume, input factors and prices as well.

Gordon derives the value of h and u which maximizes P_t, but this is not done simultaneously. On the other hand, simulations are performed in which optimal combinations of values for u and h are derived for various exogenously given levels of the discount rate (k) and the rate of return (r). Also the influence of taxes on the firm's share value and on its optimal dividend policy is shown.

(b) *Marris' theory*

Marris also assumes balanced growth of the firm. His model may be written concisely:

$$r_E = (r - ih')/(1-h') \qquad (2{:}\ 23)$$

$$v_E = (1-u)r_E \qquad (2{:}\ 24)$$

$$v = v_K = v_E \qquad (2{:}\ 25)$$

$$r = r(v_K) \qquad (2{:}\ 26)$$

$$P_t/K_{Et} = ur_E(k-v)^{-1}. \qquad (2{:}\ 27)$$

If there is no taxation of profits (i.e., $t_V = 0$) equations (2: 23)–(2: 25) are obtained from equations (2: 12), (2: 14), and (2: 15) in our model. Marris' leverage ratio is formulated as $h' = K_{Ft}/K_t$. Equation (2: 26) is obtained by substituting our model's production function into the identity for the rate of return on total capital (r). If Marris' relation (2: 26) is to specify r unambiguously as a function of capital growth rate (v_K), it is necessary to assume that prices are exogenously given and that the chosen capital intensity is not affected by v_K.

Marris' model, like Gordon's, gives no possibility of analyzing how the choice of input factors influences the firm's profitability and growth market value. Nor does Marris consider the interest rate to be an increasing function of the extent of the firm's reliance on debt finance. Another important difference is that Marris assumes that the firm's objective is to maximize a utility function in which, in addition to P_t, the growth rate (v_K) is an argument so that both owner and management objectives are considered.

(c) *Vickers' theory*

Vickers' model of the firm can be simplified

$$\hat{F}_t = F(\hat{L}_t; \hat{K}_t) \tag{2: 28}$$

$$p = p(\hat{F}_t) \tag{2: 29}$$

$$V_{Et} = p\hat{F}_t - p_1\hat{L}_t - p_2 a\hat{K}_t - iK_{Ft} \tag{2: 30}$$

$$i = i(K_{Ft}; \bar{K}_{Et}) \tag{2: 31}$$

$$k = k(K_{Ft}; \bar{K}_{Et}) \tag{2: 32}$$

$$P_t = V_{Et}/k \tag{2: 33}$$

$\partial\hat{F}/\partial\hat{L} > 0$, $\partial\hat{F}/\partial\hat{K} > 0$, $\partial p/\partial\hat{F} < 0$, $\partial i/\partial K_F > 0$ and $\partial k/\partial K_F > 0$.

If we ignore profit taxes (i.e. $t_V = 0$) and multiply (2: 12) by K_{Et}, we obtain $r_E K_{Et} = V_{Et} = K_t r - iK_{Ft}$.[1] Since according to (2: 9) $rK_t = rp_2\hat{K}_t = p\hat{F}_t - p_1\hat{L}_t - p_2 a\hat{K}_t$, Vickers' (2: 30) is then obtained. Equations (2: 31) and (2: 32) correspond to our functions for the interest rate and discount rate, except that Vickers allows borrowed capital to be an explanatory variable in the discount rate function while, we instead, assume that the pay-out ratio is the explanatory variable.[2]

Vickers assumes that the entire profit is distributed, that no new issue of shares takes place and that no changes occur in the firm's conditions of production. It therefore follows that no growth of either the firm's real or financial variables takes place so that the share value formula is reduced to equation (2: 33).

On the other hand, Vickers does take into account the effect of a changed level of external financing on both the borrowing and discount rates. The purpose of his study is also to illuminate the interplay between optimizing decisions which involve the choice of factor inputs and financing with borrowed capital. The firm's objective is the maximization of the share value (P_t).

[1] Recall the identities $K_t = K_{Ft} + K_{Et}$ and $K_{Ft} = hK_{Et}$.

[2] The influence of the level of indebtedness on the discount rate is discussed in chapter 7, p. 98.

CHAPTER 3

Empirical analysis of the relationship between profitability and growth

In the preceding chapters we argued that a higher rate of growth of the firm can be expected to affect its profitability unfavorably due to increasing growth costs. At the same time increased profitability and the consequent possibility of increased retained profit enables the firm to finance more rapid growth. This implies a two-way causal relationship between profitability and growth. The values of profitability and growth which one observes in cross sectional data are in fact intersection points (different for different firms) of a profitability function in which profitability is negatively related to growth and a growth function in which growth is positively related to profitability. It is thus impossible to identify either of these functions only on the basis of cross sectional observations.[1]

There are many studies in which growth functions have been estimated. In the first instance the purpose has been to test various accelerator and liquidity theories of the determination of a firm's investment level. However, only simple cross sectional estimations have been carried out (e.g., Kuh [1963], Singh & Whittington [1968], and Jones [1969]). Since significantly positive regression coefficients have been obtained for the profitability variable, this may be taken as a sign that one has succeeded in capturing the effect which profitability has on the firm's rate of expansion through changes in the inflow of funds.

There are only a few researchers, including Weiss [1963] and Marris [1966], who have tried to establish empirically the relationship between profitability and growth, with growth as an explanatory variable in an ordinary least squares regression. However, these studies also find a positive covariation between profitability and rate of growth which seems to indicate that the

[1] Even if profitability had no effect at all on growth, there would be in general estimation difficulties due to the conditions of expansion not being the same in all firms. The firms affect each other's expansion possibilities within limited markets. Hence the typical relationship between profitability and rate of growth for individual firms should diverge from that which one observes in cross sectional data.

estimated relationships show mainly the influence of profitability on growth instead.

As far as we are aware there have been no earlier attempts at estimating profitability functions that explicitly take account of the two-way causation between profitability and growth. To do so with the aid of the two stage least squares method, is indeed the principal objective of this chapter.[1] First, we give a brief outline of some well-known hypotheses about the influence of growth on profitability in section 3.1. Then, the variables which enter our regressions are defined and the estimation method described in sections 3.2 and 3.3 and finally, the regression results are presented in section 3.4.

3.1. Theories of the influence of growth on profitability

The factors which make for a systematic dependence of profitability on growth seem principally to affect profitability negatively—i.e., to create costs of growth (see Marris [1964]).

3.1.1. Growth costs

The firm's growth costs are of two kinds: internal costs which arise from the installation of new capital equipment, recruiting labor and training workers; and external costs which are related to advertizing existing products, developing new products and geographically spreading production through establishing new plants. Through growth new tasks are created which demand retraining of labor within the firm. Growth also requires the adjustment of capital equipment. If the installed equipment cannot be adjusted to the new technology one would have to select an optimal useful life of the capital stock. This has been shown to vary inversely with the rate of technological progress (Brems [1973]).

An important question is whether the rate of increase of growth costs varies systematically with a rising rate of growth. With regard to internal growth costs one can argue that they should increase at a declining rate because the labor and capital resources which the firm uses are not perfectly divisible. For example, the number of persons required to instruct one newly hired worker is the same as that required for two or three. Also the shutdowns that can be caused in a plant when new machines are installed should typically be independent of how many and how expensive the machines are. Indivisibilities are also inherent in the knowledge which is necessary for the instruction of

[1] In the steady state growth model above the production function (2: 8) together with the identity (2: 9) for total profitability gives a function which shows how total profitability is affected by the growth of capital. We have not sought to estimate a production function with growth rate as an explanatory variable directly, because of difficulties of constructing a uniform measure of the volume of production for each firm.

newly hired workers. When one has found a good method for teaching it can be used to train an unlimited number of workers (see Rothschild [1971]).

However, these phenomena would seem to affect the growth–cost relationship primarily at lower rates of growth. As the growth rate continues to increase it seems likely that adjustment costs begin to accelerate. The most obvious factor which would cause accelerating growth costs is that the supply of management services is limited. As has been pointed out in chapter 2, the additional tasks necessitated by growth are particularly likely to require such services. If the use of management services in order to plan and organize growth is an increasing function of the growth rate and if the amount of these services used for other (production) activities is in addition to labor and capital, an input factor in a production function with the usual neoclassical properties, one can show that as the rate of growth increases growth costs, sooner or later, begin to rise at an increasing rate.

Assume that the maximum available supply of management services ($\bar{T}$), is given. Of this amount T_1 is used in growth activities, and T_2 is used for other activities. Assume further that the firm's volume of production ($\hat{F}$) is influenced positively by the factor T_2, with declining marginal productivity. The other factors of production (X) are assumed to stand in a multiplicative relation to T_2 in the production function. Finally the use of the factor T_1 is a monotonically increasing function of the rate of growth ($\hat{v}$). These assumptions give us the equations.[1]

$$\bar{T} = T_1 + T_2 \tag{3: 1}$$

$$\hat{F} = f(X)g(T_2) \tag{3: 2}$$

$$T_1 = h(\hat{v}), \tag{3: 3}$$

where $\partial\hat{F}/\partial\hat{T}_2 > 0$, $\partial^2\hat{F}/\partial\hat{T}_2^2 < 0$ and $\partial T_1/\partial\hat{v} > 0$. All variables are assumed to take positive values.

Case 1. T_1 is an increasing function of $\hat{v}$ with $\partial^2 T_1/\partial\hat{v}^2 \geqslant 0$. If (3: 3) is differentiated with respect to $\hat{v}$ and (3: 1) and (3: 2) are taken into consideration, we obtain[2]

$$\frac{\partial\hat{F}}{\partial\hat{v}} = \left(\frac{\partial\hat{F}}{\partial T_2}\right)\left(\frac{\partial T_2}{\partial T_1}\right)\left(\frac{\partial T_1}{\partial\hat{v}}\right) \tag{3: 4}$$

$$\frac{\partial^2\hat{F}}{\partial\hat{v}^2} = \left(\frac{\partial^2\hat{F}}{\partial T_2^2}\right)\left(\frac{\partial T_1}{\partial\hat{v}}\right)^2 - \left(\frac{\partial\hat{F}}{\partial T_2}\right)\left(\frac{\partial^2 T_1}{\partial\hat{v}^2}\right). \tag{3: 5}$$

From (3: 4) and (3: 5) it is clear that $\partial\hat{F}/\partial\hat{v} < 0$ and that $\partial^2\hat{F}/\partial\hat{v}^2 < 0$. This means that the internal growth costs increase at a more rapid rate with higher growth. These costs are expressed by the reduction of production $f(X)[g(T) - g(\bar{T}_2)]$.

---

[1] In order to simplify the notation, time-subscripts are dropped from the variables.

[2] Note that $\partial T_2/\partial T_1 = -1$.

Case 2. T_1 is an increasing function of $\hat{v}$ with $\partial^2 T_1/\partial\hat{v}^2 < 0$. One cannot directly determine the sign of $\partial^2\hat{F}/\partial\hat{v}^2$ from (3: 5). However, if (3: 2) and (3: 3) are constant elasticity functions, one obtains[1]

$$\frac{\partial\hat{F}^2}{\partial\hat{v}^2} = \alpha_1(\alpha_1 - 1)\left(\frac{\hat{F}}{T_2^2}\right)\pi^2\left(\frac{T_1}{\hat{v}}\right)^2\left[1 - \frac{(\pi - 1)\,T_2}{\pi(\alpha_1 - 1)\,T_1}\right]. \tag{3: 6}$$

According to (3: 6) the sign of $\partial^2\hat{F}/\partial\hat{v}^2$ shifts from positive to negative as $\hat{v}$ increases from zero. Note: $0 < \alpha_1 < 1$; $0 < \pi < 1$; and the ratio $T_2/T_1 = [\bar{T} - h(\hat{v})]/h(\hat{v})$ declines with increasing $\hat{v}$. This means that the internal growth costs increase first at a declining rate and then at an accelerating rate as growth increases.

The relationship between external growth costs and the rate of growth would seem to be more complicated. The way in which these costs react to the faster growth depends on the extent to which the market is limited for both the firm's products and its input factors—i.e., on the slopes of its product and factor price functions. Naturally these costs are determined by the level of resources that the firm must expend in each period in order to achieve any given increase in the product-price functions and any given decrease in the factor-price functions. The greater the market, the lower the external costs of growth ought to be at any given rate of growth. If, for example, the market were unlimited—i.e., if the price functions for the firm's products and input factors were completely elastic, which is the case in perfectly competitive markets—then there would be no external growth costs.

The size of the market for potential new products which the firm can begin to manufacture profitably is also of significance. It determines how much of its resource capacity the firm must allocate to achieve a desired expansion of demand when introducing new products. Hence the way in which external growth costs change as the rate of growth increases is dependent on both the rate at which the prices of existing products decline and of existing factors' increase when the firm increases its supply of products and demand for factors, as well as on the share of the labor and capital resources within the firm which must be devoted to research on and the development of new products in order to counteract the unfavorable price influences at any given rate of growth.[2]

---

[1] α_1 is the constant elasticity $(\partial\hat{F}/\partial T_2)/(\hat{F}/T_2)$, and π is the constant elasticity $(\partial T_1/\partial\hat{v})/(T_1/\hat{v})$ where

$$\frac{\partial\hat{F}}{\partial T_2} = \alpha_1\frac{\hat{F}}{T_2} \quad\text{and}\quad \frac{\partial^2\hat{F}}{\partial T_2^2} = \alpha_1(\alpha_1 - 1)\frac{\hat{F}}{T_2^2}$$

$$\frac{\partial T_1}{\partial\hat{v}} = \pi\frac{T_1}{\hat{v}} \quad\text{and}\quad \frac{\partial^2 T_1}{\partial\hat{v}^2} = \pi(\pi - 1)\frac{T_1}{\hat{v}^2}.$$

[2] We conceive of the length of each time period being fixed so that a higher rate of growth implies both an increased speed of growth and a greater increase in size of the firm.

3.1.2. Growth benefits

In certain situations a faster expansion of the firm can be expected to affect its profitability favorably, i.e., to give rise to growth revenues. This matter has been analyzed thoroughly by Penrose [1959]. Her basic theory is that unutilized capacity, or slack, in the firm constitutes an incentive to expand. Perhaps of imperfect divisibility, labor or capital resources may not be utilized fully. Through growth the firm can increase the degree of utilization of these resources or else redirect them to tasks where they have a comparative advantage.

The reason that continued expansion does not automatically imply the gradual elimination of unutilized capacity is that new unused capacity arises from changes in the firm's external environment. Another benefit of growth is that it provides the firm with new personnel bringing in new initiatives, abilities and ideas. Furthermore, the inflow of capital-embodied technology to the firm ought to increase with faster growth.

It would seem less likely that the above mentioned advantages of growth, in general, should contribute to an ever more quickly increasing profitability as the rate of growth increases. Rather, the possibilities of efficiently assimilating a certain amount of unutilized capacity or inflow of knowledge would seem to vary inversely with the length of the time, since it always takes time to find new tasks suitable for those persons who previously were underemployed and exploit the new knowledge for specific purposes.

It is clear from the above discussion that efficiency and profitability are influenced by both the advantages and disadvantages of growth but that the latter can be expected to dominate as the firm successively increases its rate of growth. However, it is not possible to confirm these *a priori* arguments. In the end it must be an empirical question.

3.2. The empirical data and definition of variables

The source of the data we use is the profit statistics of the Swedish Engineering Employers' Association, in which information concerning profits and capital given by the firms' official annual reports has been corrected for excessive depreciation, writing down of inventories and other book-keeping "distortions". The statistics began to be collected in 1963 and cover all manufacturing firms with at least fifty employees in the engineering industry (metal products, non-electrical and electrical machinery, transportation equipment and instruments). However, our data include only sixty-two firms that have submitted information to the Association, covering the period 1963–68. The definition of a firm, the principles of valuation, etc., are described in appendix B, p. 129.

The relationship between profitability and the rate of growth in the theoretical model outlined in chapter 2 applies to firms growing at a steady state rate. This means that we are interested in establishing, empirically, the effect that various rates of long-run stable growth have on profitability.

In order to obtain estimates which approximate as closely as possible to the values of profitability and growth that are valid in the long run, we have calculated for each firm a weighted average of several successive annual values.[1] The more annual values on which the averages are based, the less they are affected by shortrun fluctuations in the annual values. This is important, particularly since occasional variations in the growth variable ought to lead to systematic underestimation of its influence on profitability. We have therefore utilized data for all years during the period 1963–68.

(a) *Profitability*

Two profitability variables are defined: the rate of profit on working capital and the rate of profit on total capital.

The *rate of profit on working capital* is obtained by dividing operating profits by working capital. We calculate operating profits as gross profit minus financial revenues and depreciation, where gross profit is equal to sales after deductions for costs of production, marketing and administration. Working capital is defined as physical capital assets plus cash assets. Physical capital consists of property, plant, equipment and inventories, while cash assets consist of cash on hand plus bank accounts.

The inclusion of cash assets in working capital is justified by the fact that cash reserves are necessary for the firm's current operations. It would obviously have been more satisfactory if only those cash assets necessary for transaction purposes had been included. It would also have been preferable to have been able to assign to working capital such financial assets as can be regarded as necessary for operations (e.g., trade credit which the firm grants in exchange for higher prices for its products).

The *rate of profit on total capital* is obtained by dividing total profit by total capital. Total profit is defined as operating profit plus financial revenues. Total capital is equal to working capital plus interest-yielding financial capital.

These two measures of profitability are measured prior to taxes. Included in both measures of capital are expenditures for plants under construction and a number of minor items. These are described in appendix B, p. 131.

The firms' profits are probably significantly influenced by costs for research and development work and sales promoting efforts. These expenditures can be regarded as investments just like purchases of physical assets. It would therefore be justifiable to include such cumulated expenditures, i.e., non-physical investment in the concept of capital. However, lack of data precluded this.

---

[1] Unweighted averages have also been calculated on the basis of the annual values, but they differ relatively little from the corresponding weighted variables.

(b) *Growth*

There are also several possible measures of the rate of growth, such as the relative change in any of the following variables: number of employees, equity capital, total capital, sales and value added. The three first mentioned measures of growth have the weakness that they only partially describe the expansion of the firm; they show the growth of only one particular factor of production. With respect to the last two sales would seem preferable to value added inasmuch as it ought to be affected less by exogenous changes in the firms' prices. We have therefore chosen sales in defining the growth of the firm.

In fact, the choice between these measures of growth is not very important, since there exists a strong covariation between them in our cross sectional data. None of the pairwise correlation coefficients between the measures which we calculated is less than 0.650.

(c) *Other explanatory variables*

Every firm has two important possibilities for expanding at a rate which exceeds the growth of demand for its products and supply of its input factors which are exogenously given. It can expand both by initiating manufacture of new products and locally dispersing production by setting up new plants. It is reasonable to assume that a faster growth of the firm requires a faster diversification both of new products and new plants. Therefore, in the calculations in this chapter we have also defined two dynamic explanatory variables. The *rate of product diversification* measured by the value of final sales in 1968 from eight-digit statistical classifications in which the firm had started production during the period 1963–68 divided by the total value of its sales in 1963. The *rate of plant dispersion* measured as value added in 1968 from plants built by the firm during the period 1963–68 divided by its total value added in 1963.

Information on the value of final sales distributed among various statistical classifications and value added distributed among various plants (i.e., places of employment) has been obtained for our sixty-two engineering firms from the industrial statistics of the Swedish Central Bureau of Statistics. In the industrial statistics[1] different levels of aggregation are given for products which correspond to different statistical classifications. A more detailed definition of the concept of a place of employment is also given.

Finally, it should be noted that two further explanatory variables have been introduced into the regressions. First *firm size* which is measured by sales. Of course, several alternative measures of size are possible, among them value added, profits, number of employees, etc. We have chosen sales because we believe that it gives a good estimate of the size of the firm's total operation while being comparatively less affected by autonomously caused changes in

---

[1] *SOS*, Industri 1968, part I. The data are classified according to the standard Swedish industrial classification (Standard för svensk näringsgrensindelning).

product prices. Second, *capital intensity* which is measured by the ratio of total capital assets to the number of employees. Here total capital assets are equal to total assets given in the firm's balance sheet.

3.3. Regression model

Our hypothesis is that the profitability of the firm depends on the explanatory variables defined above according to the following functional relationships.

$$r = f_1(v_O, p_d, a_d, s, k_I), \tag{3: 7}$$

where r = the rate of profit on working capital or total capital,
v_O = the rate of growth of sales,
p_d = the rate of product diversification,
a_d = the rate of plant dispersion,
s = the size of the firm and
k_I = capital intensity.

Growth should also be influenced by profitability because higher profitability makes it possible for the firm to finance a higher rate of growth through retained profits. This implies that v_O is explained by r according to the relationship

$$v_O = g_1(r, Z), \tag{3: 8}$$

where Z is a vector of financial variables (pay-out ratio, leverage ratio, rate of interest on borrowed capital, etc.).

In order to obtain a regression coefficient for v_O in (3: 7) which is not biased by this feedback from r, we employ a stepwise estimation procedure. First, for each firm a growth variable ($\hat{v}_O$) which is a function of only the explanatory variables (Z) is calculated according to the function

$$\hat{v}_O = g_2(Z). \tag{3: 9}$$

Then, $\hat{v}_O$ is substituted for v_O in (3: 7), and an ordinary least squares regression is performed on the entire cross section of firms. Thus we estimate the relationship

$$r = f_2(\hat{v}_O, p_d, a_d, s, k_I). \tag{3: 10}$$

Both linear and loglinear functional forms are estimated. A more detailed description of the estimation procedure is given in appendix B, p. 134.

As far as the other explanatory variables in (3: 10) are concerned, it would appear that size (s) and capital intensity (k_I) can be regarded as exogenously determined, since we are measuring them with values observed at the beginning of the sample period, i.e., 1963. On the other hand, the dynamic market adjustment variables (p_d and a_d) ought to be endogenously determined. There is reason to believe that the incentive for the firm to diversify and geographically disperse its production is dependent on its profitability. We will return to this question in section 3.4.2.

3.4. The results

3.4.1. Growth as the only explanatory variable

It is likely that the firm's costs of expansion are practically negligible when no positive growth occurs. Few resources need then be devoted to training new personnel, developing and marketing new products, etc. We have therefore carried out separate regressions for the two groups of firms with sales growth less than and greater than zero, group 1 and group 2, respectively. Group 1 consists of twelve and group 2 of fifty firms (see table 1). It is clear from the table that for firms with positive growth, the rate of profit on both working capital and total capital is influenced negatively by an increased rate of growth. This result is in line with the theory of growth costs we expounded above.

We have also performed separate regressions with a finer classification of the data into five groups with twelve to thirteen firms in each (see appendix B, table B: 3). These show that profitability does not decline at an increasing speed as the rate of growth increases. These estimates therefore give no support to our hypothesis of accelerating growth costs.

It is also clear from table 1 that for firms in Group 1, with negative growth rates, we get significant positive regression coefficients. This can be interpreted to mean that not only costs but also benefits are associated with expansion. It thus seems, as we assumed earlier, that it is the benefits from growth that primarily influence profitability when the firms are cutting back their operations at a slower rate.

In appendix B, tables B: 7–B: 9, are shown the regression results obtained using the logarithmic form. Also according to these results significant (at the 5 % level) regression coefficients are obtained which are positive for the firms in Group 1 and negative for those in Group 2. Furthermore, we have estimated linear functions in which all firms are included in the same regression. We then find, not unexpectedly, a significantly weaker negative relationship between profitability and rate of growth (see appendix B, table B: 2).

Finally, we have estimated linear functions for all firms on the basis of their actual rates of growth of sales. This reveals a strong positive covariation between profitability and the actual rate of growth of sales (see appendix B, table B: 1). This result agrees with those of Weiss [1963] and Marris [1966] which were mentioned at the beginning of this chapter.

Table 1. *Regression estimates for the influence of the growth of sales on the rate of profit on working capital and total capital*

Two growth categories. Linear specifications

	Rate of profit on working capital		Rate of profit on total capital	
	Group 1	Group 2	Group 1	Group 2
B	0.1072	0.0818	0.0782	0.0823
b	0.7785**	−0.4920**	0.5104**	−0.3868***
σ	0.3246	0.1869	0.1960	0.1312
e	0.5183	−0.6467	0.4307	−0.5243
R^2	0.3652	0.1262	0.4042	0.1534
$\bar{v}_0$	−0.0477	0.0653	−0.0457	0.0650
a	12	50	12	50

Group 1 includes firms with growth rates less than zero; Group 2 includes firms with growth rates greater than zero.

Note: B is the intercept term, b is the regression coefficient, σ is its standard deviation, e is the elasticity calculated at the mean. If $\bar{r}$ and $\bar{v}_0$ are the means of profitability and growth, respectively, then $e = b(\bar{v}_0/\bar{r})$. R^2 is the coefficient of multiple correlation and a is the number of firms.

Significant regression coefficients according to a two-tailed t-test at the 10 %, 5 % and 1 % confidence levels are indicated by *, ** and ***, respectively.

3.4.2. Growth as one of several explanatory variables

Table 2 presents the results of the regressions for the rate of profit on working capital as a function of growth and the other previously defined explanatory variables. These estimates are, for linear specifications, applied to firms with positive rates of growth.

As is clear from table 2, the numerical values of the regression coefficients for the growth variable are reduced when the dynamic market adjustment variables (the rate of product diversification and the rate of plant dispersion) are introduced as additional explanatory variables. The growth coefficient is reduced most when the rate of product diversification is included. Note that the growth coefficients in those equations in which both market adjustment variables are present (equations 3–5) ought to reflect the influence of growth on profitability for firms which have the same values for the market adjustment variables.

Since the costs of expanding the market on both the product and factor sides (the external costs of growth) are dependent on the rate at which the firm diversifies its product line and disperses its manufacture through establishing new plants, the values of the diversification variables (p_d and a_d) should also be capable of reflecting the size of the external growth costs. If this is

Table 2. *Regression estimates for the influence of growth of sales, rate of product diversification, etc., on the rate of profit on working capital*

Firms with positive growth rates. Linear specifications

Equation number		Rate of growth of sales	Rate of product diversification	Rate of plant dispersion	Size	Capital intensity	B, R^2 and F_R
1	b	−0.4920**					0.0818
	σ	0.1869					0.1262
	e	−0.6467					6.930
2	b	−0.4075**	−0.0406				0.0808
	σ	0.2040	0.0393				0.1455
	e	−0.5355	−0.0899				4.002
3	b	−0.4054**	−0.0474	0.0059			0.0805
	σ	0.2062	0.0485	0.0241			0.1466
	e	−0.5328	−0.1085	0.0171			2.634
4	b	−0.4282**	−0.0359	0.0018	0.0029*		0.0742
	σ	0.2006	0.0475	0.0235	0.0015		0.2127
	e	−0.5628	−0.0795	0.0051	0.1447		3.039
5	b	−0.3937*	−0.0406	0.0031	0.0036**	−0.0002	0.0740
	σ	0.2012	0.0473	0.0234	0.0016	0.0001	0.2502
	e	−0.5174	−0.0899	0.0091	0.1777	−0.2879	2.781

Note: The interpretation of b, σ and e and the statistical significance levels of b denoted by *, ** and *** respectively are given in table 1, p. 41.

the case, the growth coefficients in equations 3–5 may show the negative influence on profitability which follows only from the internal costs of growth.

However, this interpretation of the growth coefficients in the equations in which the rate of product diversification and the rate of plant dispersion are explanatory variables is disputable. In the first place, the costs of diversification do not constitute all of the external costs of growth. In the second place, it may be questioned whether our measures of the diversification variables really show the speed with which the firm initiates the manufacture of new products and disperses production geographically.[1]

As for the last two explanatory variables, it can be seen that the coefficient of the size variable in equation 5 is positive and significant at the 5 % level. This suggests the existence of economies of scale in production and monopoly power which favorably influence the firm's profitability. That the capital-intensity variable in equation 5 received a negative coefficient would further suggest that firms can achieve a higher rate of return on their invested capital if they introduce less capital-intensive methods of production.

[1] What is said here implies that one can hardly draw the conclusion on the basis of, for example, the negative coefficient of the product diversification variable that an increased rate of product diversification in general leads to lower profitability.

3.4.3. Growth costs and the firm's optimal rate of growth

(a) *The growth costs*

On the basis of the relationships estimated above, one should be able to quantify the costs (in terms of reduced profitability) which follow from the expansion of the firm.

The intercept term and coefficient of the growth variable in table 2 give, when only growth is an explanatory variable, the equation

$$r_p = 0.082 - 0.492\ v_O, \tag{3: 11}$$

where r_p is the rate of profit on working capital and v_O is the rate of growth of sales. Assume—and this would not seem unreasonable—that the growth costs are negligible when the firm's sales are not growing. We then obtain from (3:11) that profitability declines by 0.492 percentage points as a result of one percentage point increase in the growth rate. Hence, when v_O increases from zero, growth will have reduced profitability by half at $v_O = 0.084$ and will have eliminated it at $v_O = 0.167$.

It should be noted that we have not assigned to growth costs the expenditures which the firm undertakes in the form of net investment in physical and non-physical capital.[1] Since net investment is drawn from the fund which is used in each period for dividends, and considering that we have assumed that the firm's objective is the maximization of the present value of all future dividends, it would seem to be incorrect to let the concept of growth costs include net investment as well. To do so would allow such expenditures to affect dividend capacity negatively twice.

If perfect competition prevails, no external growth costs exist. Then the coefficient of growth in the profitability function would receive a lower negative value. If it should be possible to approximate such a value for the growth coefficient by the value which we estimated in equation 3 in table 2—i.e., the profitability function is $r_p = 0.082 - 0.405 v_O$. If no growth costs exist at all, the growth coefficient ought to be zero, and the profitability function would be $r_p = 0.082$.

In figure 2 three cases which include both external and internal growth costs, only internal growth costs and no growth costs are represented by the profitability lines A_0B_2, A_0B_3 and A_0B_4, respectively. However, these lines are all intended to show how profitability is affected by the rate of growth for each individual firm under the assumption that the economic behavior of other firms is given.

The relationship between profitability and the rate of growth of all firms is also determined by how they affect each other's growth within a given market. If some of them increase their growth rate it is done partly at the

[1] A growth cost variable which includes purchases of investment goods is being used, for example by Lucas [1967].

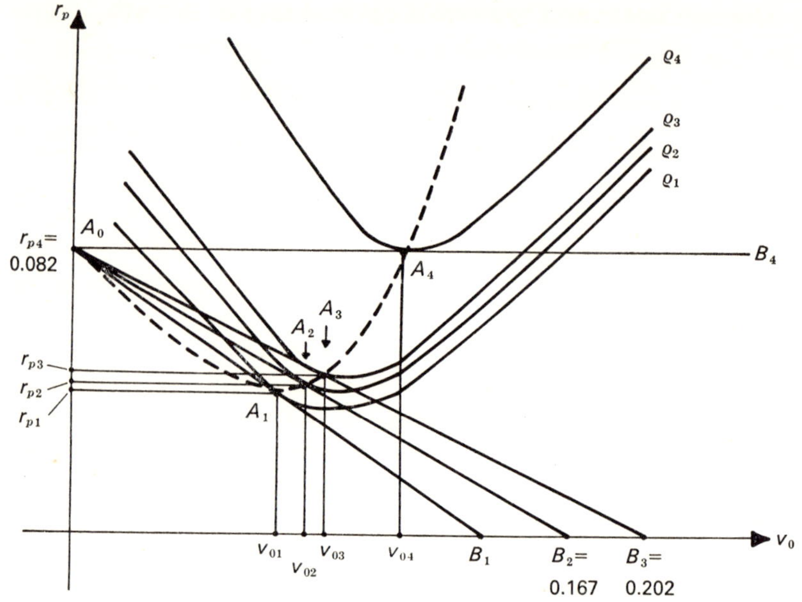

Figure 2. *Optimal rates of growth in the presence of various growth–cost constraints*

expense of others since they take a larger share of the market from these firms. Therefore, the macro relationship for profitability may show a steeper negative slope than the average of the corresponding micro relationships. In the figure A_0B_1 illustrates this hypothetical macro relationship.

(b) *The optimal rate of growth*

As negative growth accelerates our empirical results indicate that profitability is reduced.[1] Thus, it is obviously irrational for firms to choose negative growth. It must also be irrational for them to choose a rate of growth so high that profitability becomes negative. Assume that the profitability function (3: 11) applies to each firm. All rates of growth outside of the interval from 0.0 to 0.167, where the line A_0B_2 cuts the axes of the coordinate system, should in such a case be excluded from consideration as expansion alternatives. But which of the growth rates within this area is optimal? We will use figure 2 to answer this question.

For a firm which maximizes the market value of its shares the optimal rate of growth will be where the line A_0B_2 is tangent to a share-value isoquant. Such an isoquant is a curve connecting points representing combinations of growth rate and profitability which give the same share value. We have drawn four isoquants labelled ϱ_1 to ϱ_4 corresponding to four different levels of share

[1] See the estimates in table 1 concerning firms in Group 1, for which rates of growth were negative.

value, where the share value of ϱ_2 is greater than that of ϱ_1, that of ϱ_3 greater than that of ϱ_2, etc. The line A_0B_2 is tangent to the ϱ_2 isoquant at point A_2. The optimal rate of growth we seek should therefore be v_{02} and the corresponding profitability r_{p2}.

We have also indicated in the figure the optimal combinations of profitability and growth rate which correspond to the dynamic constraint lines A_0B_1, A_0B_2, A_0B_3, and A_0B_4 (points A_1, A_2, A_3, and A_4, respectively). The dashed curve $A_0A_1A_2A_3A_4$ shows how the optimal profitability and growth rate are changed as the slope of the constraint line is successively reduced from the point at which costs of growth are very high to the point at which they do not exist.

The different share-value isoquants which we have drawn into the figure can be derived from the growth model of the firm presented in chapter 2; see equations (2: 9)–(2: 17). The derivation of an isoquant involves first fixing the share-value so that $P_t = \bar{P}_t$, then eliminating from these equations all endogenous variables except profitability and growth. This leaves one equation, which is the isoquant corresponding to $\bar{P}_t$.

In order to simplify the derivation of the isoquants, it is assumed that

(1) the firm makes no financial investments, from which it follows that the rate of profit on total capital (r) equals the rate of profit on working capital (r_p),
(2) no profit tax and no debt finance exist, from which it follows that the rate of profit on equity equals the rate of profit on total capital ($r_E = r$),
(3) the rate of discount (k) is a function of the pay-out ratio of the form $k = \varkappa_1(1/u) + \varkappa_2$.

We then obtain (see appendix B, p. 140) the isoquant function

$$\{r + (\varrho - 1)v_0 - [\varkappa_1(\varrho - 1) + \varkappa_2\varrho]\}\{r - v_0 - \varkappa_1\} = \varkappa_1[\varkappa_1(\varrho - 1) + \varkappa_2\varrho], \qquad (3: 12)$$

where

$\varrho = P/K_E$ is the valuation ratio,
P = the share value and
K_E = equity, which is a given magnitude.

The higher P is, the higher ϱ will be. The function (3: 12) is a hyperbola with asymptotes $r = -(\varrho - 1)v_0 + \varkappa_1(\varrho - 1) + \varkappa_2\varrho$ and $r = v_0 + \varkappa_1$. The constant term $\varkappa_1^2(\varrho - 1) + \varkappa_1\varkappa_2\varrho$ states the distance of the function from these two asymptotes. When ϱ is increased, the negatively sloped asymptote is shifted to the right at the same time as the constant term is increased.

The positive curvature of the isoquants—i.e., their U-shape—is due to the rate of discount being assumed to be a decreasing function (with a positive second derivative) of the pay-out ratio. If instead it is assumed that the rate of discount is not affected by the dividend percentage—i.e., $\varkappa_1 = 0$—the isoquants become straight lines (see appendix B, p. 141). This means that no "internal" optimum solution with finite and positive values of profitability and growth exists. We will return to this problem in chapter 5.

CHAPTER 4

The financial costs of the firm

4.1. Introduction

In this chapter the effect of the financial structure of the firm on its financial (capital) costs are investigated empirically. The point of departure for the analysis is provided by the equations of our growth model for the interest rate on borrowed capital and the stockholders' required rate of return.

No uniform or generally accepted definition of capital costs exists. In the finance literature there are several different measures of capital costs. They all have in common the fact that they are defined on the basis of the market value of the firm's shares and/or its borrowed capital.[1] The use of different measures of the cost of capital seems to have been an important cause of the differing opinions as to how capital costs are affected by financial variables such as the pay-out and the leverage ratios.

A group of researchers (Lutz & Lutz [1951], Solomon [1955], Modigliani & Miller [1958], Kuh [1960] and Weston [1961]), have claimed that changes in the pay-out ratio, given the firm's investment policy, do not affect capital costs defined as the ratio of the firm's current earnings to the market value of its shares. They assume that the market value of the shares is a function only of the expected future earnings of the firm, independent of dividends.

On the other hand, several researchers have asserted that the firm's dividend policy influences its capital costs. Given a fluctuating earnings stream and risk-minimizing stockholders this is explained by the fact that the variance of the growth of expected future dividends increases more than proportionately to dividend growth as the pay-out ratio is reduced. (See Walter [1956], Gordon [1962], Lerner & Carleton [1964], Brigham & Gordon [1968] and Bennet, Graham & Tran Van Hoa [1969].)

Concerning the influence of the leverage ratio on the costs of capital, there are also two clearly divergent lines of thought represented in the literature. The best known proponents of the first are Modigliani & Miller [1958], who

[1] The most common capital-cost measures are the current earnings divided by the market value of the shares, dividends divided by the market value of the shares plus the expected rate of growth of dividends and a weighted average of the stockholders required rate of return and interest rate on borrowed capital, where the weights are the relative shares of equity and borrowed capital in the total market value of the firm. For a more detailed survey, see Lintner [1963].

assert that the choice between debt and equity is of no significance for these costs. This claim is founded on the notion that the market mechanism leads to capital costs being the same for all firms in a given risk class under the assumptions of a perfect market for shares, equal borrowing possibilities for firms and individuals, no tax differentials between dividends and capital gains and no transaction costs.[1]

According to the other line of thought, which is propounded, among others, by Gordon [1962] and Lerner & Carleton [1964], an increased leverage ratio raises capital costs. The reason is that an increased debt to equity ratio increases the relative variability of the rate of return on equity given the uncertainty attaching to the gross earnings stream, and thereby increases the likelihood of insolvency for the firm due to inability to meet the interest charges and the amortization payments. This is regarded by the firm's owners and lenders as involving an increased financial risk for which they wish to be compensated through a higher rate of return on their invested capital.

In view of the considerable attention which earlier studies have devoted to the factors determining the firm's cost of capital, it is of interest to explore empirically the extent to which these costs are influenced by the leverage ratio and the pay-out ratio. We adopt the same definition of the cost of capital as Modigliani & Miller [1958]. Total capital costs are assumed to consist of two components: the stockholders required rate of return (the discount rate) and the interest rate on borrowed capital (the interest rate). Since there is reason to believe that these two rate variables are affected differently by the pay-out ratio and the leverage ratio, they will be analyzed separately.

We recall that our growth model of the firm includes both a function for the interest rate in which the interest rate depends on the leverage ratio and a function for the discount rate in which the discount rate depends on the pay-out ratio. For the regression calculations of these functions in this chapter, we also include, as explanatory variables, the new issue ratio and firm size. The calculations are carried out as cross-section estimates. The sample employed consists of fifty-six Swedish industrial firms listed on the stock exchange for the years 1963–70. The data sources are *Svenska Aktiebolag* and *Finanstidningen*. Appendix C, p. 142, contains a more detailed presentation of this statistical material.

[1] If a firm with given earnings stream can increase the market value of its shares by higher leverage the rate of return on the market value of its total capital (equity plus debt) is reduced. It is then profitable for the stockholders of the firm to sell their shares in this firm and buy shares in other firms (belonging to the same risk class) which have a higher rate of return on total capital. The stockholders can now borrow on personal account so that their own leverage is the same as that of equity of the old firm. In this way the stockholders obtain a higher yield on their new investment than before. However, sales of the firm's shares depress their price. Only when their price has sunk so that the rate of return on their total capital again equals that of other firms does the incentive for the stockholders to redistribute their wealth in this manner cease to exist (Robichek & Myers [1965] chapter 3).

4.2. The interest rate on borrowing

4.2.1. Hypotheses concerning the effect of debt finance on the interest rate

There is reason to believe that a change of the ratio of debt to equity as well as a change of the composition of debt between long- and short-term debt systematically influence the rate which the firm must pay on its borrowed capital.

(a) *The leverage ratio*

Two factors seem to be of particular importance for how the interest rate is affected by the ratio of total debt to equity (the leverage ratio): (1) the risk that the firm may go bankrupt, and (2) the lender's risk aversion.

(1) According to empirical experience the interest rate varies from year to year to a much lesser extent than does the rate of return on total capital. If the leverage ratio is raised, therefore, the relative variability over time of the rate of return on equity (r_E) is increased. This increases the probability that r_E will be less than zero. If r_E is less than zero for a longer period of time, the firm may not be able to meet its obligations and thus, be forced to declare bankruptcy, in which case lenders run the risk of losing all or a part of their invested capital.[1]

Note that lenders ought to be indifferent to the level of r_E provided that it is positive since they can then always count on getting back their principal and interest income. How the probability that the rate of return on equity is less than zero, $P(r_E<0)$, varies with the leverage ratio can be illustrated mathematically as follows.

Assume that the total rate of return (r) is in every period a normally distributed random variable with expected value $E(r)$ and standard deviation $\sigma(r)$. Assume further that the interest rate (i) and the leverage ratio (h) are non-stochastic variables and that there is no profit tax ($t_V=0$). We then obtain from the identity relation $r_E=(1+h)r-ih$ that $E(r_E)=(1+h)\,E(r)-ih$ and that $\sigma(r_E)=(1+h)\sigma(r)$. We construct the variable $Z=[r_E-E(r_E)]/\sigma(r_E)$ which is normally distributed with an expected value of zero and a standard deviation of one where $Z'=-E(r_E)/\sigma(r_E)$. This gives us the equations

$$Z' = -E(r_E)/\sigma(r_E) = [ih/(1+h)-E(r)]/\sigma(r) \qquad (4{:}\,1)$$

$$\mu = P(r_E<0) = P(Z<Z') = \int_{-\infty}^{Z'} \frac{1}{\sqrt{2\pi}\sigma_Z}\exp(-Z^2/2\sigma_Z^2)dZ \qquad (4{:}\,2)$$

[1] A bankruptcy should lead to extra costs for the firm due to change of management, administration expenses and the need to secure new venture capital at high rates of interest. But most important seems to be that the bankruptcy may have an adverse effect on the firm's earnings capacity. The admission of the firm's financial difficulties reduces the confidence of its customers, suppliers and extenders of credit. Studies of firms which have declared bankruptcy have shown that sales and profits have sunk markedly once the bankruptcy has become generally known (Baxter [1967]).

If the interest rate is fixed it is clear from (4: 1) and (4: 2) that an increase of h increases Z', which in turn increases μ. If μ is differentiated with respect to h, we obtain $d\mu/dh = (d\mu/dZ')(dZ'/dh) > 0$, and $d^2\mu/dh^2 = (d^2\mu/dZ'^2)(dZ'/dh)^2 + (d\mu/dZ')(d^2Z'/dh^2)$. It is true that $d^2\mu/dZ'^2 < 0$ when $Z' > 0$. Furthermore it is clear that $d^2Z'/dh^2 = -2i/[(1+h)^3\sigma(r)] < 0$. This means that when the leverage ratio is increased, μ increases at a decreasing rate for positive values of Z'.

However, the interest rate should be positively affected by the bankruptcy-risk variable (μ) (see below). At the same time it is clear from (4: 1) and (4: 2) that a higher interest rate increases μ. This positive feedback from a rise in borrowing costs to the risk of bankruptcy will reinforce the increase in financial risk involved in greater reliance on debt finance.

(2) Lenders' required return (the interest rate) is affected by not only the risk of bankruptcy (μ) but also by the dispersion of lenders' expected net revenues from lending.[1] It is shown in appendix C, pp. 143 f., that under certain simplifying assumptions an increased leverage ratio increases the dispersion of the expected net revenues and that this leads to a rising interest rate if lenders are risk averse. Thus, if lenders are risk averse, the interest rate always rises with an increasing leverage ratio and can even do so if lenders do not display risk aversion, due to higher probability of bankruptcy.

As to the question of how quickly the interest rate rises with increased debt, it seems hardly possible to reach any unambiguous conclusions on the basis of theoretical considerations alone. To do so would require knowledge of the exact shape of lenders' utility functions and of the relationship between the risk of bankruptcy and the leverage ratio. It should be clear, however, that the slower the rate of increase of the risk of bankruptcy with an increase in the leverage ratio, and the slower the rate of decline of lenders' marginal utility with rising income, the slower the interest rate will increase as the leverage ratio is raised.

(b) *The share of long term debt and the size of the firm*

The longer the term to maturity of the debt, the greater its liquidity for the firm, i.e., the less should be the probability that the debt must be refinanced during an adverse time. This may make the firm willing to pay a higher interest rate on its debt. A change in the composition of debt which lengthens its average maturity may also make the lenders increase their required rates of return. A variable which reflects the average maturity of debt is the share of long-term debt. We therefore expect the interest rate to be an increasing function of the share of long-term debt.

In addition, the interest rate can be expected to depend on the size of the firm. The fixed costs of making a loan are independent of the size of the loan. Also the production of large firms is more diversified than that of small firms,

[1] These net revenues are here assumed to be equal to the expected mean value of the loss taken by the lenders if the firm goes bankrupt and their interest income obtained if bankruptcy does not occur. See appendix C, p. 143.

so that the rate of return on total capital is expected to vary inversely with the size of the firm. Other reasons for why the variability of the rate of return of larger firms may be lower are that they have their production concentrated in less risky industries and that they possess some monopoly power in setting prices (Alexander [1949] and Hymer & Pashigian [1962]).

A negative relationship can therefore be expected between the interest rate and size. Earlier empirical investigations (Leverson [1962] and Laudadio [1963]) have also supported this view.

4.2.2. Regression model

On the basis of the preceding theoretical discussion, the following explanatory variables are incorporated in the regressions for the interest rate which is measured by interest costs divided by debt.

Leverage ratio. This is defined as the ratio of debt to equity. Equity consists of share capital reserve fund, debt adjustment fund, etc. plus half of untaxed reserves (e.g., investment funds). Debt is equal to total capital less equity. Note that this includes all forms of debt, such as, commercial paper, debt to suppliers, prepayments from customers, liabilities to subsidiaries, liabilities to pension funds, etc.

Share of long-term debt. This variable is obtained by dividing long-term debt by total debt. Long-term debt consists of bonds, debentures, pension funds, mortgage loans, etc. As a rule of thumb we have regarded as long-term debt that wich has average maturity in excess of one year.

Firm size. This is measured by sales, the justification for which has been given in chapter 3, p. 38.

Since our purpose is to capture the expected long-run influence on the interest rate of these explanatory variables, it ought to be unsatisfactory to utilize only one annual cross-sectional value for them since, if an explanatory variable fluctuates around a given trend and if only individual annual values are utilized in the regression calculation, coefficients are obtained which systematically underestimate the influence of the explanatory variable on the dependent variable (see, for example, Johnston [1960]). Therefore we use in the regression calculations averages of the actual annual values of the variables during the whole period 1963–70.

The function for the interest rate on borrowed capital is run both in a simple linear and in a combined additive-multiplicative form with a non-zero intercept. Accordingly, the regression equations are:

$$i = B_{i0} + b_{ih}h + b_{im}m + b_{is}s \qquad (4:3)$$

$$i = E_{i0} + E_{i1}h^{e_{ih}}m^{e_{im}}s^{e_{is}}, \qquad (4:4)$$

where i is the interest rate, h is the leverage ratio, m is the share of long-term debt, and s is the size of the firm. B, b, E and e are the coefficients. According to the hypotheses given above, $b_{ih}>0$, $b_{im}>0$, $b_{is}<0$, $E_{i1}>0$, $e_{ih}>0$, $e_{im}>0$, and $e_{is}<0$.

In the estimation of equation (4: 4) an iterative procedure is employed. For various given values of the intercept coefficient E_{i0} regressions are performed. Then the regression is selected which has obtained the highest explanatory power as measured by the coefficient of multiple determination (R^2). The interval of given values of E_{i0} runs from -0.015 to 0.035 with a distance of 0.005 between each value.

The estimation technique which is used is ordinary least squares (OLS). A weakness of OLS is that it does not give consistent estimates if the explanatory variables are influenced by the dependent variable. The share of long-term debt and the size of the firm should not be influenced to any appreciable extent by the dependent variable, i.e., the interest rate. On the other hand, the interest rate may have a significant negative influence on the leverage ratio—see p. 71 below—from which it follows that in the cross section of firm observations the positive relationship between these two variables is weakened.[1]

In order to reduce this source of simultaneous equations bias, we also apply two-stage least squares (TSLS). This involves first calculating for each firm a leverage-ratio variable which is independent of the interest rate and then estimating, on a cross-sectional basis with OLS, the functions (4: 3) and (4: 4), where the calculated leverage variable replaces the original leverage variable. In appendix C, p. 144, this two stage technique is described in greater detail.

4.2.3. Results

4.2.3.1. REGRESSION ESTIMATES

In tables 3 and 4 are presented the estimates for the linear and linear-multiplicative interest-rate functions, respectively. As is clear from the tables, there is a significant positive relationship between the interest rate and the leverage ratio. This is in line with the hypothesis above that an increased degree of debt finance raises the financial risk for lenders of the firm. The fact that the coefficient of the leverage ratio in equation 1 estimated with OLS is less than

---

[1] Let $\tau_1 C_1$, $\tau_2 C_2$ and $\tau_3 C_3$ in the figure to the right be interest rate functions for three different firms. If a shift upward in the exogenous part of the interest rate reduces their optimal leverage ratios (h) this may be illustrated by the optimum combination of interest rates and leverage ratios C_1, C_2 and C_3, respectively. The relationship between the interest rate and the leverage ratio in the cross section of firms may then be equal to the line connecting the points C_1, C_2 and C_3 instead of being an average of the lines $\tau_1 C_1$, $\tau_2 C_2$ and $\tau_3 C_3$.

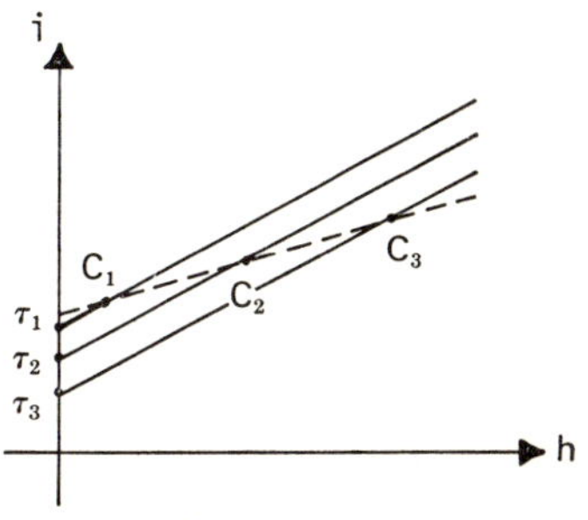

Table 3. *Estimated regressions of the interest rate on the leverage ratio, the share of long-term debt, and the size of the firm*

Linear specifications

Equation number		Leverage ratio	Share of long-term debt	Firm size	
1	b	0.0031***	0.0102**	−0.0001	B_0 = 0.0192
(OLS)	σ	0.0009	0.0047	0.0016	R^2 = 0.2085
					F_R = 4.565
2	b	0.0059**	0.0082*	−0.0001	B_0 = 0.0158
(TSLS)	σ	0.0023	0.0047	0.0017	R^2 = 0.1438
					F_R = 2.912

Note: b is the regression coefficient and σ is its standard error. Regression coefficients which are significantly different from zero at the 10 %, 5 % and 1 % confidence levels are indicated *, **, and *** respectively. B_0 is the intercept term, R^2 is the coefficient of multiple determination and F_R is the F-ratio with respect to the regression as a whole.

that in equation 2 estimated with the TSLS may be interpreted that our two-stage technique gives regression coefficients which show the influence of debt on the interest rate without feedback from the latter.

For the linear-multiplicative form of the interest-rate function in table 4, the leverage-ratio elasticity is less than unity, which shows that the interest rate increases at a declining rate as the leverage ratio increases. Note that this result is not inconsistent with the often mentioned view that a continued increase in the ratio of debt to total capital exerts an increasing positive influence on the risk of bankruptcy of the firm (see Baxter [1967]). The leverage ratio elasticities of about 0.40 estimated by us imply that the interest rate rises with the share of debt in total capital first at a decreasing rate but then rises at an increasing rate.[1]

We have performed regressions with only the leverage ratio as an explanatory variable for two different groups of 28 firms each, in which all firms in Group 1 have a lower leverage ratio than those in Group 2. The results are

[1] If the share of debt to total capital is h_K and the leverage ratio is h, then $h = h_K/(1-h_K)$. With a leverage elasticity of 0.40, the interest-rate function is $i = E_1[h_K/(1-h_K)]^{0.40} + E_0$. The given values of the remaining two explanatory variables, the share of long-term debt and the size of the firm, are included in the constant term E_1.

Differentiation of this function gives:

$$\partial i/\partial h_K = E_1 0.40[h_K^{0.40-1}/(1-h_K)^{0.40+1}]$$

$$\frac{\partial^2 i}{\partial h_K^2} = \frac{E_1 0.40 h_K^{0.40-2}(1-h_k)^{0.40}}{(1-h_K)^{2(0.40+1)}}[(0.40-1)(1-h_K)+(0.40+1)h_K].$$

When h_K takes values from zero to unity, $\partial^2 i/\partial h_K^2$ changes sign from negative to positive. The change of sign occurs when $[(0.40-1)(1-h_K)+1.40h_K]=0$, i.e., when h_K equals 0.30.

Table 4. *Estimated regressions of the interest rate on the leverage ratio, the share of long-term debt and the size of the firm*

Linear-multiplicative specifications

Equation number		Leverage ratio	Share of long-term debt	Firm size	
1	e	0.2300***	0.0565**	0.0112	$E_0 = -0.0150$ $E_1 = 0.0305$
(OLS)	σ	0.0636	0.0202	0.0260	$R^2 = 0.3181$ $F_R = 8.087$
2	e	0.4689***	0.0535	0.0547	$E_0 = 0.0000$ $E_1 = 0.0202$
(TSLS)	σ	0.1582	0.0378	0.0509	$R^2 = 0.1631$ $F_R = 3.378$

Note: E_0 is the intercept term, E_1 the constant term and e is the regression coefficient (elasticity). The other estimates are analogous to those in table 3.

presented in appendix C, table C: 1. As is clear from these that coefficient of the leverage ratio is notably smaller in Group 2 than in Group 1, which also suggests that the influence of the leverage ratio on the interest rate is less the greater the leverage ratio.

The share of long-term debt has a positive coefficient which is significant at the 5 % level in the equation estimated with OLS. The sign of the coefficient also agrees with the hypothesis above that the longer the term to maturity of loans, the less liquidity they have from the lender's viewpoint. However, the positive relationship between the interest rate and the share of long-term debt can also be explained by the fact that short-term debt includes, e.g., commercial credits which suppliers give to the firm in exchange for a higher price on their goods. For these debts the firm pays a very low or zero nominal interest rate. It has not been possible to separate out these types of debt in our data.

It appears that firm size hardly influences the interest rate, which may seem surprising since there is reason to expect a negative relationship between the interest rate and the size of the firm—see pp. 49 f. A conceivable explanation may be that the reduction of risk which follows from the greater size of the borrower, for the most part, operates in the size interval in which small and medium-sized firms are found. The data used here include mostly large firms (those which are listed on the A-list of the Stockholm Stock Exchange).

As far as the ability of all of the explanatory variables to explain the variations in the interest rate between firms is concerned—i.e., the explanatory power of the whole regression equation—one finds that the linear-multiplicative specification is superior to the linear specification. The values of F_R, which are corrected for degrees of freedom, are higher in table 4 than in table 3.

4.2.3.2. EFFECTS OF AN ALTERED LEVERAGE RATIO

If the rate of return required by shareholders is independent of debt finance, the leverage ratio which maximizes the rate of return on equity will also maximize the present value of the firm's future dividends (see chapter 5). Now we shall show diagrammatically how changes in the leverage ratio affect the rate of return on equity; on the basis of the regression estimates above, we may quantify these relationships.

Let us make the following assumptions:

(1) The function for the interest rate is linear, and the rate of tax on profits (t_V) is zero.[1]

(2) The intercept term in the interest-rate function (B'_{i0}) is equal to 0.0400. This value has been chosen since it should correspond approximately to the interest rate which the firms are expected to pay for their least expensive loans (e.g., liabilities to pension funds).

(3) The coefficient of the leverage ratio in the interest-rate function b_{ih} is 0.0059, which is the coefficient estimated with the two-stage method in table 3.

These assumptions and the identity (2: 12) give the equations:

$$i = 0.0400 + 0.0059\, h \tag{4: 5}$$

$$r_E = r + h(r - i). \tag{4: 6}$$

As in chapter 2 we assume constant returns to scale and fixed prices. When no costs of growth exist, total profitability r will then be independent of the leverage ratio (h). In figure 3 the given total profitability, the interest-rate function and the marginal borrowing-cost function are illustrated by the lines r_1,[2] $i(h)$ and $MC(h)$, respectively. The area $y = h(r-i)$ shows the increased return on equity (r_E) due to borrowing.[3]

When the leverage ratio (h) is increased from zero, the area $y = h(r-i)$ increases due to the percentage increase of h being greater than the percentage decrease of $(r-i)$. Since the interest-rate function is linear, this occurs as long as $(r-i) > (i - B'_{i0})$. Then we can find one h where $(r-i) = (i - B'_{i0})$, i.e., where total profitability (r_1) is equal to the marginal borrowing cost $MC(h)$—see point R_1—and y is maximized. If h is increased further, $(r-i) < (i - B'_{i0})$ and y begins to decline. The value of h which maximizes the rate of return on equity (r_E) is thus obtained from the condition $(r-i) = (i - B'_{i0})$. This value is $h_1^* = (r_1 - B'_{i0})/2b_{ih} = (0.076 - 0.0400)/(2 \times 0.0059) = 3.034$[4] and the corresponding value of r_E is $r_{Ei}^* = r_1 + h_1^*(r_1 - i^*) = 0.130$.

In addition, figure 3 can be used to show how h^* and r_E^* are affected by changes in r. If r is increased from r_1 to r_2, the point of intersection between the r-line and the $MC(h)$-curve falls further to the right, and h^* increases to

[1] In principle these two assumptions do not change the analysis and conclusions which follow below compared with the case in which the interest-rate function is logarithmic and $t_V > 0$.

[2] The value of $r_1 = 0.0758$, is the average for firms in our data.

[3] These relationships have been discussed earlier by Jensen & Johansson [1969].

[4] Observe that $\partial r_E/\partial h = [r_1 - (i + h\partial i/\partial h)] = [0.0758 - 0.0400 - 2 \times 0.0059h] = 0$ also give $h = h_1^* = 3.034$.

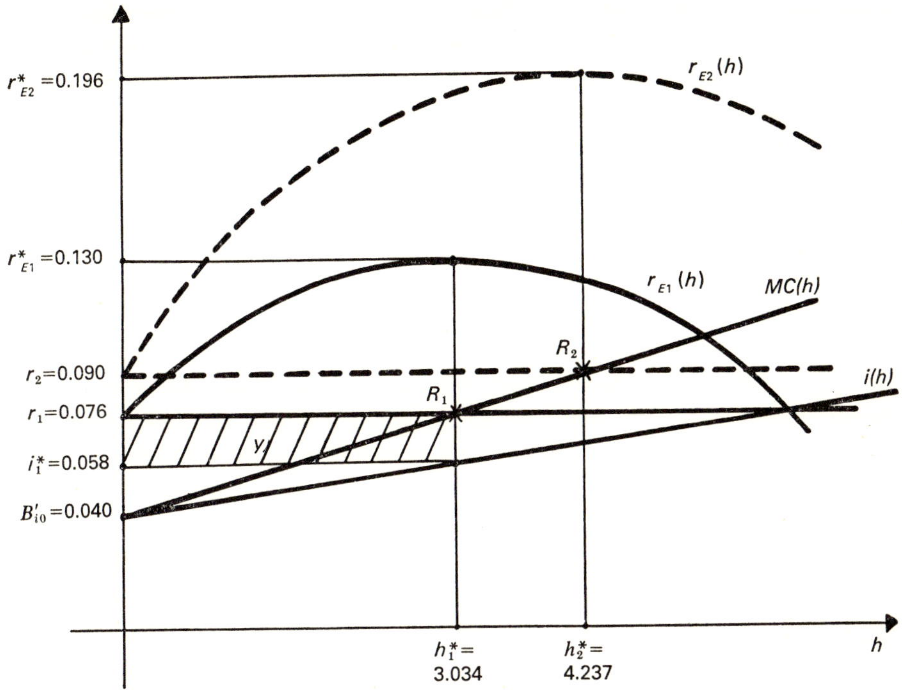

Figure 3. *The influence of the leverage ratio on the interest rate and on the rate of return on equity*

h^*_2. At the same time the $r_E(h)$-curve is shifted upward, and r^*_E increases to r^*_{E2}. Note that h^* and r^*_E also increase if the interest-rate function is shifted downwards—i.e., if the intercept of the function is reduced.

Hitherto we have assumed that the leverage ratio does not influence the shareholders' required rate of return. But if this rate of return is a positive function of the degree of debt financing, the leverage ratio which is optimal for the shareholder—i.e., that which maximizes the value of the shares of the firm—will be lower than that which maximizes the expected rate of return on equity (see section 7.2).

4.3. The discount rate

4.3.1. Hypotheses concerning the influences of internal and external finance on the discount rate

The discount rate is here defined as the rate of return the shareholders require on money they have invested in the firm, i.e., the rate at which they discount future dividends from their shareholdings. Shares and loans are both financial claims which the stockholders and lenders have on the firm. If the firm becomes insolvent, the holders of shares and bonds risk are losing their invested funds. There are, however, certain essential differences between these two types of financial claims as regards liquidity, risk and other characteristics. The value of the shares is not fixed at any nominal amount on the basis of earlier agreements.[1] At every point in time their value is affected by the firm's future dividends, which in turn are dependent on its future profits. Since profits are uncertain, uncertainty is also attached to dividends. In addition, the dividends are directly affected by the firm's financing through retained earnings and issue of new shares.

(a) *Finance through retained earnings*

By assigning different values to the retention rate the owners of the firm can choose alternative growth paths for dividends. We assume that every growth path can be described by a given expected trend value for dividends and a given expected deviation of dividends around the trend in each future time period. The greater the dispersion of dividends, the greater the uncertainty connected with the whole expected stream of dividends. We also assume that stockholders are risk averse and that their required rate of return, i.e., the average rate of discount for all future dividends, is a positive function of the variability of the dividend stream.

Whatever the risk associated with expected future dividends (U_t) one imagines that there is some factor x_t, where $0 < x_t < 1$, by which U_t is multiplied. $x_t U_t$ is then defined as the certainty equivalent which corresponds to dividends paid out with full certainty (discounted with a riskless rate of interest) and which, for the stockholders, is worth the same as U_t (discounted with a risk-adjusted rate of interest). It should be pointed out—see Robichek & Myers [1965]—that x_t must fall exponentially over time if the risk-adjusted discount rates for every future dividend are to be of equal size. This in turn puts restrictions on how the variance of dividends may change over time and on how the stockholders' valuation of the dividends is affected by changes in the variance. See appendix C.4.

What, then, is the influence of the dividend policy on the discount rate? When a firm reduces the pay-out ratio this may be done in order to grow at a more rapid rate. If the market for the products which the firm sells is limited, a higher rate of expansion may be expected to provoke countermeasures from competing firms and even to attract entry of new firms. The uncertainty concerning how the competitive situation will be affected by the firm increasing its rate of growth would seem to imply an increase in the relative variability of the dividend stream and thus to lead to the stockholders demanding a higher discount rate (Lerner & Carleton [1966]).

---

[1] This is, of course, not the case with preferred shares which in many respects resemble long-term bonds. We mean by shares only common shares, and it is the required rate of return on these which is analyzed here.

In addition, the discount rate may differ between industries. It is likely that the discount rate is higher in a risky industry, such as oil exploration, than in a less risky industry, such as textiles. When the firm attempts to increase its growth rate by lowering the pay-out ratio it redirects its production from less risky to more risky industries. At the same time the firm ought to devote more resources to development and marketing of new products, which in itself involves greater risk-taking. By doing that the firm in fact switches from a lower to a higher discount rate (Brems [1976]).[1]

Reduction of the pay-out ratio also means that dividends in the near future are reduced, which delays the point of time when the funds which the owners have invested in the firm will be paid back through dividends. This effect is analogous to that on the income of lenders when the average maturity of their lending is extended. As loans are repaid more slowly, lenders' income from them becomes more spread out in time. As has been maintained earlier, this delay of repayment of principal and payment of interest is expected to lead to an increase of lenders' required rate of return.

(b) *Finance with share issuing and borrowed funds*

Finance through issue of new shares can be regarded as a negative payout. For the same reasons given under point (a) above, a higher rate of expansion of the firm, due to increased finance through new issues, should imply a greater financial risk for the stockholders. In addition, a more extensive reliance on new issues also means that the near future net dividends (dividends minus the inflow of funds obtained due to the new issues) are reduced. Thus we expect the stockholders' discount rate to be positively affected by increased financing through new issues.

In section 4.2.1 it was shown that increased finance through borrowed capital increases the probability of bankruptcy of the firm. The stockholders run, to at least the same degree as lenders, the risk of not getting back the funds which they have invested in the firm if a bankruptcy takes place. In addition an increased indebtedness should raise the variability of the dividend stream from the firm. Thus, our hypothesis is that the discount rate is affected positively by the leverage ratio.

This hypothesis seems to be in conflict with Modigliani & Miller's [1958] assertion that the amount of debt does not affect the firm's total cost of capital. In particular, if their assertion were valid, given a rise in the leverage

[1] These arguments for a negative relationship between the discount rate and the pay-out ratio have been taken from a review of the Swedish edition of this book by Professor Hans Brems. I then justified this relationship by assuming that distant dividends are discounted at a higher rate than those in the near future. I am very grateful for Brem's observation that such an assumption is inconsistent with an average discount rate being constant over time—which was assumed in the derivation of the present value formula (2: 4).

ratio sooner or later the stockholders discount rate would begin to fall, assuming that the interest rate is an increasing function of the leverage ratio. According to Modigliani & Miller's "Proposition I", the firm's total capital costs ($\varkappa$) are constant and independent of the relative amount of debt. Also according to their "Proposition II" the discount rate $k = \varkappa + (\varkappa - i)h$, where i is the interest rate and h is the leverage ratio.

If $i = E_{i0} + E'_{i1} h^{e_{ih}}$—see equation (4: 4) above—one obtains upon differentiation with respect to h

$$\partial k/\partial h = \varkappa - E_{i0} - (1 + e_{ih}) E'_{i1} h^{e_{ih}}$$

$$\partial^2 k/\partial h^2 = -e_{ih}(1 + e_{ih}) E'_{i1} h^{e_{ih}-1}.$$

If the interest rate is positively dependent on the leverage ratio ($E'_{i1} > 0$ and $e_{ih} > 0$), as our regression estimates indicate, it follows that $\partial^2 k/\partial h^2$ is negative. This implies that when $\varkappa$ is greater than i for $h = 0$, the rate of discount (k) is first a rising and then a declining function of the leverage ratio.

4.3.2. Regression model

We define each firm's explanatory variables in the regression for the discount rate as follows.

Pay-out ratio. This variable is measured by the ratio of paid out dividends to profit on equity; the latter being equal to gross profit net of depreciation costs, interest payments and profit taxes. Note that gross profit in turn is equal to total revenue minus the cost of labor and commodity inputs.

New issue ratio. This variable is measured by the ratio of inflow of funds acquired through share issues to the book value of equity. Equity capital consists of share capital, taxed reserves and half of untaxed reserves.

Leverage ratio. The measurement of this variable has been described on p. 50 above.

These three financial explanatory variables fluctuate from year to year. Therefore, in the regressions we use averages of the annual values for the period 1963–70 for which we have individual firm data. The justification for using such normalized, time-invariant variable values instead of actual annual values are the same as that advanced on p. 37.

The rate of discount, which is the dependent variable, cannot be observed as a statistical magnitude. We have therefore measured this variable indirectly. If k is the discount rate, d is dividends divided by the market value of shares and v is the percentage rate of growth of dividends, it follows from the present-value formula (2: 17) above that

$$k = d + v. \qquad (4: 7)$$

However, in order that (4: 7) shall hold exactly, it is necessary that the stockmarket is perfect and that firms grow at a steady rate. If deviations from the perfect market situation and steady state growth only cause non-systematic variations in the variables d and v, then the calculated discount rate (k) may be regarded as varying randomly about the long-run expected value of k at any point in time.[1]

The v component of the rate of discount can, due to occasional fluctuations in firms' profits, be expected to vary sharply from year to year. We have therefore approximated a time-invariant rate of growth by a weighted average of dividend growth during the period 1963–70. The denominator in the d component is the market value of the firm's shares. The most suitable point in time at which to measure the market value would seem to be the end of 1970 which is the last cross-sectional year. Concerning the numerator in d, i.e., the dividends, the firms seem to adjust them only in response to long-run changes in profits and growth of product demand. Therefore, it would also seem most proper to use actual values for the same year (1970).[2]

Procedures for measuring the variables (d and v) resembling those described have been used earlier by Gordon [1962] and by Bennet, Graham & Tran Van Hoa [1969].

The same functional forms are used as in the estimation of the interest-rate function. Thus coefficients are estimated for the following two discounting functions:

$$k = B_{k0} + b_{ku}u + b_{kn}n + b_{kh}h \tag{4: 8}$$

$$k = E_{k0} + E_{k1}u^{e_{ku}}n^{e_{kn}}h^{e_{kh}} \tag{4: 9}$$

where k is the rate of discount, u is the pay-out ratio, n is the new issue ratio and h is the leverage ratio. According to the hypotheses above, we expect the coefficients $b_{ku}<0$, $b_{kn}>0$, $b_{kh}>0$, $E_{k1}>0$, $e_{ku}<0$, $e_{kn}>0$, and $e_{kh}>0$.

The method of estimation is ordinary least squares (OLS). As is shown in chapter 5, there are reasons to expect that an exogenous increase of the discount rate leads firms to increase their pay-out ratios. If the discount rate affects the pay-out ratio positively, the effect of the pay-out ratio on the discount rate will be underestimated in the cross section of firm observations.

In order to eliminate this source of simultaneous equations bias, regressions are also carried out using two-stage least squares (TSLS). This involves first

---

[1] For the larger firms listed on the stock-exchange which we are studying, the market seems to function relatively well. The shares of these firms are as a rule spread among a significant number of owners and are traded daily. In addition, the public ought to be rather well informed about the firms' profit situation, liquidity and future prospects through the publishing of their reports and through the analyses which are made by the press.

[2] In our data dividends have been quite stable over time. Experience also seems to indicate that the firms, as a rule, strive to prevent dividends from being affected by short-run fluctuations in profits.

Table 5. *Estimated regressions of the discount rate on the pay-out ratio, the new issue ratio and the leverage ratio*

Linear specifications

Equation number		Pay-out ratio	New issue percentage	Leverage ratio	
1	b	−0.0748***	−0.3705	0.0076**	$B_0 = 0.1390$
(OLS)	σ	0.0160	0.3028	0.0039	$R^2 = 0.3355$
					$F_R = 8.752$
2	b	−0.0834***	−0.4964	0.0012	$B_0 = 0.1597$
(TSLS)	σ	0.0177	0.3059	0.0030	$R^2 = 0.3379$
					$F_R = 8.847$

Note: See the note to table 3.

computing for every firm a calculated pay-out ratio which is independent of the discount rate and then estimating the functions (4: 8) and (4: 9) on the basis of this calculated pay-out ratio. (For a more detailed presentation, see appendix C, p. 148.) In estimating of the linear-multiplicative specification (4: 9) the same iterative procedure is used as was described on p. 51.

4.3.3. Results

4.3.3.1. REGRESSION ESTIMATES

In tables 5 and 6 are given the estimates of the linear and linear-multiplicative discount rate functions, respectively.

As is clear from the tables, there is a strongly negative relationship between the discount rate and the pay-out ratio. This result agrees with the view advanced above that a redistribution of dividends ahead of time increases the financial risk of the owners of the firm and thus makes them discount their dividend income at a higher rate. The result is also in line with what Gordon [1962], Walter [1963], and others have maintained, that the firm's capital costs increase with the rate of growth in its dividends, but it conflicts with the contention of Modigliani & Miller [1958] and Solomon [1955] that capital costs are independent of internal financing decisions (see pp. 46 f.).

The coefficient of dividends is numerically greater in equation 2 estimated with the TSLS than in equation 1 estimated with OLS. This difference seems to confirm what we have assumed earlier, that the relationship between the discount rate and the pay-out ratio is weakened in the cross section of firm observations due to the discount rate affecting the pay-out ratio positively.

The negative coefficients for dividends in the linear-multiplicative regression specifications in table 6 suggest that the discount rate rises at an increasing rate as the pay-out ratio is lowered. In addition we have run separate linear

Table 6. *Estimated regressions of the discount rate on the pay-out ratio, the new issue ratio and the leverage ratio*

Linear-multiplicative specifications

Equation number		Pay-out ratio	New issue percentage	Leverage ratio		
1	e	−0.5313***	0.0313	−0.0169	$E_0 = -0.0200$	$E_1 = 0.0933$
(OLS)	σ	0.0984	0.0403	0.0775	$R^2 = 0.3923$	$F_R = 11.187$
2	e	−0.6062***	0.0015	−0.0849	$E_0 = -0.0050$	$E_1 = 0.0745$
(TSLS)	σ	0.1503	0.0547	0.1015	$R^2 = 0.2827$	$F_R = 6.830$

Note: E_0 is the asymptote approached as u tends to infinity, E_1 is the constant term, and e is the regression coefficient (elasticity). Concerning the other regression estimates, see the note to table 3.

regressions, for two groups of firms ranked according to the value of the pay-out ratio (see appendix C, table C: 2); these also indicate that the effect of the pay-out ratio on the discount rate is strengthened as the pay-out ratio is lowered. A reason for this could be that the lower the pay-out ratio, the greater (relatively) the shift forward in time of the major part of the dividend stream which follows with every given percentage reduction of the pay-out ratio. For example, a reduction of one percentage point from the value 0.10 reduces the near-term dividends much more than a similar reduction from the value 1.0.

As far as the two remaining explanatory variables are concerned, we may note that the new issue ratio has insignificant coefficients in both specifications. Furthermore, in one case it is positive and in the other it is negative. A conceivable explanation for this "unsuccessful" result may be that in our cross-sectional data new issues occur, to a greater extent, among firms whose pay-out ratio has sunk during the period 1963–70. Since a reduced pay-out ratio immediately leads to a slower rate of growth of dividends, this implies a negative bias in our estimated new issue coefficients.

The result obtained for the leverage ratio, is also ambiguous, i.e., we have not been able to verify the hypothesis stated that an expanded debt finance raises the discount rate. On the other hand, that no relation exists between the discount rate and the leverage ratio over the whole range of values of the leverage ratio may be consistent with Modigliani & Miller's "Proposition II" provided that the interest rate is a rising function of the leverage ratio. Then, according to their proposition the discount rate first rises and then falls as the leverage ratio is increased (see pp. 57 f.).[1]

[1] In addition we have estimated with OLS, linear and logarithmic discount-rate functions with the rate of profit on equity as a fourth explanatory variable. The estimated coefficient of this profitability variable was barely significant in the linear function and insignificant

Finally, it may be of interest to compare our results with those of Brigham & Gordon [1968] and Bennet, Graham & Tran Van Hoa [1969], who have attempted to determine empirically the effects of internal and external finance on the discount rate.

Brigham & Gordon (B–G)

B–G estimate cross sectionally for a sample of sixty-nine firms in the US electrical engineering industry the influence on the dividend yield on shares (d) of internally financed growth (v_I) and of the leverage ratio (h). They measure d as the ratio of current dividends to the market value of shares, and v_I is defined to equal internally generated profits divided by equity. Several sequential annual values are used to approximate a time-stable expected growth rate without errors of measurements.

Their regression estimates show that d is influenced negatively by v_I and only slightly positively by h. The regression coefficient of v_I is clearly significant, while that of h is barely significant (at the 5% level). According to B–G, the sizes of the estimated coefficients for v_I and h provides a basis for determining their influence on the rate of discount (k)[1]. The authors came to the conclusion that v_I and h both affect the discount rate positively but that the influence of the former is statistically much more certain.

Bennet, Graham & Tran Van Hoa (B–G–T)

Like B–G, B–G–T estimate, using cross sectional data, relationships with the dividend yield on shares (d) as the dependent variable and internal growth (v_I) and the leverage ratio (h) as explanatory variables. In addition, B–G–T allow external equity growth (v_N) to be an explanatory variable. It is measured as the ratio of capital acquired through share issues to equity capital. The regressions are carried out on a sample of fifty-eight Australian industrial firms.

Their results show that d is affected negatively by v_I and v_N but positively by h. Highly significant coefficients are obtained for the explanatory variable v_I, which has a coefficient approximately ten times greater than its standard error. The coefficients of the other two explanatory variables have much lower precision, with standard errors of approximately the same size as the coefficients. The numerical values of the coefficients are then used by B–G–T in order to determine the influence of v_I, v_N and h on the discount rate, and they find at least statistical support for the theory, that the discount rate is a rising function of v_I.

---

in the logarithmic function, and the numerical value of the coefficient of profitability was several times smaller than that of the pay-out ratio. We interpret this result to suggest that profitability—as long as the pay-out ratio is also included as an explanatory variable—ought not to have any effect worth mentioning on the discount rate.

[1] To do this the identity $k = d + v$ is used.

4.3.3.2. EFFECTS OF A CHANGED PAY-OUT RATIO

The choice of the pay-out ratio affects the market value of the firm's shares (i.e., the present value of its dividends) as the pay-out ratio determines both the dividends in the initial period and the growth of dividends as well as the rate of discount. In what follows, these effects on the firm's share value will be illustrated diagrammatically and also quantified by using our regression estimates of the discount-rate function.

Assume that the influence of the pay-out ratio (u) on the discount rate (k) is described by the TSLS estimated equation in table 6. With given average values of the two remaining explanatory variables in this function: the new issue ratio (n) and the leverage ratio (h),[1] we then obtain

$$k = -0.0050 + 0.0745\, u^{-0.606}. \tag{4: 10}$$

We have from chapter 2 the identities

$$v = (1-u) r_E \tag{4: 11}$$

$$\varrho = P_t / K_{Et} = u r_E / (k - v), \tag{4: 12}$$

where r_E is the rate of return on equity, v is the rate of growth of dividends, P_t is the share value and K_{Et} is equity capital.

Observe that K_{Et} is a predetermined magnitude. Assume further that there are no costs of growth. Then it follows that r_E is independent of u. In figure 4 the given average value of r_{E1}[1] is represented by the line r_{E1}, the discount-rate function (4: 10) by the curve $k(u)$, and the growth identity (4: 11) by the line $v(u)$.

In order to find the pay-out ratio (u) maximizing the valuation ratio $\varrho = P_t / K_{Et}$ we construct a line $A'A$ which goes through any point (u, k) on the k-curve and through the point (0, r_{E1}) on the r_{E1}-line. The tangent of the angle α between the r_{E1}-line and this line, is equal to $(r_{E1} - k)/u$, and the tangent of the angle β between the r_{E1}-line and the $v(u)$-line, is equal to $(r_{E1} - v)/u = r_{E1}$.

Now it follows according to equation (4: 12), that the valuation ratio is $\varrho = u r_{E1}/(k - v) = \operatorname{tg}\beta / (\operatorname{tg}\beta - \operatorname{tg}\alpha)$. Since $\operatorname{tg}\beta$ is fixed, ϱ is a monotonically increasing function of $\operatorname{tg}\alpha$. When u rises from 0, ϱ rises at first, reaches a maximum at $u = u_1^*$ when the line $A'A$ is tangent to the $k(u)$-curve and then declines. The tangency implies that $\operatorname{tg}\alpha = (r_{E1} - k_1^*)/u_1^* = -\partial k/\partial u$.[2] From (4: 10)–(4: 12) we then obtaine $u_1^* = 0.763$, $k_1^* = 0.083$ and $\varrho_1^* = 2.053$.

One can also see from figure 4 that an increase of the rate of return on equity

---

[1] The average values of n and h for our sample of firms are 0.012 and 1.727, respectively. The average value of r_{E1} is 0.136.

[2] Note that this optimal condition $u^* = (r_E - k)/-\partial k/\partial u$ follows directly from the maximization of the share value (P_t) with respect to the pay-out ratio. See chapter 5.

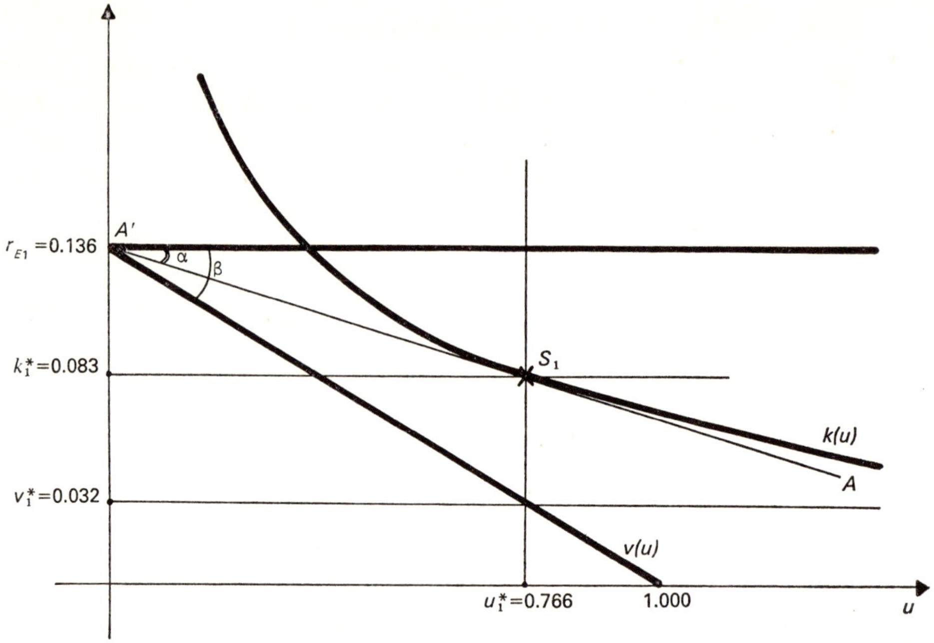

Figure 4. *The influence of the pay-out ratio on the discount rate, the growth of dividends and the valuation ratio*

(r_E) reduces the optimal pay-out ratio (u^*) but raises the optimal growth of dividends (v^*) and the maximal valuation ratio (ϱ^*). Furthermore, it is clear from the figure that the variables u^*, v^* and ϱ^* are affected in the same direction by the discount-rate function being shifted downward in a parallel fashion.

CHAPTER 5

The behavior of the firm: real and financial

5.1. Introduction

Two questions are dealt with in this chapter. The first is how the firm determines its optimal decisions about production, finance and investment, and the second is how changes in the firm's environment affect these decisions.

The analysis is based on the steady-state growth model presented in chapter 2. In this model we introduced three basic behavior functions: a production function in which production depends on labor, capital and the growth of capital, an interest rate function in which the interest rate depends on the leverage ratio and a discount rate function which makes the discount rate a function of the pay-out ratio. We assumed that the firm's objective is to maximize its capital value, i.e., the present value of all future dividends. To this end the firm has three decision variables—labor intensity, the leverage ratio and the pay-out ratio. It is further assumed that equity capital in the initial period $t=0$—the period which begins the firm's equilibrium growth—is predetermined from earlier periods.

Our optimization problem is to find the values of the decision variables which maximize the firm's capital value under the assumption of steady-state growth and that the initial size of equity is given. The solution gives the necessary first-order conditions which form the basis of the production, finance and investment decisions of the firm. The optimality conditions together with the other equations in the model give the relationships which show how the firm reacts to changes in its environment.

The basic analysis is simplified if we begin by ignoring growth costs in deriving the optimality conditions and the influence of various external factors on the firm's behavior. Subsequently, we investigate how these results are changed by the introduction of growth costs into the model. The chapter ends with a diagrammatic summary of the results.

5.2. Optimal labor intensity, the leverage ratio and retention ratio

5.2.1. The optimality conditions

The assumption of steady-state and balanced growth implies that the optimum conditions and the optimal values of all monetary ratio variables which hold for the initial period also hold for all future periods. The first-order conditions for a maximization of the firm's capital value are obtained by differentiating the capital value formula (2: 17) with respect to labor intensity ($\hat{l}$), the leverage ratio (h), and the pay-out ratio (u) and setting the partial derivatives equal to zero. Recalling that equity capital (K_{Et}) is given in the initial period (t), we then obtain

$$\frac{\partial P}{\partial \hat{l}} = (k-v)^{-2} u r_E K_{Et} \left\{ \frac{\partial r_E}{\partial \hat{l}} r_E^{-1}(k-v) + (1-u)\frac{\partial r_E}{\partial \hat{l}} \right\} = 0 \qquad (5:1)$$

$$\frac{\partial P}{\partial h} = (k-v)^{-2} u r_E K_{Et} \left\{ \frac{\partial r_E}{\partial h} r_E^{-1}(k-v) + (1-u)\frac{\partial r_E}{\partial h} \right\} = 0 \qquad (5:2)$$

$$\frac{\partial P}{\partial u} = (k-v)^{-2} r_E K_{Et} \left\{ (k-v) + u\left(\frac{\partial v}{\partial u} - \frac{\partial k}{\partial u}\right) \right\} = 0. \qquad (5:3)$$

Note that the assumption that the discount rate (k) is independent of $\hat{l}$ and h but is affected negatively by u—i.e., $\partial k/\partial \hat{l} = \partial k/\partial h = 0$ and $\partial k/\partial u < 0$. Note also that the growth rate of the monetary variables (v) is determined by the relationship $v = (1-u)r_E$, where r_E is the rate of return on equity. In addition it follows from the assumption of no growth costs that neither total profitability nor the rate of return on equity is affected by changes in the pay-out ratio (u)—i.e., $\partial r/\partial u = \partial r_E/\partial u = 0$.

(5: 1)–(5: 3) are also sufficient conditions for a maximum, if d^2P_t is negative for all variations in $\hat{l}$, h and u around the values of these variables which satisfy (5: 1)–(5: 3). This means that the determinants

$$D = \begin{vmatrix} \frac{\partial^2 P}{\partial \hat{l}^2} & \frac{\partial^2 P}{\partial \hat{l}\,\partial h} & \frac{\partial^2 P}{\partial \hat{l}\,\partial u} \\ \frac{\partial^2 P}{\partial h\,\partial \hat{l}} & \frac{\partial^2 P}{\partial h^2} & \frac{\partial^2 P}{\partial h\,\partial u} \\ \frac{\partial^2 P}{\partial u\,\partial \hat{l}} & \frac{\partial^2 P}{\partial u\,\partial h} & \frac{\partial^2 P}{\partial u^2} \end{vmatrix} < 0 \quad \text{and} \quad D_{33} = \begin{vmatrix} \frac{\partial^2 P}{\partial \hat{l}^2} & \frac{\partial^2 P}{\partial \hat{l}\,\partial h} \\ \frac{\partial^2 P}{\partial h\,\partial \hat{l}} & \frac{\partial^2 P}{\partial h^2} \end{vmatrix} > 0$$

as well as $\partial^2 P/\partial \hat{l}^2 < 0$

In appendix D, p. 151, it is shown that $\partial^2 P/\partial \hat{l}\partial u = \partial^2 P/\partial h \partial u = 0$ which simplifies these second-order conditions. After solving the three-by-three and two-by-two determinants we obtain

$$D = (\partial^2 P/\partial \hat{l}^2 \cdot \partial^2 P/\partial h^2 \cdot \partial^2 P/\partial u^2 - \partial^2 P/\partial \hat{l}\partial h \cdot \partial^2 P/\partial h \partial \hat{l} \cdot \partial^2 P/\partial u^2) < 0.$$

$$D_{33} = (\partial^2 P/\partial \hat{l}^2 \cdot \partial^2 P/\partial h^2 - \partial^2 P/\partial \hat{l} \partial h \cdot \partial^2 P/\partial h \partial \hat{l}) > 0;$$

$$\partial^2 P/\partial \hat{l}^2 < 0; \quad \partial^2 P/\partial h^2 < 0 \quad \text{and} \quad \partial^2 P/\partial u^2 < 0.$$

In appendix D, p. 154, it is also shown that satisfaction of the sufficient second-order conditions ultimately depend on the interest rate being a positive function of the leverage ratio and on the discount rate being a negative function (with a positive second derivative) of the pay-out ratio. If for example these two rate variables were constant, i.e. exogenously determined, there would be no determinate optimum solution as long as there were no growth costs in the model.

(a) *Labor intensity and the leverage ratio*

According to (5: 1) and (5: 2), $\partial P/\partial \hat{l} = 0$ when $\partial r_E/\partial \hat{l} = 0$, and $\partial P/\partial h = 0$ when $\partial r_E/\partial h = 0$. The values of $\hat{l}$ and h which maximize the rate of return on equity (r_E) consequently also maximize the capital value (P_t). The maximization of the rate of return gives (see appendix D, p. 155)[1]

$$\frac{\partial r_E}{\partial \hat{l}} = p\frac{\partial \hat{F}}{\partial \hat{L}} - p_1 = 0 \tag{5: 1)'}$$

$$\frac{\partial r_E}{\partial h} = p\frac{\partial \hat{F}}{\partial \hat{K}} - p_2\left(a + i + \hat{K}_{Ft}\frac{\partial i}{\partial \hat{K}}\right) = 0. \tag{5: 2)'}$$

These optimality conditions are the same as in the static profit maximization theory. $p\partial \hat{F}/\partial \hat{L}$ is the value of the marginal product of labor, p_1 is its marginal cost, $p\partial \hat{F}/\partial \hat{K}$ is the value of the marginal product of capital and $p_2(a+i+\hat{K}_{Ft}\partial i/\partial \hat{K})$ is its marginal cost. (Note that all prices are given.) The term $p_2 a$ states the depreciation cost per unit of capital and $p_2(i+\hat{K}_{Ft}\partial i/\partial \hat{K})$ states the marginal borrowing cost per unit of capital. Due to our assumption of constant returns to scale in production and exogenously given prices, from (5: 1)′ and (5: 2)′ is obtained (see appendix D, p. 155)

$$r - (i + h\partial i/\partial h) = 0. \tag{5: 4}$$

Thus an optimal level of debt requires that the rate of return on total capital (r) equals the marginal cost of borrowing.

In chapter 4 we came to the conclusion that the following functional form provides a good description of how the interest rate is affected by the leverage ratio h:

$$i = E_{i0} + E_{i1}h^{e_{ih}}, \tag{5: 5}$$

where E_{i1} and e_{ih} are positive constants.

---

[1] Maximization of r_E is the same as maximizing in every period the return on equity because K_{Et} is predetermined at the outset of every period.

Combining (5: 4) and (5: 5), one obtains $r - E_{i0} = (1 + e_{ih}) E_{i1} h^{e_{ih}}$. From this equation it is clear that the smaller E_{i1} and e_{ih} are, the greater h will be. Consequently, the leverage ratio (h) which maximizes the rate of return on equity is positively influenced by the total profitability (r) and negatively influenced by the exogenously given interest rate (E_{i0}). It is also evident that for h to be positive r must be greater than E_{i0}. An optimal solution with positive leverage ratio thus requires that when the leverage ratio is zero the interest rate should be less than total profitability.

Since $\partial i/\partial h$ is positive, it follows from (5: 4) that r must be greater than the interest rate (i) if h is positive. Consequently, an increasing interest rate with a higher leverage ratio implies that the firm will not push it's debt finance so far that the interest rate equals the profitability on total capital. Disregarding profit taxes, it further follows that if r exceeds i—see equation (2: 12)— r_E exceeds r. Maximization of the capital value of the firm with respect to borrowing then implies that total profitability is greater than the interest rate and that the return on equity in turn is greater than total profitability—i.e., that the inequality $r_E > r > i$ holds.

(b) *The pay-out ratio*

The marginal condition (5: 3) for the pay-out ratio may be written

$$k - u\frac{\partial k}{\partial u} = v - u\frac{\partial v}{\partial u}. \qquad (5\text{: }3)'$$

An optimal distribution of dividends over time clearly requires that the "marginal cost" in terms of an increasing discount rate ($k - u\partial k/\partial u$) be equal to the "marginal revenue" in terms of increasing growth of dividends ($v - u\partial v/\partial u$) due to an increased retention of profits. Since $v = (1-u) r_E$ and $\partial r_E/\partial u = 0$—see above—we obtain

$$k - u\frac{\partial k}{\partial u} = r_E. \qquad (5\text{: }3)''$$

The analysis in chapter 4 gave support to the discount-rate being a function of the pay-out ratio according to the form

$$k = E_{k0} + E_{k1} u^{e_{ku}} \qquad (5\text{: }6)$$

where E_{k1} is positive and e_{ku} is negative.

Combining (5: 3)″ with (5: 6), one obtains $r_E - E_{k0} = (1 - e_{ku}) E_{k1} u^{e_{ku}}$. It is clear from this equation that u is affected negatively by r_E and positively by E_{k0}. The higher the rate of return on equity and the lower the exogenously given component of the discount rate, the lower is the optimum value of the pay-out ratio. It is also clear that in order for the optimum value of the pay-out ratio to be finite and positive, it is necessary that r_E be greater than E_{k0}.

Since $\partial k/\partial u<0$, it follows from (5: 3)″ that $r_E>k$ for positive u. The rising discount rate associated with increased retentions clearly implies—contrary to what is often assumed in traditional investment theory—that the firm will not retain profits to such an extent that the discount rate becomes equal to the rate of return on equity. In addition, from $r_E>k$ it follows that $k>y$, where y is the earnings-price ratio[1]—see appendix D, p. 156. Thus maximization of capital value with respect to the pay-out ratio implies not only that the rate of return on equity will be greater than the discount rate, but also that the discount rate in turn will be greater than the earnings-price ratio, i.e., that the inequality $r_E>k>y$ holds.[2]

5.2.2. The explicit solutions

If the firm's production function is of the Cobb–Douglas type $\hat{F}_t=\psi\hat{L}_t^{\alpha}\hat{K}_t^{1-\alpha}$ and if the interest-rate and discount-rate functions have the form indicated in the previous section, we get the following relationships which show how the optimal values of the endogenous variables are determined by the exogenous variables of the model (* denotes optimal values).[3]

$$\hat{l}^*=\left[\frac{p}{p_1}\alpha\psi\right]^{1/1-\alpha} \tag{5: 7}$$

$$r^*=\frac{p}{p_2}\psi(\hat{l}^*)^{\alpha}-\frac{p_1}{p_2}\hat{l}^*-a \tag{5: 8}$$

$$h^*=\{(r^*-E_{i0})/[E_{i1}(1+e_{ih})]\}^{1/e_{ih}} \tag{5: 9}$$

$$i^*=E_{i0}+E_{i1}(h^*)^{e_{ih}} \tag{5: 10}$$

$$r_E^*=(1-t_V)\{(1+h^*)r^*-i^*h^*\} \tag{5: 11}$$

$$u^*=[(r_E^*-E_{k0})/E_{k1}(1-e_{ku})]^{1/e_{ku}} \tag{5: 12}$$

$$k^*=E_{k0}+E_{k1}(u^*)^{e_{ku}} \tag{5: 13}$$

$$v^*=(1-u^*)r_E^* \tag{5: 14}$$

$$P_t^*=\frac{u^*r_E^*K_{Et}}{k^*-v^*}, \tag{5: 15}$$

where the coefficients are subject to the restrictions:

$$0<\alpha<1,\ \psi>0,\ E_{i1}>0,\ e_{ih}>0,\ E_{k1}>0,\quad \text{and } e_{ku}<0.$$

---

[1] The earnings-price ratio equals profit on equity divided by the capital value (V_{Et}/P_t).

[2] This inequality has been derived, in a different way, by Lintner [1964].

[3] The directional changes which we derive below are also obtained for all production functions which are linearly homogeneous (see section 5.5 below).

The relationships in the system above are derived as follows. By combining the optimum condition for labor (5: 1)′ with the production function, we obtain (5: 7). The identity (2: 9) in chapter 2 and the production function give (5: 8). Substitution of (5: 5) in the optimum condition (5: 4) for the leverage ratio and substitution of (5: 6) in the optimum condition (5: 3)″ for the pay-out ratio give (5: 9) and (5: 12), respectively. (5: 10), (5: 11), (5: 13), (5: 14) and (5: 15) correspond to the earlier defined equations (5: 5), (2: 12), (5: 6), (2: 14) and (2: 17), respectively.

(5: 7)–(5: 15) form a recursive system in which the endogenous variables are determined one by one in the same order as that given by the numbers of the equations in the system. First, the optimal labor intensity ($\hat{l}^*$) determined by (5: 7). When the labor intensity has been determined, the rate of return on total capital is obtained by (5: 8), which then forms the basis of optimization of indebtedness, from which is obtained the optimal leverage ratio (h^*) by (5: 9) and so on.

This step-by-step determination of the optimal values of the endogenous variables is due to the assumptions of constant returns to scale, exogenously given product and factor prices and absence of growth costs. Later it will be shown that this recursivity in the model disappears when we introduce growth costs.

5.3. The influence of exogenous factors on the behavior of the firm

In this section, we investigate the effects of changes in the exogenous factors of the model. These are the variables p, p_1, p_2, a and t_V and the shift parameters ψ, E_{i0} and E_{k0} in the production function, interest-rate function and discount-rate function, respectively.

The assumption of steady-state and balanced growth implies that when changes during the initial period occur in the exogenous factors, the new values of these factors are expected to persist indefinitely. The optimal ratios of the firm's endogenous variables which are thereby determined are also assumed to last for ever. We thus compare different dynamic equilibrium situations for the firm which follow from different sets of values of the exogenous factors. The assumption of no growth costs further implies that the firm's adjustment to external disturbances takes place immediately. In other words the firm switches from one set of optimal ratios and an optimal steady-state growth rate to another, instantaneously.

5.3.1. Changes of direction in the endogenous variables

The recursivity of the system (5: 7)–(5: 15) means that a given exogenous factor change which concerns a certain equation only affects the endogenous variables in that equation and in those which have higher ranking numbers.

Let us first study equations (5: 7)–(5: 10). When the product price (p) or total productivity (ψ) is raised, or when the wage (p_1) is reduced, the optimal labor intensity ($\hat{l}^*$) increases. The rise in p or ψ implies together with the higher $\hat{l}^*$ that the optimal rate of return on total capital (r^*) increases. We note that r^* also increases when the price of capital p_2 or the rate of depreciation a is reduced. On the other hand, p_2 and a have no effect on labor intensity. When r^* increases, the optimal leverage ratio (h^*) increases, from which it follows that the interest rate (i^*) becomes higher. A shift downwards of the interest-rate function (a reduction of the intercept E_{i0} in that function) also raises h^*. However, the change in E_{i0} leaves r^* and $\hat{l}^*$ unaffected.

According to equations (5: 11) and (5: 12), an increase in the rate of return on total capital like an increase in the leverage ratio, raises the rate of return on equity (r_E^*). Note that r_E^* also increases if the profits tax rate (t_V) is reduced. On the other hand, t_V has no influence on $\hat{l}^*$, r^*, h^*, and i^*. When the rate of return on equity rises, the optimal pay-out ratio (u^*) declines. In addition we see that a downward shift of the discount-rate function (a reduction of the intercept E_{k0} in that function) affects u^* in the same direction. However, the change of E_{k0} does not affect $\hat{l}^*$, r^*, h^*, i^*, and r_E^*.

Finally, as concerns the equations (5: 13)–(5: 15), it can be seen that a reduced pay-out ratio (u^*) increases the optimal discount rate (k^*). On the other hand, k^* declines as a result of a reduction of E_{k0}. The lower the pay-out ratio and the higher the rate of return on equity the higher is the optimal growth rate of dividends (v^*). These changes in the pay-out ratio (u^*), the rate of return on equity (r_E^*), and the growth of dividends (v^*) then imply that the capital value (P_t^*) increases.

From what has been said it is clear in which directions the optimal values of the endogenous variables are affected by an increase in every exogenous factor. These results are summarized in table 7.

5.3.2. Comments

(a) *Factor mix and debt finance*

Despite the assumption of fixed prices and constant returns to scale, we obtain a determinate optimum solution for both the labor input ($\hat{L}_t^*$) and the capital input ($\hat{K}_t^*$). The reasons are: The optimal labor intensity ($\hat{l}^*$) is determined only by the optimization with respect to the labor input (see (5: 7)). $\hat{l}^*$ determines the marginal revenue of $\hat{K}_t$, which is $MR_K = p\partial\hat{F}/\partial\hat{K} = (1-\alpha)p\psi(\hat{l}^*)^{\alpha}$. The rising interest rate which accompanies an increased leverage ratio ($\partial i/\partial h > 0$) implies at the same time that the firm maximizes its capital value through assigning the leverage ratio a value such that the marginal cost of capital $MC_K = p_2(a + i^* + h^*\partial i/\partial h) = MR_K$. The fact that equity capital is given implies that once $\hat{l}^*$ and h^* have been set, $\hat{L}_t^*$ and $\hat{K}_t^*$ are determined.[1] If for

[1] Note the identities $p_2\hat{K}_t = (1+h)K_{Et}$ and $\hat{L}_t = \hat{l}\hat{K}_t$.

Table 7. *Changes in the optimal values of the endogenous variables associated with increases in the exogenous factors when no growth costs exist*

Exogenous factor	Endogenous variable $\hat{l}^*$	r^*	h^*	i^*	r_E^*	u^*	k^*	v^*	P_t^*
ψ	+	+	+	+	+	−	+	+	+
p	+	+	+	+	+	−	+	+	+
p_1	−	−	−	−	−	+	−	−	−
p_2	0	−	−	−	−	+	−	−	−
a	0	−	−	−	−	+	−	−	−
E_{i0}	0	0	−	+	−	+	−	−	−
t_V	0	0	0	0	−	+	−	−	−
E_{k0}	0	0	0	0	0	+	+	−	−

Note: The signs +, − and 0 denote an increase, a decrease and no change, respectively.

example the rate of interest were independent of the leverage ratio ($\partial i/\partial h = 0$), the marginal cost of capital would become instead, $MC_K = p_2(a+i)$. Consequently no optimal solution with respect to both the labor and real capital inputs can be attained.

We found above that a rise in the total productivity (ψ) or the product price (p) leads the firm to use a more labor-intensive technique of production, while a reduction in the price of capital (p_2) or in the rate of depreciation of capital (a) has no effect at all on the labor intensity. These results—which differ from those of the neoclassical theory of production—can also be explained by the assumptions of given equity capital, a rising interest-rate function and exogenously given prices.

In addition we maintained that changes in the rate of profit tax (t_V) influenced neither the firm's choice of factor intensity nor its relative indebtedness. The base of the profit tax is value added after labor and interest costs have been subtracted which explains why we come to the same conclusion as that offered by the static profit-maximization models that the optimal labor intensity and leverage ratio are not affected by the rate of profit tax. Our model differs of course from the static ones in that changes in the profits tax rate during a given period affect the volume of labor and capital inputs and the amount of borrowed capital in the following periods.

The discount rate has been assumed to be independent of the leverage ratio. Thus exogenous changes in this rate do not influence the total marginal cost of borrowing, which explains why it does not influence the optimal leverage ratio either. If on the other hand the discount rate were an increasing function of indebtedness, the firm's marginal borrowing cost and its optimal leverage ratio would be affected by externally caused changes in the discount rate (see chapter 7, p. 100).[1]

[1] Both the profit tax and the exogenously determined discount rate always influence the

(b) *Internal finance and growth*

In section 5.3.1 we found that all changes in the exogenous factors which increase the rate of return on equity capital (r_E^*), i.e., a rise in the product price, a reduction of the labor price, etc., lead to the firm reducing its optimal pay-out ratio u^*. We also found that u^* is affected negatively by a decrease in the externally given discount rate (E_{k0}). Furthermore a reduction in E_{k0} or an increase in r_E^* implies that the growth of equity capital, total capital dividends, etc., increase. In contrast to E_{k0}, r_E^* not only influences the growth rate through its effect on u but also affects it directly. This means that if r_E^* and E_{k0} are increased by an equal number of percentage units, the growth rate increases despite the fact that no change occurs in the pay-out ratio.

A reduced profit tax rate is one of the exogenous factors in our model which through an increased rate of return on equity leads to a lower pay-out ratio. In two recent studies by Stiglitz [1973] and King [1974] which used capital-value models of the same type as our own the conclusion has been reached that the profit tax rate does not influence the firm's investment decisions. A crucial reason for Stiglitz' and King's findings seems to be that they assume that the volume of investment itself, rather than the pay-out ratio, is a control variable which the firm manipulates. From this it follows that investment decisions can take place independently of how the firm divides its profits between dividends and retained earnings.

According to Stiglitz and King, the condition which determines optimal investment volume is the same as in neoclassical investment theory—i.e., $MR_K = p\partial\hat{F}/\partial\hat{K} = MC_K = p_2(a+i)$. If the firm's investment policy is determined by this marginal condition, the profit tax naturally will not affect the share of profits which firms are willing to retain for continued expansion. In our model it is instead optimal indebtedness which is determined by the marginal condition, though with the difference that for us $MC_K = p_2(a+i+h\partial i/\partial h)$.

Finally it may be noted that Solow [1971] has analyzed the influence of profit taxation on the investment behavior of the firm using a capital-value model. He assumes that firms grow at a steady state rate and that depreciations for tax purposes are equal to true economic depreciation. In contrast to Stiglitz and King, Solow assumes the pay-out ratio simultaneously determine the dividends and investments in each period. This should explain why he obtained the same result as we do, namely, that an increase in the profits tax rate reduces the firm's rate of growth. Moreover, Solow's results are analogous to ours in that he finds that a higher product price, a lower capital-goods price and a lower discount rate increase the rate of investment and the rate of growth.

---

optimal labor intensity and leverage ratio as soon as costs of growth in production arise —see section 5.4.

5.4. Growth costs

The simplest way to take account of internal costs of growth is to let the growth rate of real capital enter the production function as an independent variable. Using the Cobb–Douglas production function, we have

$$\hat{F}_t = \psi \hat{L}_t^{\alpha} \hat{K}_t^{1-\alpha} f(\hat{v}_K), \tag{5: 16}$$

where $\hat{F}_t$ is the volume of production, ψ is the total productivity factor, $\hat{L}_t$ is the amount of labor, $\hat{K}_t$ is the amount of real capital, $\hat{v}_K$ is the rate of growth of $\hat{K}$ and $f(\hat{v}_K)$ is the growth factor. Note that according to the assumption of accelerating internal costs of growth, $\partial f/\partial \hat{v}_K < 0$ and $\partial^2 f/\partial \hat{v}_K^2 < 0$.

5.4.1. The optimization

When the growth of real capital is assumed to influence the productivity of labor and capital inputs, respectively, the firm's choice of labor intensity and leverage ratio no longer take place independently of the value which is assigned to the pay-out ratio. Maximization of capital value with respect to these three decision variables now gives the following optimum conditions (see appendix D, pp. 156–8).

$$p\alpha\psi \hat{l}^{\alpha-1} f(\hat{v}_K) = p_1 \tag{5: 17}$$

$$r = i + h\partial i/\partial h \tag{5: 18}$$

$$r_E - k\frac{\partial r_E}{\partial u}\frac{u}{r_E} = k - u\frac{\partial k}{\partial u}. \tag{5: 19}$$

From (5: 17) it is clear that the labor intensity ($\hat{l}$) is reduced when $\hat{v}_K$ increases since $\partial f/\partial \hat{v}_K < 0$. This means that, a reduction in the pay-out ratio implying an increased $\hat{v}_K$ leads to a reduction in $\hat{l}$. It is also clear that $\hat{l}$ is affected by changes in the leverage ratio (h). If for example h is less than the value of it, which maximizes the rate of return on equity, an increase in h will increase $\hat{v}_K$, which in turn leads to a decline of $\hat{l}$.

From this follows that the values of the three decision variables ($\hat{l}$, h and u) are determined simultaneously or, in other words that the firm's production finance and investment decisions are completely interdependent. This also means that the recursivity demonstrated earlier in the solution of the optimal values of the endogenous variables ceases to hold.

In (5: 19) the term $k(\partial r_E/\partial u)(u/r_E)$ expresses the marginal negative growth effect—i.e., when the pay-out ratio is reduced, the growth of real capital rises ($\partial \hat{v}_K/\partial u < 0$), which in turn reduces the rate of return on equity ($\partial r_E/\partial \hat{v}_K < 0$). Since $\partial r_E/\partial u$ is positive, it follows from (5: 19) that $r_E > k - u(\partial k/\partial u)$. As soon as costs are associated with the expansion of the firm it is obviously in the interest of its owners that the firm does not retain profits to such an extent that the marginal cost of doing so equals the rate of return on equity (note that this is in contrast to the optimum condition (5: 3)″ above).

5.4.2. The influence of the exogenous factors

The equations showing how the optimal values of endogenous variables are affected by the exogenous factors in the model are the same as before with three exceptions. As a result of the new optimum conditions, equations (5: 7) and (5: 8) are replaced by

$$\hat{l}^* = \left[\frac{p\alpha\psi f(\hat{v}_K^*)}{p_1}\right]^{1/(1-\alpha)} \tag{5: 20}$$

$$r = \frac{p^*}{p_2}\psi(l^*)^\alpha f(\hat{v}_K^*) - \frac{p_1}{p_2}l^* - a, \tag{5: 21}$$

and equation (5: 12) by[1]

$$u = \left[\frac{r_E - (1+e_{ru})E_{k0}}{(1-e_{ku}+e_{ru})E_{k1}}\right]^{1/e_{ku}}, \tag{5: 22}$$

where $e_{ru} = (\partial r_E/\partial u)(u/r_E)$.

Due to the assumption of balanced expansion of the firm and constant prices the rate of growth of real capital ($\hat{v}_K$) equals the rate of growth of all monetary non-ratio variables (v), i.e., at an optimum we have

$$v^* = \hat{v}_K^*. \tag{5: 23}$$

From (5: 20)–(5: 23), (5: 9)–(5: 11) and (5: 13)–(5: 15), it is clear that every exogenous change which leads to an increase of the optimal value of any of the endogenous variables $\hat{l}^*$, r^*, h^*, i^*, r_E^*, $(1-u^*)$, k^*, v^*, and P_t^* also increases $\hat{v}_K^*$. (See also the comments to the diagrammatic representation on p. 79.) The increasing $\hat{v}_K^*$ reduces the factor productivities, which in turn reduces the increases in the optimal values of these variables.[2] Obviously, the existence of such a negative growth effect decreases the sensitivity with which the firm reacts to changes in its environment.

It should be pointed out that the insertion of the growth rate of real capital ($\hat{v}_K$) into the production function cannot imply that the influence of the exogenous factors on the optimal values of the endogenous variables changes sign. The extra influence that follows from changed $\hat{v}_K$ is present only once an adjustment of the endogenous variables takes place. This growth effect can only theoretically be a cause of no adjustment being undertaken, which would happen if an initial increase in $\hat{v}_K$ immediately generated such extensive growth

---

[1] Note $k = E_{k0} + E_{k1}u^{e_{ku}}$ and $k - u(\partial k/\partial u) = E_{k0} + (1-e_{ku})E_{k1}u^{e_{ku}}$.

[2] What is said here holds with the exception of the influence of E_{t0} on i^* and of E_{i_0} on k^*.

Table 8. *Changes in the optimal values of certain endogenous variables associated with increases in the exogenous factors when growth costs exist*

Exogenous factor	Endogenous variable $\hat{l}^*$	r^*	h^*	i^*	r_E^*
p_2	+	−	−	−	−
a	+	−	−	−	−
E_{i0}	+	+	−	+	−
t_V	+	+	+	+	−
E_{k0}	+	+	+	+	+

Note: The signs + and − indicate increase and decrease, respectively. The signs to the left of the zig-zag line in the table show combinations where no influence existed when growth costs were assumed not to exist; the other changes of direction are the same as in the case with no growth costs. Table 8 constitutes a segment of table 7 covering lines 4–8 and columns 1–5.

costs that no increase is ever achieved. However, it seems unlikely that this would happen.

The simultaneity which is introduced into the model due to growth costs also gives us relationships between the optimal values of endogenous variables and exogenous factors where no such relationships existed before. In table 8 are summarized these relationships that merely concern the influence of p_2, a, E_{i0}, t_V and E_{k0} on $\hat{l}^*$, r^*, h^*, i^*, and r_E^*. When p_2, a, E_{i0}, t_V or E_{k0} is raised, growth (v_K^*) declines, which is the cause of the new relationships given in the table to the left of the zig-zag line.

5.5. A diagrammatic illustration

In this section the optimization analysis and the results of effects on the endogenous variables presented in sections 5.2–5.4 are summarized diagrammatically. We begin by assuming that there are no growth costs but later introduce them as a generalization of the model. In the figures we also let the profit tax rate equal zero.

(a) *The optimization procedure*

Figure 5*a* describes how the firm determines its optimal labor-capital ratio ($\hat{l}$).[1] The value of production per unit of capital and labor costs per unit of capital are represented by the curve $pF(\hat{l})/p_2$ and the line $p_1\hat{l}/p_2$, respectively. At the value of $\hat{l}$ where the production value curve has the same slope as the labor-cost line, i.e., where the distance between $pF(\hat{l})/p_2$ and $p_1\hat{l}/p_2$ is greatest, the optimum condition for labor input, $pF'(\hat{l})=p_1$, is satisfied (see point Q_1 on

[1] In order to simplify the symbols, the asterisks are here dropped from the optimal values.

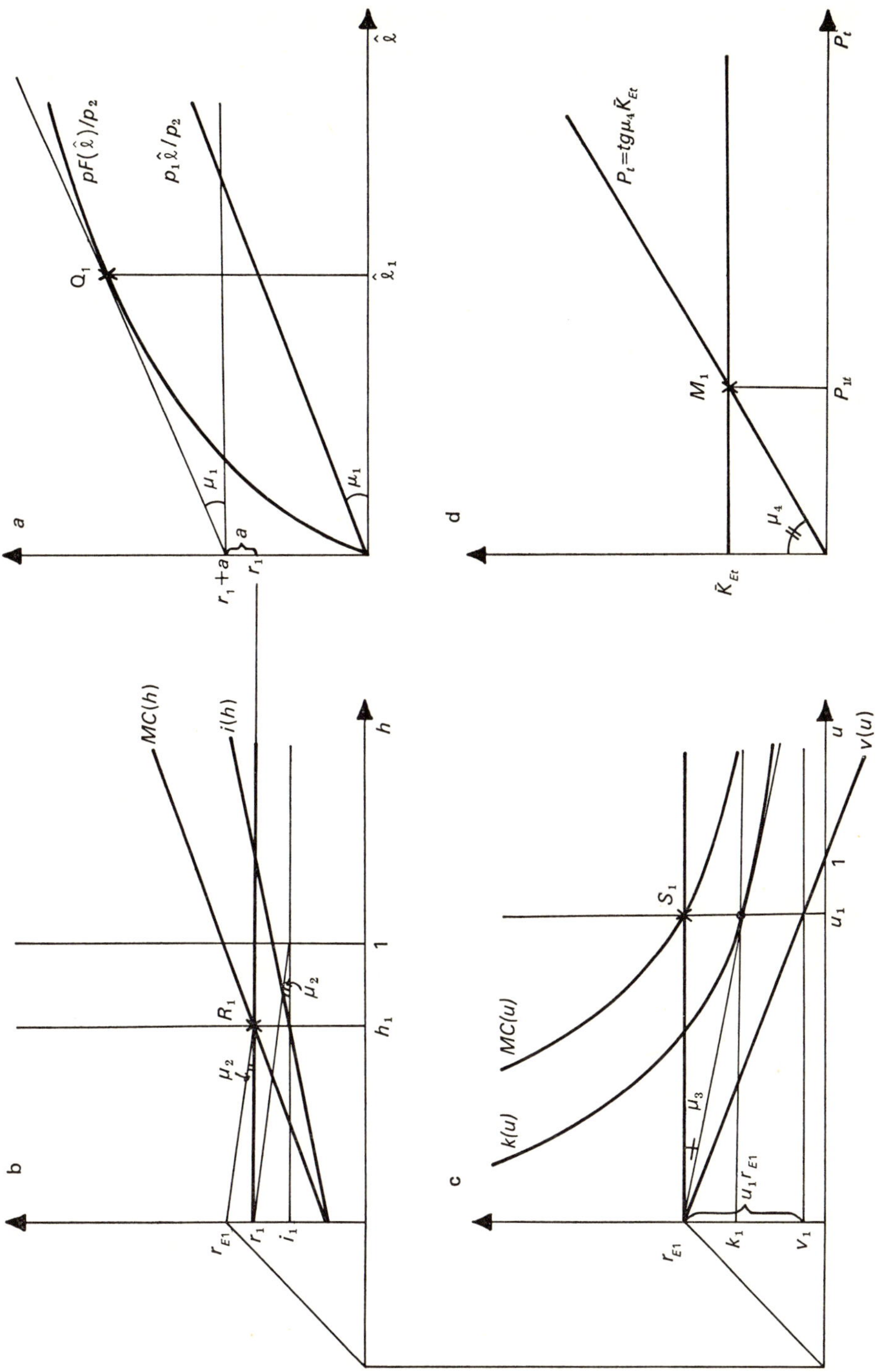

Figure 5. *Determination of the firm's production, finance and investment decisions*

the $pF(\hat{l})/p_2$-curve). We obtain in this way the optimal labor intensity $(\hat{l}_1)$. The identity (5: 8) then gives the maximum total profitability as $r_1 = pF(\hat{l}_1)/p_2 - p_1\hat{l}/p_2 - a$.

Figure 5*b* describes the firm's decision concerning debt finance. From figure 5*a* is carried over the total profitability line (r_1). The interest-rate function (5: 10) and its marginal cost function, $MC_h = i + h\partial i/\partial h$ are indicated by the lines $i(h)$ and $MC(h)$, respectively.[1] At the value of the leverage ratio (h) where the area $h(r-i)$ is greatest, the optimum condition for indebtedness $r = MC(h) = i + h\partial i/\partial h$ is satisfied (see point R_1 on the $MR(h)$-curve). This gives us the optimal leverage ratio (h_1). From the interest-rate curve is then obtained the interest rate (i_1). From the identity (5: 11) we get the maximum rate of return on equity (r_{E1}) through the construction tg $\mu_2 = (r_1 - i_1)/1 = (r_{E1} - r_1)/h_1$, since we have assumed that $t_V = 0$.

Figure 5*c* describes how the firm determines its optimal pay-out ratio. From figure 5*b* is carried over the rate of return line r_{E1}. The discount-rate function (5: 13) and its marginal cost function $MC_u = k - u\partial k/\partial u$ are indicated by the curves $k(u)$ and $MC(u)$, respectively. Also the growth identity (5: 14) is illustrated by the line $v(u)$. For every given pay-out ratio (u) we can draw a line which goes through the point $(0, r_{E1})$ and cuts the $k(u)$ curve. At the value of u where this line is tangent to the $k(u)$ curve, i.e., where the angle μ_3 between these lines is greatest, the optimum condition for pay-out $r_E = MC(u) = k - u\partial k/\partial u$ is satisfied (see point S_1 on the $MC(u)$-curve). In this way we obtain the optimal pay-out ratio (u_1). Then the discount rate (k_1) and the rate of growth (v_1) are obtained from the discount-rate curve $(k(u))$ and the growth line $v(u)$, respectively.

Finally the determination of the firm's capital value is described in figure 5*d*. The predetermined value of equity capital is depicted by the horizontal line $\bar{K}_{Et}$. The distances $u_1 r_{E1}$ and $(k_1 - v_1)$ are carried over from figure 5*c* thus giving us tg $\mu_4 = u_1 r_{E1}/(k_1 - v_1) = \varrho_1$. The highest valuation ratio (ϱ_1)[2] obtained at the point of intersection of the lines $K_{Et} = \bar{K}_{Et}$ and $P_t = \text{tg}\,\mu_4 \bar{K}_{Et}$.

The recursivity in the firm's decision process which was derived earlier, now stands out clearly in the figure. First, is determined the optimal labor intensity $(\hat{l}_1)$ which gives the maximum total profitability (r_1). Then, on the basis of r_1, the optimal leverage ratio (h_1) is obtained which gives the maximum return on equity (r_{E1}). On the basis of r_{E1} is determined at last the optimal pay-out ratio (u_1) which gives the maximum capital value (P_{1t}). We may also read off the inequalities $r_E > r > i$ and $r_E > k$ in figures 5*b* and 5*c*, respectively. Furthermore, since $\varrho = 1/(1-\delta)$, where $\delta = (r_E - k)/ur_E$ it follows that $\varrho > 1$ for $r_E > k$.

---

[1] In this diagrammatic presentation it is assumed that the interest-rate function is linear, i.e., $e_{ih} = 1$.

[2] This is clear from the fact that $\varrho = ur_E/(k-v)$ is maximized when the angle (μ_3) is greatest.

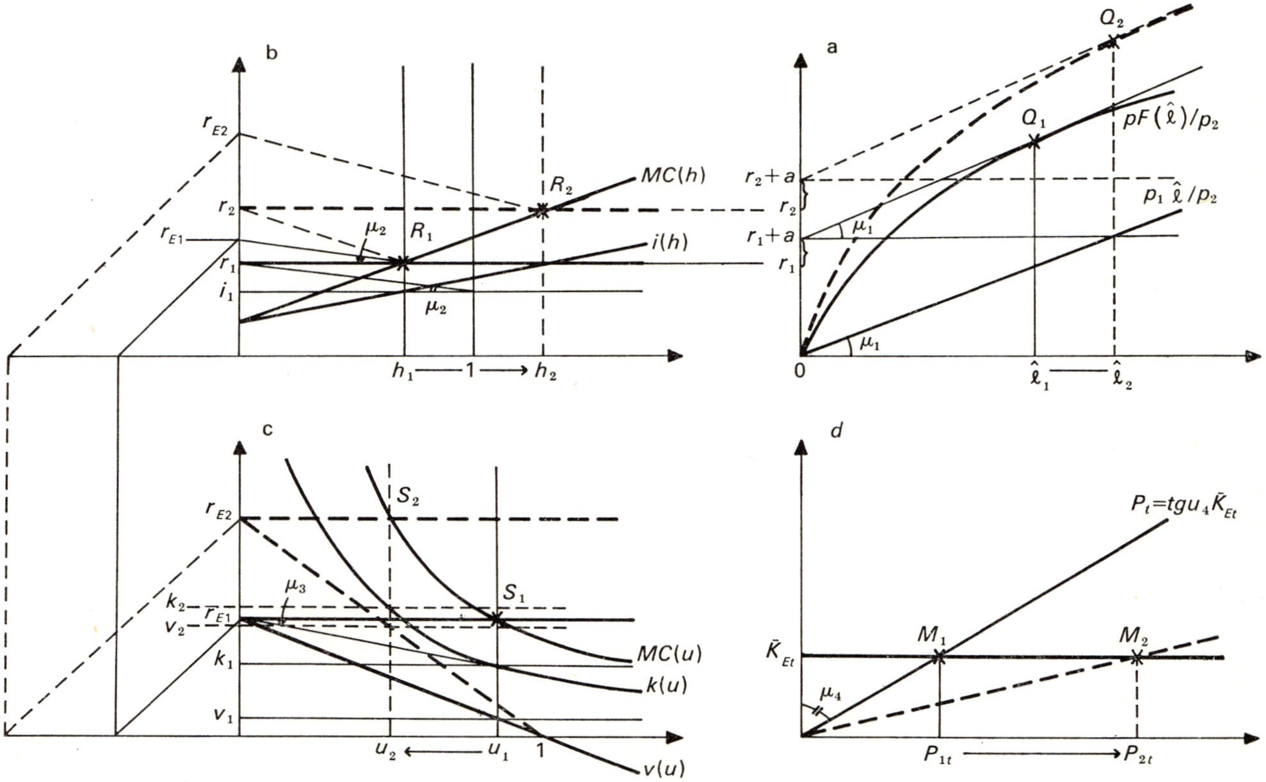

Figure 6. *Influence of external changes on the firm's production, finance and investment decisions*

(b) *The influence on firm behavior of changes in the exogenous factors*
In figures 6*a*–6*d* below is illustrated what happens when total productivity (ψ) or the product price (p) is raised. The function giving the value of production per unit of capital, $pF(\hat{l})/p_2$, is then twisted upward around its origin 0 and the new dashed curve $0Q_2$ is obtained. It has the same slope as the line $p_1\hat{l}/p_2$ at point Q_2 on the latter, from which it follows that the labor intensity increases to $\hat{l}_2$. The upward shift in the $pF(\hat{l})/p_2$-curve also implies that total profitability increases to r_2. The new higher, dashed total profitability line (r_2) cuts the MC_h-curve at point R_2, from which is obtained the leverage ratio (h_2). The interest rate is then raised to i_2.

The changes in these last three variables imply that the rate of return on equity rises. The new higher dashed line for the rate of return on equity r_{E2}, intersects the $MC(u)$-curve at S_2, which gives the pay-out ratio u_2. The variables u_2 and r_{E2} give a higher rate of growth of dividends and a higher discount rate corresponding to v_2 and k_2, respectively. Finally, u_2r_{E2} and (k_2-v_2) result in a higher valuation ratio. This is $\varrho_2=u_2r_{E2}/(k_2-v_2)$, which gives the capital value P_{2t} (given $\bar{K}_{Et}$).

It can also be shown that a reduction in the price of labor (p_1) causes changes in the optimal values of the endogenous variables in the same direction. When p_1 is reduced, the line $p_1\hat{l}/p_2$ is twisted downward around its origin 0, so that $\hat{l}$ increases since the point where this line and the curve $pF(\hat{l})/p_2$ have the same slope is shifted to the right. It then follows that r rises, h rises, etc.

In addition we see that a reduction in the price of capital (p_2) twists both the $pF(\hat{l})/p_2$-curve and the $p_1\hat{l}/p_2$-line upward by the same proportion, so that the value of $\hat{l}$ where they have the same slope is not moved. A reduction of the rate of depreciation of capital (a) twists neither $pF(\hat{l})/p_2$ nor $p_1\hat{l}/p_2$. This explains why changes in p_2 and a do not affect the firm's optimal factor intensity ($\hat{l}$). On the other hand, a reduction in either p_2 or a will raise the r-line, from which the same changes of direction then follow as when ψ or p is increased.

When the exogenously given rate of interest (E_{i0}) is reduced, a parallel shift downward of the $i(h)$- and $MC(h)$-lines in figure 6*b* takes place. Hence the $MC(h)$-line intersects the r-line further to the right, which causes h to increase and the distance $(r-i)$ to increase, which in turn leads to an increase of r_E, etc. But since the changes in the functions $i(h)$ and $MC(h)$ affect neither $pF(\hat{l})/p_2$ nor $p_1\hat{l}/p_2$, $\hat{l}$ and r remain unchanged.

A reduction of the profit tax rate (t_V) can be illustrated by raising the r_E-line. The point of intersection between this line and the $MC(u)$-curve in figure 6*c* is shifted to the left, so that the optimal pay-out ratio (u) declines, etc. Finally we find that a reduction of the exogenously given discount rate (E_{k0}) causes a parallel downward shift of the $MC(u)$-curve, from which it follows that u declines, etc. On the other hand none of the curves r, $i(h)$, $MC(h)$, $pF(\hat{l})/p_2$ or $p_1\hat{l}/p_2$ is shifted due to the changes in t_V or E_{k0}, which explains why they do not have any impact on $\hat{l}$, r and h.

(c) *Growth costs*

We have taken account of growth costs by allowing the growth rate of real capital to influence the firm's production volume negatively. Since all prices have been assumed exogenously given it follows from that the rate of growth of the volume of capital ($\hat{v}_K$) is equal to that of all monetary non-ratio variables (v). The curve for the value of production per unit of capital in figure 5a can then be written $pF(\hat{l}, v)/p_2$, where $\partial F/\partial v < 0$.

The interdependence of production, borrowing and pay-out decisions of the firm which now follow may be seen by the fact that the assigned values of the decision variables h and u determine the location of the $pF(\hat{l}, v)p_2$-curve through their influence on v. Only when this curve has been fixed can the optimal labor intensity ($\hat{l}$) be determined and thus also the optimal h and u. The lower the value assigned to u, the higher v will be, and the less will be the slope of this curve. In addition if, for example, h is lower than its optimum value which maximizes r_E and v, an increase in h implies that v increases, from which it follows that the curve for the value of production per capital unit becomes less steep.

It is also now clear that this negative growth effect brings about a feed back effect on the endogenous variables going in an opposite direction to that caused by the various external disturbances. Consider for example an autonomous shift downwards in the interest-rate function and its marginal cost function. Then the optimal leverage ratio, the rate of return on equity and the rate of growth increase. But the increased rate of growth reduces the slope of the $pF(\hat{l}, v)/p_2$-curve, which moderates the increase in the leverage ratio, rate of return on equity, etc.

CHAPTER 6

The model applied to empirical data

6.1. Introduction

In this chapter certain results derived theoretically from our dynamic steady-state model are tested empirically. We test marginal conditions for the maximization of the capital value of the firm with respect to its decision variables as well as the conclusions concerning the effects, on the optimum values of the decision variables, of changes in factors exogenous to the firm. We also carry out simulation studies in order to investigate how sensitive the optimal solutions are to exogenous changes. Furthermore we try to determine the "costs" in the form of a reduced capital value following from nonoptimal financial behavior.

The individual firm data which are utilized are the same as those used for the regressions of chapter 4—i.e., a cross section of 56 manufacturing firms quoted on the Stockholm stock exchange. The variables for each firm are the average of annual values for the period 1963–70, for which we have been able to obtain statistical data for identical firms.

6.2. Tests of inequality relations and marginal conditions

6.2.1. The inequality relations

We recall from chapter 5, pp. 68 f., that the maximization of capital value with respect to the leverage ratio and pay-out-ratio gives the following inequality relations:

$$r_E > r > i \tag{6: 1}$$

$$r_E > k > y, \tag{6: 2}$$

where r_E is the rate of return on equity, r is the rate of return on total capital, i is the interest rate, k is the discount rate, and y is the earnings-price relation.[1]

The first and the second column in table 9 show how many firms in our

[1] Definitions of the variables r_E, r, i, k and y are given in the list of variables, p. 123.

Table 9. *Firms satisfying the financing inequalities*

Inequality	Number of firms satisfying the inequality	Percentage of firms satisfying the inequality	Critical percentage value for random distribution
(1) $r>i$	53	95	66
(2) $r_E>r$	54	96	66
(3) $r_E>r>i$	52	93	29
(4) $k>y$	41	73	66
(5) $r_E>k$	43	77	66
(6) $r_E>k>y$	29	52	29

sample satisfy either the double inequalities (6: 1) and (6: 2) or the simple inequalities obtained from them. According to a common zero-one test the probability is 1 % that more than 66 % of the firms satisfy the simple inequalities and more than 29 % satisfy the double inequalities. These critical values are given in the third column of the table. For all inequalities the percentages in column 2 are greater than those in column 3. We interpret this result as indicating that the inequalities are satisfied to such an extent that one cannot explain it by chance.

The critical percentage values are calculated as follows: Every firm which satisfies a given inequality is assigned a value of unity; the others receive a value of zero. Consequently, for the simple inequalities the probability is 0.5 that a firm receives the value unity which is equal to the probability that it receives the value of zero assuming the operation of only random factors. For the double inequalities the corresponding probabilities are 1/6 and 5/6. Considering that the number of firms in one sample is 56, the simple inequalities have an expected mean value of 0.5 with a standard deviation $\sqrt{0.5\cdot 0.5/56}\approx 0.0671$, and the double inequalities have an expected mean value of 0.167 with standard deviation $\sqrt{0.167\cdot 0.833/56}\approx 0.0500$. These mean values of the zero-one observations may be regarded as approximately normally distributed. This means that only 1 % of the sample means for the simple inequalities will exceed $0.5+2.33\cdot 0.0671=0.6561$ by chance. The corresponding critical value for the double inequalities is $0.167+2.33\cdot 0.0500=0.2835$.

We have also calculated the percentage in our sample and the critical percentage (at the 1 % level) for simultaneous satisfaction of the double-inequalities (3) and (6), which follow from the model when capital value is simultaneously maximized with respect to the leverage ratio and the payout ratio. The sample percentage is 50 % and the critical percentage is $0.05+2.33\sqrt{0.05\cdot 0.95/56}\approx 12$ %.[1]

The statistical measures of the rate of return and the discount rate which

[1] The figure 0.05 has been obtained by taking into account the number of possible rank orderings between the five variables in the inequalities (3) and (6) which is $5!=120$. Of these only six simultaneously fulfill the inequalities mentioned.

we use are influenced by firms depreciating capital assets in excess of the true economic depreciation (to obtain tax credits) and revaluing them over time. Since the inequalities were derived under the assumption that the profitability and discount-rate variables were not influenced by such factors, the same tests are carried out on the basis of corrected variable values—i.e., values which one would obtain if neither excessive depreciation nor revaluations occurred—in appendix E, p. 160. We then find that all inequalities are still satisfied at the 1 % confidence level.

It should be pointed out that the inequalities are very weak conditions for an optimum. First, inequalities can hold for values of the leverage ratio and pay-out ratio which diverge from the optimal. (See pp. 76–8.) Second, if the optimum solution should imply a non-positive leverage ratio or a pay-out ratio greater than one, it can be shown that instead the following inequalities hold:[1]

$$r \leqslant i \tag{6: 3}$$

$$k \leqslant y. \tag{6: 4}$$

All firms in our sample have a leverage ratio which is greater than zero but six firms have a pay-out ratio which is greater than one. Of these six firms four have a discount rate (k) which is less than their earnings-price ratio (y). Since the actual values of all the financial variables given here for each firm are calculated as the average of annual values for the period 1963–70, external disturbances during this period might be a cause of these firms having dividends temporarily greater than the net earnings.

6.2.2. The marginal conditions

In chapter 5, pp. 67 f., we derived the following marginal (first-order necessary) conditions with respect to the leverage ratio and the pay-out ratio.[2]

$$r = i + h\partial i/\partial h \tag{6: 5}$$

$$r_E = k - u\partial k/\partial u. \tag{6: 6}$$

[1] According to our optimal borrowing condition (5: 4) $r = i + h\partial i/\partial h$, $h \leqslant 0$ implies $r \leqslant i$. According to the identity $k - y = (1-u)(r_E - k)/u$, $u \geqslant 1$ implies $k \leqslant y$. Observe $r_E > k$ and $y = r_E K_E/P = (k - (1-u)r_E)/u$.

[2] The definitions of the variables in equations (6: 5) and (6: 6) are given in the variable list, pp. 122 f.

The reason why we do not test the marginal condition for the optimal labor intensity is that it has not been possible to obtain for every firm satisfactory measures of the volume of production and of the product price, which enter this optimum condition. Nor has it seemed possible to obtain a reliable regression estimate of the partial derivative ($\partial r_E/\partial u$), which enters the marginal condition for the optimal pay-out ratio (5: 19) when growth costs are assumed to exist. This is the reason why we do not test this optimum condition empirically either.

Table 10. *Calculated normalized deviations from the marginal conditions*

Marginal conditions	Normalized deviation ($\hat{d}_i$)
1. $r - i = b_{ih} h$	7.31
2. $r - i = e_{ih}(i - E_{i0})$	6.98
3. $r_E - k = -b_{ku} u$	−1.58
4. $r_E - k = -e_{ku}(k - E_{k0})$	−1.35

Note: In the first two rows the normalized deviation is calculated on the basis of the linear and linear-multiplicative interest-rate functions, respectively, and in the last two rows on the basis of the linear and linear-multiplicative discount-rate functions, respectively.

From a random distribution the confidence interval for $\hat{d}_i$ around zero at 95 % is (0 ± 1.96) or at 99 per cent is (0 ± 2.58).

In order to determine the extent to which there exists in our sample of firms a systematic difference between the left and right sides of (6: 5) and (6: 6), the normalized differences ($\hat{d}_i$) are calculated for both of these marginal conditions. In doing so, we use the regression coefficients in the interest-rate and the discount-rate function estimated by the two-stage method in chapter 4. Table 10 presents the calculated values of $\hat{d}_i$. It is clear from the table that $\hat{d}_1$ and $\hat{d}_2$ are significantly different from zero at the 1 % confidence level, while $\hat{d}_3$ and $\hat{d}_4$ are not significant at even the 5 % level.

With respect to the calculation of the $\hat{d}_i$, this may be said: For the linear regression of the interest-rate and discount-rate functions $\partial i/\partial h = b_{ih} = 0.0059$ and $\partial k/\partial u = b_{ku} = -0.0834$, and for the linear-multiplicative regression of these functions $\partial i/\partial h = e_{ih}(\bar{i} - E_{i0})/\bar{h}$ and $\partial k/\partial u = e_{ku}(\bar{k} - E_{k0})/\bar{u}$, where $E_{i0} = 0.0000$, $e_{ih} = 0.4689$, $E_{k0} = -0.0050$ and $e_{ku} = -0.6062$ see tables 3–6. We have $\bar{h} = 1.7268$, $\bar{i} = 0.0283$, $\bar{u} = 0.7638$, $\bar{k} = 0.0906$, $\bar{r} = 0.0758$ and $\bar{r}_E = 0.1356$.

If the b- and e-coefficients are the same for each firm, the following average differences $\bar{d}_i$ are obtained for all firms:

$$\bar{d}_1 = (\bar{r} - \bar{i}) - \bar{h} b_{ih} = 0.0373$$
$$\bar{d}_2 = (\bar{r} - \bar{i}) - (\bar{i} - E_{i0}) e_{ih} = 0.0342$$
$$\bar{d}_3 = (\bar{r}_E - \bar{k}) + \bar{u} b_{ku} = -0.0187$$
$$\bar{d}_4 = (\bar{r}_E - \bar{k}) + (\bar{k} - E_{k0}) e_{ku} = -0.0130.$$

Then we estimate the standard error of every $\bar{d}_i$ which are $\bar{\sigma}_1 = 0.0051$, $\bar{\sigma}_2 = 0.0049$, $\bar{\sigma}_3 = 0.0118$ and $\bar{\sigma}_4 = 0.0096$. Finally, we estimate $\hat{d}_i = \bar{d}_i / \bar{\sigma}_i$, since $E(\hat{d}_i) = 0$ according to the null hypothesis which we are testing here.

We have also, in appendix E, p. 161, calculated the differences $\hat{d}_i$ on the basis of values of the rate of return and discount-rate variables which have been corrected for excess depreciation and capital revaluation. It then turns out that $\hat{d}_1$ and $\hat{d}_2$ lie outside the 1 % confidence interval, and $\hat{d}_3$ and $\hat{d}_4$ lie within it.

Concerning the marginal borrowing condition, it should be pointed out that the firms may take into account that an increased indebtedness increases the financial risk for their owners. This means increasing the discount rate with higher leverage ratio. In optimum total profitability (r) will then exceed the marginal cost ($i+h\partial i/\partial h$) as our test results suggest.[1] In addition the value of ($i+h\partial i/\partial h$), which we have calculated can be expected to underestimate the actual marginal borrowing cost of the firm, our measure of borrowed capital includes commercial short term credits which the suppliers of the goods to the firm receive in exchange for higher prices. For these debts the firms often pay a very low interest or none at all.

6.3. Tests of certain effects of exogenous changes

Here, we test empirically our earlier derived results concerning the influence on the firm's financial decision of exogenously caused changes in the rate of return on total capital, the interest rate and the discount rate. The influence of the other exogenous factors in the model (the product price, the prices of labor and real capital, the rate of depreciation of capital, etc.) have not been tested due to lack of statistical measures.

6.3.1. The leverage-ratio relationship

In chapter 5, p. 71, we showed that firms increase their optimal leverage ratio (h) if the exogenously given rate of return on total capital ($\check{r}$) is raised or the exogenously given interest rate ($\check{i}$) is reduced. For the empirical testing of these conclusions we use the following relationship

$$h=\beta_1+\beta_2\check{i}+\beta_3\check{r}, \tag{6: 7}$$

where $\check{i}$ and $\check{r}$ are defined as that part of the interest rate and total rate of return, respectively, which according to our model is affected neither directly nor indirectly by the decisions of the firm. This means that $\check{r}$ and $\check{i}$ are not permitted to vary between firms as a result of differences in their growth rates, leverage ratios and pay-out ratios. When we measure $\check{r}$ and $\check{i}$, we utilize the two-stage estimated coefficients in the linear profitability and interest-rate function. Assuming that these coefficients (b_{rv} and b_{ih}) are the same for every firm, we obtain for firm j the measures $\check{r}_j=r_j-b_{rv}v_{0j}$ and $\check{i}_j=i_j-b_{ih}h_j$, where

---

[1] See the optimum condition (7: 6) in the next chapter $\partial r_E/\partial h-(\partial k/\partial h)(r_E/k)=0$, where $\partial r_E/\partial h=r-(i+h\ \partial i/\partial h)$.

The only regression coefficient for the discount rate (k) with respect to the leverage ratio (h) which was significant at the 5 % level is that in the linear equation in table 5. Since this coefficient $b_{kh}=\partial k/\partial h=0.0076$, we get $d_1=\partial r_E/\partial h-b_{kh}(\bar{r}_E/\bar{k})=0.0373-0.0114=0.0259$. In addition $\bar{\sigma}_1=0.0105$, and we obtain $\hat{d}_1=2.467$, which is insignificant at the 1 % level.

r, v_0 and i are the actual values of the rate of return on total capital, total profitability, growth rate of sales and interest rate respectively.[1]

It is clear from the regression estimates given in table 11 that the coefficient of the exogenous interest rate is negative and significantly different from zero at the 5 % level in both equation 1 and 2. The negative signs show, as we expect, that the propensity to incur debt varies inversely with the part of the interest rate which is determined by external factors. The great numerical values of the coefficients suggest that debt finance is strongly sensitive to changes in the interest rate.

We also find that the coefficient of the profitability variable is negative and highly significant. However, that profitability affects the leverage ratio negatively conflicts with our theoretical conclusion that the capital-value maximizing firms will always increase indebtedness when their profitability is raised. What, then, is the reason for this unexpected result?[2] Here will be given some conceivable explanations.

First, the firms' debt policy may be influenced by factors which we did not take into account in the estimation of (6: 7) and which vary with total profitability. For example, it is not unlikely that firms have the possibility of choosing the alternative of reducing the range of the product-mix and/or devoting resources to the development of new products which would involve both a higher expected level of profit and higher expected risk. This would explain why the more profitable firms, despite their higher profitability, are less willing to finance their operations through debt. An increased degree of risk in production ought to express itself through a higher variability of profit σ_r^2, and higher exogenous discount rate ($\breve{k}$). Therefore we have carried out regressions with these two risk variables included as independent variables in equation (6: 7).[3] While the value of the profitability coefficient fell in these regressions, it still retained its negative sign.

Second, the time period (1963–70) which our cross-sectional data cover may be too short to satisfactorily describe firms' decisions concerning long-term debt finance. If debt financing is determined residually in the short run[4] to a

---

[1] Appendix E, pp. 162 f., describes in more detail how $\breve{r}$ and $\breve{i}$ are measured.

[2] Note that a strongly negative covariation also exists between the leverage ratio and actual total profitability.

[3] The measure which we used for σ_r^2 for every firm was

$$\sigma_r^2 = \tfrac{1}{8} \sum_{i=63}^{70} (r_i - \bar{r})^2 \quad \text{where} \quad \bar{r} = \tfrac{1}{8} \sum_{i=63}^{70} r_i,$$

and r_i is total profitability in year i. Concerning the measure used for $\breve{k}$, see the next section.

[4] The decisions concerning internal finance (dividends) ought to be strongly affected by the firm's unwillingness to incur the risk of being forced to reduce dividends, since reduced dividends can involve large declines in the price of the firm's shares. Dividends should therefore not be allowed to vary due to short-run fluctuations in the firm's profits. The

Table 11. *Regression estimates for the leverage ratio with the exogenous values of the interest rate and total profitability as explanatory variables*

Equ. 1 $h = 2.642 - 46.506 \cdot \breve{\imath}$	$R^2 = 0.1070$
(18.196)	
Equ. 2 $h = 3.636 - 37.318 \cdot \breve{\imath} - 11.702 \cdot \breve{r}$	$R^2 = 0.2377$
$(17.252) \quad\;\; (3.897)$	

higher degree than internal and external equity financing and if investment is planned on a long horizon and carried out according to fixed plans, then occasional, unexpected changes in profitability will mean that firms let the leverage ratio vary inversely with profitability over time. This would be capable of causing a negative relationship between these variables in the cross section of firms for shorter time periods despite debt decisions which in the long run aim at the maximization of capital value.

Third, firms may in addition to maximization of capital value strive to achieve greater financial flexibility and independence of lenders. Then the leverage ratio would enter the firm's utility function along with capital value as a negative argument. If at the same time capital value is relatively insensitive to changes in indebtedness, it is possible that long-run optimal debt finance behavior would imply that firms reduce the leverage ratio when exogenously given profitability is raised. (In section 6.4.2 we will present results which indicate that capital value is affected relatively little by variations in the leverage ratio.)

6.3.2. The relationship for the pay-out ratio

In chapter 5, p. 71, it was shown that the firm reduces its optimal pay-out ratio (u) when the exogenously given total profitability ($\breve{r}$) rises or the exogenously given discount rate ($\breve{k}$) decreases or the exogenously given interest rate ($\breve{\imath}$) decreases.

In order to test these results empirically, we perform a regression with the following linear relationship

$$u = \beta_1' + \beta_2' \breve{\imath} + \beta_3' \breve{r} + \beta_4' \breve{k}. \tag{6:8}$$

In principle $\breve{k}$ is defined in the same way as $\breve{\imath}$ and $\breve{r}$ above—i.e. we calculate $\breve{k}$ as that part of the discount rate which should not be affected directly or in-

---

market value of shares ought also to be influenced negatively if the firm secures funds for its new investments through issuing new shares. In addition finance through new share issues is an administratively more troublesome method of finance for large firms than increased borrowings.

Table 12. *Regression estimates for the pay-out ratio with exogenous values of the interest rate, total profitability and the discount rate as explanatory variables*

Equ. 1	$u = 1.2407 - 4.7504 \cdot \check{r}$ (0.8411)	$R^2 = 0.3714$
Equ. 2	$u = 0.7653 - 4.9243 \cdot \check{r} + 3.3767 \cdot \check{k}$ $(0.7911) \quad (1.1662)$	$R^2 = 0.4572$
Equ. 3	$u = 0.7278 - 4.9836 \cdot \check{r} + 3.4954 \cdot \check{k} + 1.3272 \cdot \check{i}$ $(0.8148) \quad (1.2220) \quad (3.7191)$	$R^2 = 0.4586$

directly by the firm's decision variables. (See appendix E, pp. 162 f.) The estimations are carried out stepwise with a varying number of variables. The regression estimates of (6: 8) are presented in table 12.

From the table it is clear that all regression coefficients for $\check{r}$-, $\check{k}$- and $\check{i}$-variables have the signs we expect. However, only $\check{r}$- and $\check{k}$-coefficients are significant at the 5 % level. Note also that the values of the regression coefficients suggest that in their dividend policies firms react more strongly to a given change in profitability than to an equal change in the discount rate.

Furthermore, it may be observed that the intercept term is greater than unity when only profitability is an explanatory variable—see equation 1—which indicates that if profitability is zero but the interest rate and discount rate are greater than zero, the firm will pay out more than its profits, i.e., it will continuously reduce its size.

The values of the multiple coefficient of determination (R^2) for the three equations in the table indicate that 35–45 % of the variation in the pay-out ratio between firms is explained by the independent variables in these equations. The F-ratios of the equations (not given in the table) take values of 15–30 which indicate a rather good explanatory power of the regressions as a whole. These F-ratios exclude by a wide margin the possibility that the independent variables which we have included do not explain any of the variation in the pay-out ratio between firms.

6.4. Sensitivity analysis

In chapter 5 was shown the direction in which the firm's optimal endogenous variables are affected by external changes. However, this analysis did not say anything either about the size of the changes in endogenous variables following a given change in each exogenous factor or about the extent to which the effects on the endogenous variables are systematically changed with changed values of the exogenous factors. Therefore, we shall try to carry out such a quantitative analysis of the firm's optimal adjustment.

6.4.1. The influence of exogenous factors

(a) *Calculations*

In order to quantify the influence of the exogenous factors on the optimal values of the endogenous variables, we use equations (5: 7)–(5: 15). To simplify the calculations, it is assumed that the profitability on total capital is exogenous. This implies that equations (5: 7) and (5: 8) drop out. We also let the valuation ratio $\varrho^* = P_t^*/K_{Et}$ be a measure of the relative capacity of the firm to generate future dividends. This means that (5: 15) is replaced by the relation $\varrho^* = u^* r_E^* / (k^* - v^*)$.

The coefficients E_{i1}, e_{ih}, E_{k1} and e_{ku} in the interest-rate function (5: 10) and the discount-rate function (5: 13) are assigned the values earlier estimated with the two-stage least squares method (see tables 4 and 6). The profit tax-rate is given the value 0.30. Below we calculate only the effects on the endogenous variables of changes in the exogenously determined total profitability ($\bar{r}$), the interest rate (E_{i0}), and the discount rate E_{k0}.

(b) *Results*

In appendix E, pp. 163–6, are presented diagrammatically the values of the endogenous variables which we have computed when:

1) $\bar{r}$ is varied, given that $E_{i0} = 0.02$ and $E_{k0} = 0.00$ (Figure E: 1);
2) E_{i0} is varied, given that $\bar{r} = 0.08$ and $E_{k0} = 0.00$ (Figure E: 2);
3) E_{k0} is varied, given that $\bar{r} = 0.08$ and $E_{i0} = 0.02$ (Figure E: 3).

From figure E: 1 it is clear that the optimal leverage ratio (h^*), the rate of return on equity (r_E^*), the discount rate (k^*), the growth of dividends (v^*), and the valuation ratio (ϱ^*) increase at an increasing rate while the optimal pay-out ratio (u^*) declines at a decreasing rate when the exogenously determined total profitability ($\bar{r}$) is raised. The reverse is true according to figure E: 2 when the exogenous interest rate (E_{i0}) is raised. The influence of E_{i0} is also uniformly weaker than that of $\bar{r}$.[1]

When the exogenous discount rate (E_{k0}) is raised, u^* increases more quickly, and v^* declines more slowly. Also, ϱ^* declines at a decreasing rate. On the other hand, neither h^* nor r_E^* is affected by changes in E_{k0}. Note, however, that if we had introduced growth costs into the model by letting total profitability be a negative function of the firm's growth,[2] an increased E_{k0} would, through reduced growth, have increased total profitability, which in turn would have increased h^* and r_E^*.

In table 13 are given the average values of the changes in h^*, u^*, v^* and ϱ^*

[1] This is seen from the fact that the curves for each endogenous variable have a greater slope in figure E: 1 than in figure E: 2, at the same value of the endogenous variable.

[2] The model would then have had to be expanded with the equation $r = f(v) + E_{r0}$ where $\partial f/\partial v < 0$, and the exogenously determined total profitability equals E_{r0}.

following from a one percentage rise in $\bar{r}$, E_{i0} and E_{k0} within four different intervals of values of these exogenous rate variables. Table 13 makes quite clear the increased effect on the leverage ratio (h^*), the growth of dividends (v^*), and the valuation ratio (ϱ^*), with higher $\bar{r}$ and lower E_{i0}, respectively. In particular, observe the strong sensitivity of ϱ^*. The effect on ϱ^* of one percentage change in $\bar{r}$ is about more than seventy times stronger within the last interval of the most profitable firms than within the first interval of the least profitable firms. The differences in relative effects of a change in E_{i0} are almost as great between firms with the lowest and highest exogenous interest rates.

The partial effects of each exogenous rate variable which have been shown here are not independent of the values of the other two exogenous rate variables, which have been held constant. For example, as far as the influence from the $\bar{r}$ variable is concerned, it is clear from equations (5: 9)–(5: 15) that the greater the difference between $\bar{r}$ and E_{i0}, the more strongly h^*, v^* and ϱ^* are affected when either $\bar{r}$ or E_{i0} is changed. This can be interpreted to mean that the effect of exogenous changes on the optimal debt, growth rate and share value should be especially strong for firms which have a high profitability and which at the same time are judged by lenders to have low-risk operations.

(c) *Explanations*

Two factors make both the optimal leverage ratio and rate of return on equity rise at an increasing rate when the exogenous total profitability is raised or when the exogenous interest rate is reduced. First, the gap between total profitability ($\bar{r}$) and the exogenous part of the interest rate (E_{i0}) is increased at all values of the leverage ratio. Second, the interest rate is a rising (at a declining rate) function of the leverage ratio (i.e., the elasticity (e_{ih}) in this function has a value between zero and unity).

Two factors make the optimal pay-out ratio decline at a diminishing rate when the exogenous profitability ($\bar{r}$) is raised or the exogenous part of the discount rate (E_{k0}) is reduced; the gap between the rate of return on equity (r_E and E_{k0}) is widened at all values of the pay-out ratio, and the discount rate is a decreasing function at a declining rate of the pay-out ratio (the elasticity (e_{ku}) in this function is less than zero).

That the optimal rate of growth of dividends increases at an accelerating rate when exogenous total profitability is raised or the exogenous part of interest rate is reduced is due, in turn, to the accelerating increase in the rate of return on equity.

We also recall that the optimal valuation ratio (ϱ^*) is insignificantly affected by a change in total profitability at low values of profitability but is affected noticeably at high values. A contributing factor is the strengthened positive effect on the optimal leverage ratio. Another cause is the high sensitivity of the valuation ratio to variations in total profitability when the difference be-

Table 13. *Simulated changes in the optimal values of the endogenous variables following from changes in exogenous factors*

Endogenous variable	Average change in the optimal value of the endogenous variable with one percentage point increase of											
	total profitability ($\bar{r}$) within the interval[a]				the interest rate (E_{i0}) within the interval [b]				the discount rate (E_{k0}) within the interval[c]			
	0.040–0.055	0.060–0.075	0.080–0.095	0.100–0.115	−0.005–0.010	0.015–0.030	0.035–0.050	0.055–0.070	−0.020–−0.005	0.000–0.015	0.020–0.035	0.040–0.055
h^*	0.154	0.285	0.425	0.570	−0.533	−0.389	−0.252	−0.123	0	0	0	0
u^*	−0.328	−0.194	−0.119	−0.070	0.070	0.067	0.042	0.023	0.056	0.092	0.173	0.396
v^*	0.010	0.014	0.020	0.028	−0.018	−0.010	−0.004	−0.001	−0.005	−0.008	−0.014	−0.033
ϱ^*	0.069	0.139	0.429	5.646	−0.686	−0.168	−0.054	−0.013	−0.823	−0.225	−0.091	−0.036

[a] The variables E_{i0} and E_{k0} are held constant at the values 0.02 and 0.00, respectively.
[b] The variables $\bar{r}$ and E_{k0} are held constant at the values 0.08 and 0.00, respectively.
[c] The variables $\bar{r}$ and E_{i0} are held constant at the values 0.08 and 0.02, respectively.

tween the discount rate and the rate of growth of dividends is small. We note that high values of total profitability imply low values of this difference.[1]

Even if the leverage ratio is held constant, the rate of growth of dividends will eventually approach the discount rate as total profitability continues to increase. This means that the valuation ratio and capital value, despite the absence of a positive effect from an increasing leverage ratio, can be expected to be affected very strongly, sooner or later, by a rise in total profitability when it assumes high values.

6.4.2. Inoptimal financial behavior

The purpose of this section is to show the consequences for the wealth of stockholders which can result from inoptimal financial decisions. This is done by computing a series of values of the valuation ratio (ϱ) for various given values of the financial decision variables, the leverage ratio (h) and the pay-out ratio (u).

We use the same model here as in section 6.4.1. All three exogenous rate variables ($\bar{r}$, E_{t0} and E_{k0}) are now held constant at the values 0.08, 0.02 and 0.00, respectively. Equation (5: 9) drops out when h varies, and equation (5: 12) drops out when u varies. It should be pointed out that according to the optimal solutions in chapter 5, h and u are not given magnitudes, but are determined endogenously in the model. However, in order to examine how sensitive our results are to incorrect financial decisions, we temporarily assume that h and u are not adjusted so as to maximize the capital value of the firm.[2]

Figure 7 shows the calculated relationship between the leverage ratio (h) and the valuation ratio (ϱ). We recall that the interest rate increases very slowly with increased debt finance according to the regression results in chapter 4. As a result, the rate of return on equity, rate of growth of dividends and discount rate will not be affected markedly by changes in the leverage ratio in the neighborhood of the value of the leverage ratio maximizing the rate of return on equity. This explains in turn why the valuation ratio in figure 7 is scarcely affected by variations in the leverage ratio.

Deviation of the leverage ratio by ten percentage points above or below its optimum value gives a valuation ratio which practically agrees with its maximal value. While an increased deviation increases the effect of changed leverage ratio, even a deviation which is as great as thirty percentage points still gives an almost insignificant effect. Such a deviation in the leverage ratio would reduce the valuation ratio by a couple of hundredths of its maximum value.

These results can be interpreted to show that the welfare losses for owners due to falling capital value as a consequence of inoptimal debt decisions are

---

[1] Naturally the causal factors mentioned here also make ϱ^* rise slowly at first and then very quickly when E_{t0} is reduced.

[2] See the observations of Brems [1976].

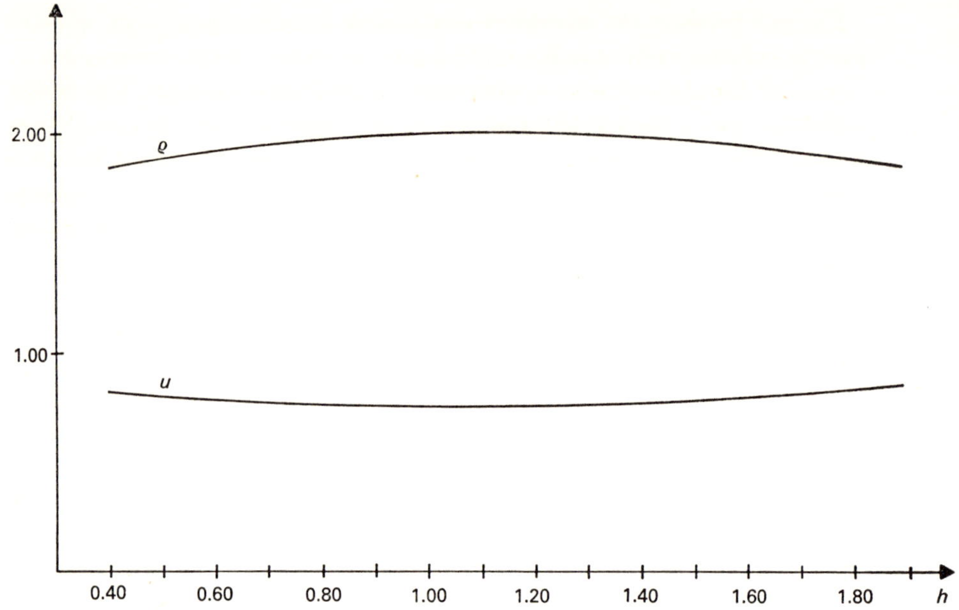

Figure 7. *Simulated relationship between the leverage ratio and the valuation ratio*

of minor significance so long as the departures from the optimal leverage ratio are held to within 40–50 percentage points in each direction. This in turn could explain why we found a negative empirical relationship between the leverage ratio and total profitability above, assuming that an increased indebtedness in itself is experienced as something undesirable by the owners—see p. 88.

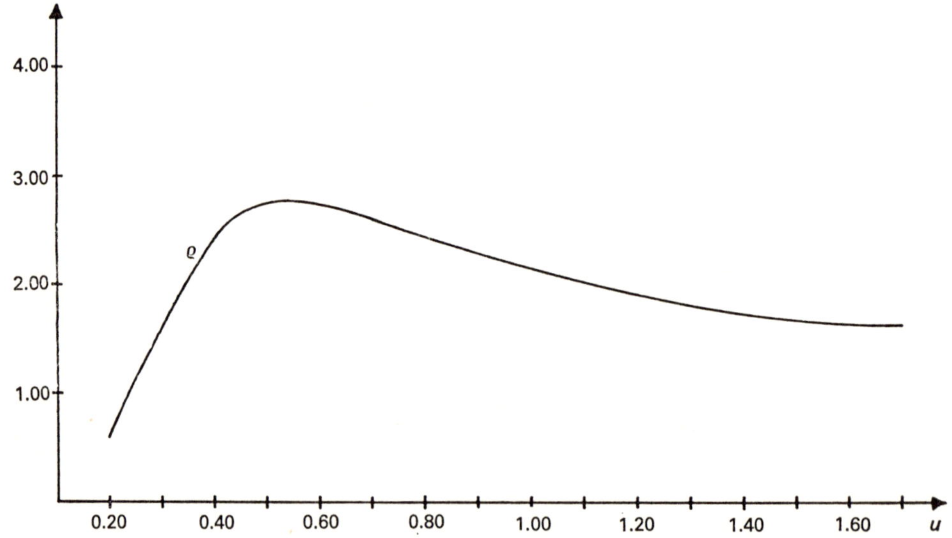

Figure 8. *Simulated relationship between the pay-out ratio and the valuation ratio*

Figure 8 presents the calculated relationship between the pay-out ratio (u) and the valuation ratio (ϱ). We see that ϱ rises quickly at first, reaches a maximum, and then falls slowly as u takes on values from zero on up. This is due to the fact that at low levels of the pay-out ratio, even a rather small reduction of this variable will involve a relatively significant decline in near-term dividends at the same time as the discount rate begins to rise sharply. In contrast to debt financing inoptimal dividend (investment) decisions can, according to the assumptions and the model which have been used here, cause the firm's owners considerable welfare losses through reduced capital value.

CHAPTER 7

Generalizations of the model

In this chapter some generalizations of the model are presented in order to make it more realistic. These are:

1) The firm acquires capital through issuing new shares.
2) The discount rate is a positive function of the leverage ratio.
3) The exogenously given product price and the prices of the factors of production, labor and capital change over time.
4) The firm has other objectives than maximization of capital value.

The same assumptions and the same model as in chapter 5 continue to apply in the analysis below except for the generalization. An important purpose of this chapter is to determine the extent to which the earlier theoretical results are changed by these generalizations.

7.1. Finance through new share issues

Increased issuing of new shares increases the inflow of cash to the firm and thus has the same effect on the distribution over time of net dividend payments from the firm as a reduced retention of profits. Finance through new issues can be regarded as negative internal finance.

7.1.1. Optimality conditions

Assume that the funds acquired through new issues in each period constitute a time-invariant proportion (c) of profit on equity. Assume further that no transaction costs are connected with the share issue, and no taxation exists. We then obtain net dividends from the firm (dividends minus the inflow of funds due to new issues) for the period t, $U'_t=(u-c)r_E K_{Et}$, the steady-state growth rate of the net dividends, $v=(1-u+c)r_E$, and the present value of all future net dividends discounted back to t[1]

$$P'_t=(u-c)r_E K_{Et}/[k-(1-u+c)r_E]. \tag{7: 1}$$

If the discount rate (k) is a function only of the net pay-out ratio ($u-c$) it is

[1] For definitions of the variables in equation (7: 1), see the variable list, pp. 122 f.

clear from (7: 1) that an equally large change in pay-out ratio (u) or new-issue ratio (c) does not affect P'_t. This means that the firm's net worth is independent of the choice between internal finance and new-issue finance and that both of these ways of acquiring capital can be regarded as perfect substitutes. Thus no determinate solution with respect to u and c which maximizes P'_t should exist. However, there is reason to believe that the discount rate (k) is affected by the chosen finance mix.[1]

Once shares are offered to new stockholders whose risk aversion, liquidity preference and valuation of the firm differ from those of the existing stockholders, the discount rate (k) should also be dependent on the relation between u and c. We therefore write

$$k = k(u, c).^{2} \tag{7: 2}$$

In chapter 5 we assumed that k rises at an increasing rate when the pay-out ratio declines—i.e., $\partial k/\partial u < 0$ and $\partial^2 k/\partial u^2 > 0$. Here we similarly assume that the discount rate is affected in the same way by an increased new-issue ratio—i.e., $\partial k/\partial c > 0$ and $\partial^2 k/\partial c^2 > 0$. It would also seem reasonable to believe that the lower the pay-out ratio, the more strongly k is positively affected by a given increase in the new-issue ratio—i.e., $\partial^2 k/\partial u \partial c < 0$.

Now the most advantageous financial policy for existing and all potential owners of the firm is given when the decision variables u and c are assigned values which maximize net capital value (P'_t). This maximization implies (see appendix F, p. 168)

$$\frac{\partial P'}{\partial u} = -B\left\{r_E - \left[k - (u-c)\frac{\partial k}{\partial u}\right]\right\} = 0 \tag{7: 3}$$

$$\frac{\partial P'}{\partial c} = B\left\{r_E - \left[k + (u-c)\frac{\partial k}{\partial c}\right]\right\} = 0, \tag{7: 4}$$

where $B = r_E K_{Et}/(k-v)^2 > 0$, since $k > v$.

Thus at the optimum there is an equality between the rate of return on equity (r_E) and the "marginal cost" of retaining profits in the firm, $MC_u = k-(u-c)\partial k/\partial u$, and the marginal cost of securing new capital through the issue of shares, $MC_c = k+(u-c)\partial k/\partial c$. From the signs of the k-function's

[1] A discount rate which is influenced by an equally large change in both u and c could provide an explanation of why firms acquire financial capital through new issues at the same time as they pay dividends although there are administrative costs of new issues and tax subsidy on capital gains.

[2] Such a discount-rate function applying to both the existing and the new stockholders has been used in earlier empirical investigations by Bennet, Graham and Tran Van Hoa [1969].

partial derivations above, it also follows that the both MC_u and MC_c increase when u is reduced or c is raised, respectively—i.e., $\partial MC_u/\partial u<0$, $\partial MC_c/\partial u<0$, $\partial MC_u/\partial c>0$, and $\partial MC_c/\partial c>0$.[1]

7.1.2. The influence of exogenous factors

If the "marginal costs" MC_u and MC_c are changed w.r.t. u and c in the way that was assumed above, then it is clear from the total differentiation of conditions (7: 3) and (7: 4) that all exogenous changes that reduce the rate of return on equity have a negative influence on the firm's financing through retained earnings and new issues, i.e., make the firm increase its optimal net pay-out ratio.

We have shown earlier—see section 5.3.1—that the rate of return on equity (r_E) is decreased by the product price or the total productivity factor (ψ) being reduced and by the wage rate (p_1), the price of capital goods (p_2), the rate of depreciation (a) or the rate of profits tax (t_V) being raised. Furthermore, if we introduce a tax on dividends which leave the discount rate unchanged this tax discriminates against new share finance. See appendix F: 1. It is also shown in appendix F: 1 that such a tax, (1) has a favorable influence on the firm's optimal net pay-out ratio ($u-c$), and (2) has no influence at all on the firm's optimal pay-out ratio (u) if there is no new-issue finance.

7.2. The discount rate as a positive function of the leverage ratio

Earlier it has been assumed that the discount rate is independent of indebtedness, which, however, seems to be rather unrealistic. Profitability on total capital can be expected to be more unstable over time than the interest rate on borrowed capital, from which it follows that the variability over time of the rate of return on equity is greater, the more extensive the reliance on external finance. This, in turn, ought to imply that share owners demand a higher yield on the capital which they invest in the firm.

That the required rate of return of the owners increases with increased indebtedness means in terms of the model that the discount-rate function (2: 16) is replaced by

$$k = k(u, h), \qquad (7:5)$$

where in addition to $\partial k/\partial u<0$ and $\partial^2 k/\partial u^2>0$, it is now assumed that $\partial k/\partial h>0$ and $\partial^2 k/\partial h^2<0$. The signs of the last two derivatives with respect to the leverage ratio (h) are the same as in the interest-rate function.

In the following we will discuss briefly (a) the inter-relatedness between the

[1] $\partial MC_u/\partial u = -(u-c)\,\partial^2 k/\partial u^2<0$, $\partial MC_c/\partial u=(u-c)\,\partial^2 k/\partial c\partial u<0$,

$\partial MC_u/\partial c = -(u-c)\,\partial^2 k/\partial u\partial c>0$, $\partial MC_c/\partial c=(u-c)\,\partial^2 k/\partial c^2>0$.

Note that $-\partial k/\partial u=\partial k/\partial c$ due to equations (7: 3) and (7: 4).

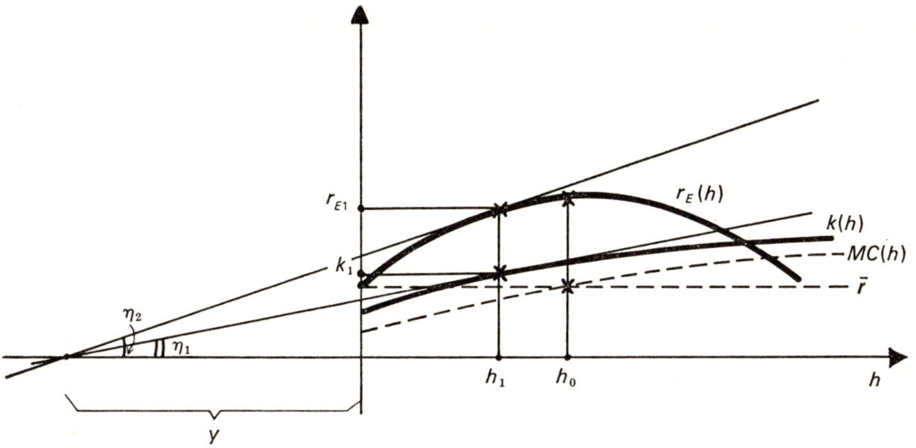

Figure 9. *Optimization of the capital value of the firm with respect to the leverage ratio*

firm's debt and retention policy and (*b*) the influence of exogenous factors on these two types of financing decisions.

7.2.1. Optimum conditions

If an optimum solution with a positive leverage ratio exists, the necessary first-order condition for maximum capital value of the firm is:[1]

$$\frac{\partial r_E}{\partial h}\frac{1}{r_E}-\frac{\partial k}{\partial h}\frac{1}{k}=0. \tag{7:6}$$

Since the rate of return on equity (r_E) has only one maximum value with respect to the leverage ratio (h), and $\partial k/\partial h$ is positive for all non-negative h, then according to (7: 6) $\partial r_E/\partial h$ must be positive. Thus capital value (P_t) is maximized for one single value of h which is less than that which maximizes r_E. It is obviously not optimal for the firm's owners to pursue borrowing to the point where the rate of return on equity reaches its highest value.

How this optimization takes place is illustrated in figure 9 where we have drawn the identity for the rate of return on equity $r_E(h)=(1+h)r-ih$, the discount-rate function $k=k(u,h)$, the total profitability line $r=\bar{r}$ and the marginal borrowing-cost function $MC_h=i+h\partial i/\partial h$. The optimum condition (7: 6) is satisfied at the value of $h=h_1$, where the tangents to the r_E- and k-curves have a common point of intersection on the negative h-axis. At that point we have $\operatorname{tg}\eta_1=k/(h+y)=\partial k/\partial h$ and $\operatorname{tg}\eta_2=r_E/(h+y)=\partial r_E/\partial h$. If h takes

[1] The assumption of a positive optimum solution implies that $(\partial r_E/\partial h)(k/r_E)>\partial k/\partial h$ for $h=0$, and that r_E/k at first rises with increased leverage ratio (h). It follows directly from the capital-value relation $P_t=\overline{K}_{Et}/(1-\delta)$, where $\delta=(r_E-k)/ur_E=(1/u)(1-k/r_E)$ that—given $u-r_E/k$, δ and P_t will increase, reach a maximum, and then fall when h is raised. Once r_E/k is maximized, we have $(\partial r_E/\partial h)/r_E=(\partial k/\partial h)/k$.

on values higher than h_1 then $(\partial r_E/\partial h)/r_E < (\partial k/\partial h)/k$ obtains, which means that the firm's capital value is declining.

If instead the discount rate were independent of the leverage ratio (i.e., $\partial k/\partial h = 0$), the k-curve would be a horizontal line. Then the optimal leverage ratio for the firm would coincide with that which maximizes the rate of return on equity (i.e., $h_1 = h_0$). We note that h_0 obtains where the $\bar{r}$-line intersects the MC-curve, which is the same thing as if the earlier optimum condition for indebtedness (5: 4) holds. This situation is identical to that which was described in figure 5*b* above.

The discount rate being a function of both the pay-out ratio and the leverage ratio also implies that the optimal leverage ratio is dependent on the value which is assigned to the pay-out ratio. This is illustrated by the k-curve in figure 9 being shifted as the pay-out ratio takes different values. In this way the firm's dividend decisions influence its debt decisions.

7.2.2. The influence of exogenous factors

The assumption of the discount rate rising with increased indebtedness also leads to certain results in the behavior analysis in chapter 5, pp. 71 f., being changed. Assuming, e.g., a linear-multiplicative discount-rate function $k = E_{k0} + E_{k1} u^{e_{ku}} h^{e_{kh}}$, where $E_{k0} > 0$, $E_{k1} > 0$, $e_{ku} < 0$ and $e_{kh} > 0$, it follows that

$$\frac{\partial[(\partial k/\partial h)/k]}{\partial E_{k0}} < 0 \quad \text{and} \quad \frac{\partial[(\partial k/\partial h)/k]}{\partial u} < 0.$$

First, when the exogenously given discount rate (E_{k0}) is raised the optimal leverage ratio (h) increases. As E_{k0} becomes higher, then for every given value of the leverage ratio (h), $(\partial k/\partial h)/k$ will decline, while $(\partial r_E/\partial h)/r_E$ is not affected. In order that (7: 6) be satisfied, h must then be increased—see also figure 9. In addition the increase of E_{k0} will lead to the optimal pay-out ratio increasing, which in turn reduces $(\partial k/\partial h)/k$.

Second, a higher rate of profits tax (t_V) increases the optimal pay-out ratio. Consequently, $(\partial k/\partial h)/k$ will decline for every given (h), which in turn increases the optimal leverage ratio. Note that a change in t_V does not change the function $(\partial r_E/\partial h)/r_E$.

Third, an increase of total productivity (ψ) or the product price (p) and a reduction of the wage (p_1), the price of capital (p_2), the rate of depreciation of capital (a), or the exogenously determined interest rate (E_{i0}) increases as before the optimal leverage ratio.[1] Since these exogenous changes lead at the same time to a lower optimal pay-out ratio, the leverage ratio will now increase less sharply; the optimal rate of return on equity, the growth of dividends and capital value will similarly be increased less sharply.

[1] This is due to the fact that these exogenous changes increase total profitability (r), which causes a shift upwards of $(\partial r_E/\partial h)/r_E = [r - (i + h\ \partial i/\partial h)]/[r + h(r - i)]$ for every given h.

7.3. Autonomous price changes

In reality the prices of the firm's products and input factors are continually changing over time. This justifies generalizing the analysis by dropping the assumption of constant prices and instead assuming changing prices. Thereby a first step is taken towards an analysis of non-balanced growth of the firm.[1] Here we restrict ourselves to study the consequences of different given rates of growth of prices for a) the development over time of the firm's real variables and its possibilities of growing with constant monetary relations, as well as b) the firms propensity to finance its operation internally or externally.

a) For the period t value added (F_t), labor costs (L_t), and the value of real capital (K_t) are defined as

$$F_t = p_t \hat{F}_t,\ L_t = p_{1t}\hat{L}_t \quad \text{and } K_t = p_{2t}\hat{K}_t, \tag{7: 7}$$

where F_t, L_t and K_t are the volumes of production, labor and capital, respectively, and p_t, p_{1t}, and p_{2t} are their respective prices. If the relations between F_t, L_t and K_t are to be unchanged over time, it follows from (7: 7) that

$$\hat{v}_F + v_p = \hat{v}_L + v_{p1} = \hat{v}_K + v_{p2}. \tag{7: 8}$$

The difference between the volume rates of growth of production and labor ($\hat{v}_F - \hat{v}_L$) must be equal to the difference between the growth rates for the labor price and the product price ($v_{p1} - v_p$), and the difference between the volume rates of growth of labor and capital ($\hat{v}_L - \hat{v}_K$) will be equal to the difference between the growth rates of the capital price and the labor price ($v_{p2} - v_{p1}$).

Let us further assume that the firm's production function is of the Cobb–Douglas type.[2] Differentiation of the production function with respect to time gives

$$\hat{v}_F = \gamma + \alpha\hat{v}_L + (1-\alpha)\hat{v}_K. \tag{7: 9}$$

Combining (7: 8) and (7: 9), we obtain

$$\gamma + v_p = \alpha v_{p1} + (1-\alpha) v_{p2}. \tag{7: 10}$$

Thus equilibrium expansion with constant wage share, capital income share, total profitability, etc. requires that the sum of the growth rates of the product price and the total productivity be equal to the weighted sum of the growth rates of the factor prices, where the weights are the elasticities of the factors

[1] Non-balanced growth is of central importance for the study of macro-economic allocation problems. This assumption makes it possible to construct more general growth models which describe how labor, capital and commodities are allocated among different industrial sectors in the conomy as a whole. See Brems [1973], chapters 7–8.

[2] $\hat{F}_t = \psi e^{\gamma t} \cdot \hat{L}_t^{\alpha} \cdot \hat{K}_t^{(1-\alpha)}$.

of production. If no autonomous increase in productivity takes place ($\gamma=0$), and the prices of capital and labor rise ($v_{p1}>0$ and $v_{p2}>0$), then the product price must continually rise ($v_p>0$). On the other hand, if the product price were constant ($v_p=0$) and an increase of factor prices took place, total productivity would have to rise ($\gamma>0$).

The relation (7: 10) should hardly be expected to hold exactly at every point in time due to short-run fluctuations in the demand for the firm's products. Therefore the relation should be regarded as a condition of equilibrium expansion of the monetary variables over longer periods of time. (7: 10) may be tested with empirical data. According to Åberg [1969] the factor elasticities for Swedish industrial firms are $\alpha=0.64$, and $(1-\alpha)=0.36$. These values also agree quite well with those which have been estimated in a number of other productivity studies (see, for example, Aukrust and Bjerke [1959] and Solow [1960]). For the period 1955–70 we have calculated on the basis of official industrial statistics the annual average growth rates of the aggregated output price (v_p), wage rate (v_{p1}) and real capital price (v_{p2}), as well as the rate of increase of total productivity (γ).[1] We then obtain

$$v_p+\gamma=0.024+0.042=0.066$$

$$\alpha v_{p1}+(1-\alpha)v_{p2}=0.64\cdot 0.088+0.36\cdot 0.036=0.069.$$

These statistical series at least do not provide grounds for any significant departure during this period of the trend rates of growth of product and factor prices and total productivity from what would be required in balanced monetary expansion.

b) Assume no autonomous increase of the total productivity ($\gamma=0$). One of the combinations of price changes then satisfying (7: 10) is that in which the rates of growth of the prices of product, labor and capital are equal. This uniform growth rate of prices ($\bar{v}_p$) can consequently vary while at the same time the monetary relations are constant over time.

Does this mean in addition that the firm's financial behavior is independent of $\bar{v}_p$? There is reason to believe that such is not the case. A higher $\bar{v}_p$ reduces the real value of the lenders' and stockholders' nominal assets. Because of this, these individuals can be expected to demand as compensation a higher nominal rate of return on their financial investments in the firm.

[1] From *SOS*; Industri (official statistics for industry) we obtain $v_p=0.024$ (the index of value added in current prices divided by the index of production volume). By using the deflators (obtained from the Central Bureau of Statistics) for investment in structures and equipment we obtain $v_{p2}=0.036$ (the weights for structures and equipment are 0.33 and 0.67, respectively).

From *SOS*; Industri and the *National Accounts* we obtain $v_{p1}=0.088$ (the index of total wages divided by the total number of working hours). Finally, $\gamma=0.042$ is the average of the growth of total productivity which was estimated for various subperiods in Nabseth, et al. [1971] p. 244.

The simplest way to take account of this phenomenon in our model is to let the intercept terms in the interest-rate and discount-rate functions be linearly dependent on $\bar{v}_p$—i.e., $E_{i0} = E^p_{i0} + \theta\bar{v}_p$ and $E_{k0} = E^p_{k0} + \theta\bar{v}_p$, where the coefficient θ is positive. We have earlier shown (see chapter 5, pp. 71 f.) that when E_{i0} and E_{k0} are increased, the optimal values of the leverage ratio, rate of return on equity and the growth rates of all real variables decline, while the optimal pay-out ratio increases. An equal rise in the rate of growth of all prices can thus, as they cause an upward shift of the interest-rate and discount-rate functions, unfavorably affect the firm's internal and external finance and its rate of real expansion.

7.4. Worker-controlled and management-controlled firms

In this section we examine the behavior of worker-controlled and management-controlled firms. We also compare their behavior with that of the owner-controlled capitalist firm. These three types of firms are assumed to be alike in all respects except in their objectives.

7.4.1. The worker-controlled firm

There are few recent studies concerning firms which are owned and managed by their workers. Among the most important works are those of Vanek [1970] and Atkinson [1973]. Vanek's model is static and has to do specifically with agricultural cooperative firms, but Atkinson's model is applicable to growing industrial firms and is the one that most resembles our own. In contrast to us, Atkinson assumes increasing returns to scale in production and no substitution between labor and capital.

Let us begin by defining some important variables for the worker-controlled firm (the L-firm).[1]

$$V'_L = \frac{p\hat{F} - p_2 a\hat{K} - ihK_E}{\hat{L}} \tag{7:11}$$

$$V'_{LN} = \frac{uV'_L}{k - v'} \tag{7:12}$$

$$v' = (1-u)r'_E \tag{7:13}$$

$$r'_E = V'/K_E. \tag{7:14}$$

V'_L is profit per employee, V'_{LN} is present value of all future paid-out profits

[1] In order to simplify the formulas, the time index is dropped from the variables.

(wages) per employee, r'_E is profit divided by equity capital and v' is growth rate of all non-ratio variables of the firm.

We follow Atkinson in assuming that the L-firm seeks to maximize the present value of wages. To realize this objective, the firm faces the problem of how to distribute its profits among a changing number of workers. One can imagine two extreme cases. The first is that current workers in the firm accept either to reduce the number of employees in their group or increase the number by employing new personnel which are paid the same wage (uV'_L) that they have themselves, (i.e. $\hat{L}$ is completely variable). The other extreme case is that all existing employees are prepared to remain in the firm but are not, however, willing to let anyone outside the firm obtain part of its earnings (i.e. $\hat{L}$ is fixed).[1]

Case 1. *$\hat{L}$ is variable*

Assuming no growth costs maximization of V'_{LN} with respect to the decision instruments labor intensity $\hat{l}$, leverage ratio h and pay-out ratio u gives the first-order conditions

$$p\partial\hat{F}/\partial\hat{K} > p_2[a+ih/(1+h)] \quad (7{:}\ 15)^2$$

$$p\partial\hat{F}/\partial\hat{K} = p_2[a+i+h\partial i/\partial h] \quad (7{:}\ 16)^3$$

$$k-u\partial k/\partial u = r'_E. \quad (7{:}\ 17)^4$$

According to (7: 15), the marginal product of capital must be greater than the average cost of capital. Since the production function is linear homogeneous, this optimum condition means that the L-firm should employ more persons than the number which gives the highest possible wage per employee. This is explained by the fact that an increase of the number of employees past the point which maximizes the wage for each of them still increases the firm's rate of growth of capital. As long as higher growth of wages increases present discounted wages by more than the reduced initial wage level decreases them, it is advantageous for the employees to hire more persons.

(7: 16) and (7: 17) are the same as the earlier derived optimum condition for indebtedness (5: 2)′ and the optimum condition for dividends (5: 3)″, respectively, for the capitalist owner-controlled firm (the C-firm) with the exception that in (5: 3)″ the rate of return on equity is included instead of r'_E.

An interesting special case is when the L-firm chooses a dividend policy which implies that all profits are paid out as wages ($u=1$)—i.e., the firm does not grow. We then obtain instead of (7: 15) and (7: 16)[4]

[1] These two types of L-firms correspond most closely to "economic associations" in which there are in principle no obstacles to new members joining the association and smaller "family firms" in which all of the owners are themselves working in the firm.

[2] See the derivation in appendix F, pp. 171 f.

[3] See the derivation in appendix F, pp. 169 f.

[4] See appendix F, pp. 169 f.

$$p\partial\hat{F}/\partial\hat{K} = p_2 a \tag{7: 18}$$

$$h = 0. \tag{7: 19}$$

With zero growth profits and the present value of wages per employee are maximized simultaneously with respect to labor intensity. The best policy for the L-firm is then to employ precisely so many persons that the marginal productivity of capital is equal to depreciation costs per unit of capital, and to not finance its operation through any debt. Constant returns to scale and given prices imply that it is not possible to influence value added per employee through changing the scale of production. Increasing the size of the firm through borrowing, for example, can only reduce profits per employee due to interest costs.

If the product price (p) rises, the L-firm will according to (7: 18) reduce its optimal labor intensity ($\hat{l} = \hat{L}/\hat{K}$).[1] Since according to (7: 19) no debt finance exists, the firm's capital input is equal to the initially given equity (K_E). The rise in product price thus also implies that the labor input and production volume decline, which is the same as the L-firm having a negatively sloped product supply curve. This firm also reduces its labor intensity, labor input and production in response to an autonomous increase of its total productivity ψ or a reduction of the price of capital p_2.[1]

We now turn to a comparison with the C-firm. There is reason to believe that the C-firm's optimization results in a positive level of indebtedness ($h > 0$). From conditions (7: 18) and (7: 19) it is then clear that (1) the L-firm has a lower marginal value product of capital and a lower labor intensity, (2) its total capital will be smaller (since equity capital (K_E) has been assumed to be the same for these two types of firms). From that it follows that (3) the size of the L-firm measured by the number of employees is also smaller.

Case 2. *$\hat{L}$ is fixed*

For the L-firm we now have the identity

$$\bar{\hat{L}} = \hat{l}(1+h)\bar{K}_E/p_2 \tag{7: 20}$$

instead of the optimum condition for labor (7: 15) where $\bar{\hat{L}}$ and $\bar{K}_E$ are assumed to be given magnitudes. On the other hand, maximization of V'_{LN} with respect to h and u gives as before the conditions (7: 16) and (7: 17). In this case without knowing p, p_1, p_2 and $\bar{\hat{L}}/\bar{K}_E$, one cannot make any statements about differences between the L- and C-firms' real and financial behavior.

If a switch to worker control leads to an increase of wages per employee—which seems likely — this ought to imply that the optimal labor intensity of the L-firm will be lower. Since the marginal value product of capital ($p\partial\hat{F}/\partial\hat{K}$) is an increasing function of the labor intensity, and since condition (7: 16)

[1] We assume the following linear homogeneous production function for the firm: $\hat{F} = \psi\tilde{L}^{\alpha}\tilde{K}^{(1-\alpha)}$, where $p\partial\hat{F}/\partial\hat{K} = p(1-\alpha)\psi\hat{l}^{\alpha}$.

holds for both these types of firms, it also follows that the relative indebtedness (h) of the L-firm will be lower.

Assuming that the L-firm does not have a significantly lower labor intensity than the C-firm, profits per unit of equity capital (r'_E) in the L-firm may be expected to be higher than the rate of return on equity (r_E) in the C-firm.[1] This would mean that the L-firm has a higher propensity to internal finance and faster growth given the same discount rate for both types of firm. It is likely, however, that the employees of the L-firm would discount their future wages at a higher average rate than that which the owners of the C-firm would use to discount their dividends. An important reason for this should be that the L-firm's investments give higher future wages for every employee only so long as he will remain in the firm.

Finally, we may mention, with regard to the influence of external factors, that since the labor input in this case has been assumed given, the L-firm increases its optimal leverage ratio, capital input, and production when the product price (p) or total productivity (ψ) is increased and when the price of capital (p_2) is reduced. See equations (7: 16) and (7: 20). Obviously, once the labor input is held constant and debt finance capital inputs are varied instead, these exogenous changes lead to the same directional effects for the worker-controlled firm as for the owner-controlled C-firm.

7.4.2. The management-controlled firm

The management-controlled firm (the M-firm) is usually assumed to maximize its growth rate, given that certain financial restrictions are satisfied. One such important restriction is that the market value of the firm's shares does not fall below a safe minimum level (Marris [1964]). According to Marris, the reason is that a firm with too low market value run the risk of being bought up by outside persons who wish to take over its management themselves. In addition the managers of the firm frequently hold significant amounts of its shares themselves. The larger these holdings are the more managers will tend to behave as stockholders.

With a balanced expansion of the firm, exogenously given prices and no new-issue finance, the growth rate of all non-ratio variables is identical and equal to the internally financed growth rate of equity capital. The objective of the M-firm may then be formulated as maximization of the growth rate (v) determined by the relationship

$$v = (1-u) r_E \qquad (7{:}\,21)$$

[1] Note the identities:

$r'_E = (p\hat{F} - p_2 a\hat{K} - ihK_E)/K_E = \{(1+h)[pF(\hat{l})/p_2 - a] - ih\}$

$r_E = (p\hat{F} - p_1\hat{L} - p_2 a\hat{K} - ihK_E)/K_E = \{(1+h)[p\hat{F}(\hat{l})/p_2 - p_1\hat{l}/p_2 - a] - ih\}$.

under the constraint

$$X \leqslant \varrho = P/K_E = ur_E/(k-v). \tag{7: 22}$$

P is the market value of shares, K_E is the predetermined equity capital, ϱ is the valuation ratio, and X is the minimum level of the valuation ratio allowed.

From chapter 5, p. 68, we have the discount-rate function

$$k = E_{k0} + E_{k1} u^{e_{ku}}. \tag{7: 23}$$

According to (7: 21), (7: 22), and (7: 23), ϱ is first an increasing and then a decreasing function of the pay-out ratio (u) as it takes on values from zero on up.[1] Thus for every given $X < \varrho_{\max}$, both a minimum value $u_{\min}$ and a maximum value $u_{\max}$ are obtained which make the constraint (7: 22) binding.

Since the growth rate (v) is a monotonically declining function of u, the M-firm's optimal pay-out ratio is $u_{\min}$. If X is increased further so that $X = \varrho_{\max}$, $u_{\min}$ will coincide with the optimal value of u for the owner-controlled C-firm. As long as X is lower than the maximum ϱ, the M-firm's pay-out ratio is lower and its growth rate is higher than that of the C-firm.

These results imply that all external changes which raise the ϱ-function, as for example an increase of the product price (p) or the total productivity factor (ψ) or a reduction of the capital price (p_2), the rate of depreciation (a), or the rate of profit tax (t_V), lead to a decline of $u_{\min}$ and an increase of v. The directional effects on the propensity to pay dividends and the rate of growth of these exogenous changes are consequently the same for the M-firm and the C-firm.

As far as the decision variables labor intensity ($\hat{l}$) and leverage ratio (h) are concerned, we have shown earlier (p. 67) that the values of these variables which maximize ϱ also maximize r_E and v at every given value of the pay-out ratio. Hence the optimal values of $\hat{l}$ and h will be the same for both the M- and C-firms. This means that the directional effects on the optimal $\hat{l}$ and h due to changed product price, total productivity, etc., will also be the same for both types of firms.

---

[1] See also pp. 94 f.

CHAPTER 8

Summary and further issues

In this chapter we summarize the model, the methods of analysis and the theoretical and empirical results presented in this book. On the last pages we raise a few issues that could be handled by further developments of our model and that we feel would be important in a more general analysis.

8.1. Summary

The main purpose of this study has been to show the optimization process behind the production, investment and financing decisions of the firm and to demonstrate the interdependencies among these three kinds of decisions. Furthermore, we wanted to show how the firm's decision variables as well as its rate of return, growth rate and capital value are affected by factors external to the firm. The point of departure for the analysis is a dynamic steady state model based on the investment and financing theories developed earlier by Gordon [1962], Marris [1964], Vickers [1968] and Solow [1971].

8.1.1. The model

The production activity of the firm was defined by a neoclassical production function with constant returns to scale. One product is produced by two homogeneous factors of production, labor and capital. Following Lucas [1967], Gould [1968] and Treadway [1967], we assume that labor is a perfectly variable resource but that capital is imperfectly variable. The latter assumption implies that investment is associated with adjustment costs which are incorporated in the model by allowing the rate of growth of capital to affect the volume of production negatively. The product price and the prices of labor and capital are exogenously given to the firm.

The firm's investments were assumed to be financed only by borrowing and retaining profits. The interest rate on borrowed capital is an increasing function of the leverage ratio. The discount rate, defined as the rate at which dividends are discounted by the stockholders, is a decreasing function of the pay-out ratio. In addition, we assumed that the former function increases and the latter decreases at a declining rate. We have followed the neoclassical tradition in assuming that the firm acts in the interest of its stockholders by maximizing the market value of equity, i.e., the discounted value of all expected future dividends.

Given these assumptions and some book keeping identities, the basic equations of the model can be stated for the period t:

$$\hat{F}_t = \hat{F}(\hat{L}_t, \hat{K}_t, \hat{v}_K) \tag{8: 1}$$

$$r = (p\hat{F}_t - p_1\hat{L}_t - p_2 a\hat{K}_t)/p_2\hat{K}_t \tag{8: 2}$$

$$i = i(h) \tag{8: 3}$$

$$r_E = (1 - t_V)\{r + h(r - i)\} \tag{8: 4}$$

$$v = \hat{v}_K = (1 - u)r_E \tag{8: 5}$$

$$k = k(u) \tag{8: 6}$$

$$P_t = ur_E K_{Et}/(k - v), \tag{8: 7}$$

where $\partial\hat{F}/\partial\hat{L} > 0$, $\partial^2\hat{F}/\partial\hat{L}^2 < 0$, $\partial\hat{F}/\partial\hat{K} > 0$, $\partial^2\hat{F}/\partial\hat{K}^2 < 0$, $\partial\hat{F}/\partial\hat{v}_K < 0$, $\partial i/\partial h > 0$, $\partial^2 i/\partial h^2 < 0$, $\partial k/\partial u < 0$ and $\partial^2 k/\partial u^2 > 0$.

$\hat{F}_t$ = volume of production
$\hat{L}_t$ = quantity of labor
$\hat{K}_t$ = quantity of capital
$\hat{v}_K$ = growth rate of capital
p = product price
p_1 = wage rate
p_2 = capital price
a = physical depreciation rate
r = rate of return on total capital
i = interest rate
h = leverage ratio
t_V = profit tax rate
r_E = rate of return on equity (after profit tax)
u = pay-out ratio
v = growth of dividends
k = discount rate
K_{Et} = equity capital
P_t = market value of the equity (the firm's capital value)

(8: 1) is the production function. (8: 2), (8: 4) and (8: 5) define the rate of return on total capital, the rate of return on equity and the growth rate of dividends respectively, (8: 3) is the interest-rate function and (8: 6) the discount-rate function. Finally, (8: 7) defines the capital value. The assumption of steady-state and balanced growth means that equity and all other monetary variables grow at an equal rate (v). Because all prices are assumed constant over time, the quantitative variables $\hat{L}_t$, $\hat{K}_t$ and $\hat{F}_t$ must also grow at the same rate.

The profit-tax rate and the physical depreciation rate are also exogenously given and take the same values in every period. The ratios $\hat{l} = \hat{L}_t/\hat{K}_t$, $h = K_{Ft}/K_{Et}$ and $u = U_t/V_{Et}$ are assumed to be the decision variables of the firm, where K_{Ft} is borrowed capital, U_t is dividends and V_{Et} is profit on equity. The equity capital (K_{Et}) is a predetermined magnitude in the initial period (t).

8.1.2. Empirical tests of some basic assumptions

In chapter 3 we tested the hypothesis that higher growth rates cause increasing costs of adjustment, which adversely affect the rate of return. Using cross sectional data based on the average values for 1963–68 of 62 firms in the Swedish engineering industry, we estimated the function

$$r = f(v_0), \qquad (8:8)$$

where r is the rate of return on total capital and v_0 is the rate of growth of sales.

However, since increased profitability provides greater possibilities for internally financed growth, v_0 also depends on r according to the relationship

$$v_0 = g(r, Z), \qquad (8:9)$$

where Z stands for a vector of financial variables such as the leverage ratio, the interest rate on borrowed capital, the pay-out ratio, etc. In order to obtain a growth coefficient which was not influenced by this feedback effect from the rate of return, we applied a two-stage least squares estimation. In the first stage we regressed v_0 on the Z-variables to obtain a growth variable $\hat{v}_0$ purged of the influence from the rate of return. In the second stage we regressed r on $\hat{v}_0$.

There is reason to believe that growth costs mainly arise at positive growth rates. Therefore we ran separate regressions for firms with positive values of $\hat{v}_0$ and for firms with negative or zero values. For the first group, consisting of 50 firms, we found a significant negative relationship between the rate of return and the rate of growth. This result seems to support the theories which state that limited markets for the firm's products and input factors and a limited capacity of management to plan and organize the firm's expansion require it to devote an ever greater share of its total resources to various growth activities as it expands at an increasing speed.

For the second group the relationship between rate of return and growth rate was found to be positive. This is not readily explained. There may be advantages from growth, such as greater ability to bring in new knowledge through the turnover of employees, which outweigh growth costs at negative and very low rates of growth.

Previous empirical studies of relation (8: 8) have, however, found a positive correlation between the rate of return and the rate of growth (see Weiss [1963] and Marris [1966]). This can probably be explained by their use of ordinary least squares (OLS), which is inappropriate in this context. It is interesting that single equation OLS estimates using our data also gave a positive and significant relationship between rate of return and growth rate. These results indicate that in cross-sectional data one observes the positive impact on the growth rate from a higher rate of return caused by increased ability to finance growth with retained profits.

In chapter 4 we tested the hypothesis that the firm's capital costs increase as a result of increased borrowing and internal financing. We estimated the behavior functions (8: 3) and (8: 6) using average values for 1963–70 of cross-sectional data for 56 industrial firms quoted on the Stockholm Stock Exchange. First, we found that the rate of interest on borrowed capital rises at a diminishing rate when the leverage ratio assumes higher values, i.e., $\partial i/\partial h > 0$ and $\partial^2 i/\partial h^2 < 0$. This result indicates that an increased use of borrowed capital increases the lender's financial risk. It should be observed that the result does not contradict the commonly accepted notion that the rate of interest rises at an increasing rate as the ratio of borrowed capital to total capital increases (as it approaches one).

Second, we found that the discount rate falls at a declining rate as the pay-out ratio is raised, i.e., $\partial k/\partial u < 0$, and $\partial^2 k/\partial u^2 > 0$. Assuming that shareholders are risk averse, this relationship may be explained by the variance of the growth of future dividends increasing at a more rapid rate than the growth of dividends. This in turn should be due to the fact that when the firm tries to increase its rate of growth by reducing its pay-out ratio, it may provoke countermeasures from competing firms (Lerner & Carleton [1966]). A negative relationship between the discount rate and the pay-out ratio may also be due to the fact that a higher growth rate would make it necessary for the firm to devote a greater proportion of its resources to innovations and more risky products (Brems [1976]).

8.1.3. The optimal decisions of the firm

Almost all theories about the firm have been concerned with either its production and investment decisions or with its investment and finance decisions. In only two studies have these three kinds of decisions been incorporated in a fully integrated model of the firm (Vickers [1968] and Turnovsky [1970]). A central problem analyzed by Vickers and Turnovsky, and which we treated in chapter 5, is the interrelatedness between production, investment and financing decisions. An important difference of approach here is that we study growing firms, whereas Vickers' and Turnovsky's theories are static.

In order to illustrate the impact of growth costs on the firm's behavior more clearly, we began by assuming that growth costs do not exist; i.e., we temporarily left out the growth rate ($\hat{v}_K$) from the firm's production function.

(a) *No growth costs*

The assumption of balanced and steady state growth means that the firm makes once-and-for-all decisions. The optimality conditions as well as the optimal value of all monetary ratios which are derived during the initial period are also valid in every future period. The maximization of the market value of the firm's shares (the capital value of the firm), with respect to the three decision variables labor-intensity ($\hat{l}$), leverage ratio (h) and pay-out ratio (u) gave the following conditions:

$$p\partial\hat{F}/\partial\hat{L} = p_1 \qquad (8{:}\ 10)$$

$$r = (i + h\partial i/\partial h) \qquad (8{:}\ 11)$$

$$r_E = (k - u\partial k/\partial u). \qquad (8{:}\ 12)$$

According to (8: 10)–(8: 12), an optimal production and financing policy implies that the firm shall

(1) employ labor to such an extent that the value of the marginal product of labor is equal to the wage rate;

(2) borrow capital until the rate of return on total capital equals the marginal cost of borrowing; and

(3) retain earnings until the rate of return on equity equals the marginal cost of retentions in terms of the increasing discount rate.

Because the interest rate is an increasing function of the leverage ratio and the discount rate is a decreasing function of the pay-out ratio, (8: 11) and (8: 12) imply that the rate of return on total capital is higher than the interest rate and that the rate of return on equity is higher than the discount rate. The latter condition means that the firm should not—in contrast to traditional theory—retain earnings to such an extent that the discount rate equals the rate of return on equity. This result conforms with the conclusion reached by Gordon [1962] and Lintner [1964].

Furthermore it can be shown that the discount rate is higher than the earnings-price ratio $y = V_{Et}/P_t$, and that the rate of return on equity is higher than the rate of return on total capital if these two rates are defined before profit tax. Thus we obtained the following two inequalities:

$$r_E > r > i \qquad (8{:}\ 13)$$

$$r_E > k > y. \qquad (8{:}\ 14)$$

The assumptions of exogenously determined prices, a linear homogeneous production function, no growth costs and no leverage effect on the discount rate make the optimal values of the labor-capital ratio and the leverage ratio independent of the pay-out ratio and also make the optimal value of the labor-capital ratio independent of the leverage ratio. In other words, a change in dividend policy does not have any impact on the optimal production and borrowing decisions; nor are the optimal production decisions influenced by borrowing decisions. Of course, in the decision process these influences always work in the other direction through the impact of a changed factor intensity on the optimal leverage and pay-out ratios.

From the optimality conditions and the model equations we could derive the optimal values of the decision variables and of all other endogenous variables as functions of the exogenous factors. The directions of once-and-for-all changes in the optimal values of endogenous variables, following an increase in every specified exogenous factor, have been summarized in table 7 in chapter 5. There we compared these results with those derived in traditional production theory and in modern investment and financing theories by Solow [1971], Stiglitz [1973] and King [1974], among others.

(b) *Growth costs*

When internal growth costs are taken into account in the model, the marginal and average factor productivities will be lower the higher the growth rate of capital is. This is true also for the rate of return on total and equity capital which, in turn, means that a decrease in the pay-out ratio reduces the rate of return on equity, i.e., $\partial r_E/\partial u > 0$. Maximizing capital value (P_t), with respect to the pay-out ratio gave the condition

$$r_E - k(\partial r_E/\partial u)(u/r_E) = k - u\partial k/\partial u. \qquad (8{:}\,15)$$

Because $\partial r_E/\partial u > 0$, a maximum occurs at a higher pay-out ratio than that given by the optimal internal financing condition (8: 12). Contrary to what we found earlier the firm now acts in the interest of its owners by not retaining earnings up to the point where the marginal cost in terms of an increasing discount rate equals the rate of return on equity.

A further consequence of growth costs is that the recursivity in the model disappears. For example, an arbitrary decrease in the pay-out ratio, which increases the growth rate, will make both the optimal labor intensity and the optimal leverage ratio lower in the new steady state solution. Similarly, an arbitrary change in the leverage ratio affects the optimal labor intensity. For example, if the leverage ratio is lower than its optimal level, an increase in this decision variable will, via a higher growth rate, lead the firm to use less labor intensive techniques.

Another consequence of growth costs is that the firm will not respond so much to changes in exogenous factors. The reason is that all exogenous changes which imply an increase in any of the optimal values of the endogenous variables $\hat{l}$, r, h, i, r_{E1}, $(1-u)$, k, v and P_t at the same time increase the real growth rate ($\hat{v}_K$). The higher $\hat{v}_K$, in turn, means that the increments in these endogenous variables are moderated compared to the case without growth costs.

Growth costs also imply that increments in certain exogenous factors which previously had no effect on the endogenous variables will now affect them. These effects have been summarized in table 8 in chapter 5. There we also gave a diagrammatic illustration both of the optimization procedure and of how changes in the exogenous factors influence the optimal values of the firm's endogenous variables.

8.1.4. Tests of certain results

In chapter 6 some implications of the model were tested with the data used in chapter 4. We estimated the percentage of firms in our sample (56 firms) which satisfied the inequalities (8: 13) and (8: 14). By applying the usual 0–1 test we found that the observed percentages are higher than can be explained by chance. The results have been given in table 9, chapter 6.

We also estimated for the same firms the average values of the left side and the right side of the marginal conditions (8: 11) and (8: 12), respectively. The deviation turned out to be significant for the former and insignificant for the latter condition at the 5 per cent level (see table 10). However, when we estimated the averages of the left and right sides of a generalized version of the borrowing condition, given the discount rate as an increasing function of the leverage ratio—see equation (8: 20) below—we did not find any significant deviation.

Furthermore, we tested the results obtained regarding the influence of exogenous changes on the optimal leverage and pay-out ratios. We regressed the leverage ratio and pay-out ratio on calculated exogenous values of the rate of return on total capital ($\check{r}$), interest rate ($\check{i}$), and discount rate ($\check{k}$). The values of $\check{r}$, $\check{i}$ and $\check{k}$ are defined as that part of the rate of return, the interest rate and the discount rate, respectively, which should not be affected by differences between firms in growth rates, leverage ratios and pay-out ratios. The results have been given in tables 11 and 12.

As expected we found that the pay-out ratio is influenced negatively by $\check{r}$ and positively by $\check{i}$ and $\check{k}$. We also found that the leverage ratio is influenced negatively by $\check{i}$ and $\check{r}$. The last mentioned relationship is not in agreement with our theory, which states that a higher value of the exogenously given part of the rate of return on total capital will induce firms to increase their borrowing. When we excluded some firms which had negative growth rates and pay-out ratios greater than one (firms may hardly be in that position permanently) the coefficient of $\check{r}$ became much lower but remained negative.

One possible explanation for the negative regression relationship between leverage and the rate of return is that leverage in the short run is determined residually by firms so that unexpected variations in their profitability on total capital induce them to make short-run changes in leverage in the opposite direction. Since our cross-section data only cover the eight year period 1963–70, such short-run changes may blur the hypothesized long-run relationship. Another possibility which cannot be overlooked is that other goals, besides maximization of the capital value, influence the firm's borrowing behavior. For example, firms may seek to achieve greater financial freedom and independence of lenders. If the capital value is relatively insensitive to variations in the leverage ratio, then optimal borrowing behavior by firms may imply lower leverage as a result of an exogenously determined improvement in profitability.

The last section of chapter 6 was devoted to a sensitivity analysis of the model solutions. Among other things, we demonstrated that the firm's optimal leverage ratio, its optimal rate of return on equity and its optimal capital value are much more strongly affected by changes in the exogenously given part of the rate of return on total capital and of the interest rate at high values of the former variable and low values of the latter. In particular, the firm's capital value increases slowly at first, then at a sharply increasing speed as the exogenously determined part of the rate of return rises or as that of the interest rate falls.

8.1.5. Some generalizations of the model

In chapter 7 we analyzed certain extensions of our basic model. To make the analysis simple we assumed no internal growth costs throughout the chapter. Here we will recapitulate only a couple of the extensions made.

(a) *External equity financing*

We assumed new shares to be continuously emitted which brings money to the firm in relation to its return on equity at a time-constant rate (c). Disregarding personal income tax on dividends and administrative costs associated with new share issues the present value of all future net dividends at the beginning of the initial period (t) could be expressed

$$P'_t = (u-c)r_E K_{Et}/(k-v), \qquad (8:16)$$

where $v=(1-u+c)r_E$.

P'_t is the present value of the net dividends which accrue to the new and old owners of the firm. If the two groups have different risk aversion and liquidity preference the discount rate function may be represented by

$$k = k(u, c), \qquad (8:17)$$

where—consistent with the empirical findings in chapter 4—we assumed $\partial k/\partial u<0$, $\partial^2 k/\partial u^2>0$, $\partial k/\partial c>0$, $\partial^2 k/\partial c^2>0$ and $\partial^2 k/\partial u \partial c<0$. The maximization of P_t' gave two necessary optimality conditions

$$r_E = k-(u-c)\partial k/\partial u = k+(u-c)\partial k/\partial c. \tag{8: 18}$$

According to (8: 18) an optimal financing policy requires equality between the rate of return on equity and the "marginal cost" of retaining earnings and of emitting new shares.

From (8: 18) and the signs of the derivatives to the $k(u, h)$-function we came to the conclusion that all external influences which increase the rate of return on equity (r_E) (a higher product price or higher total productivity or a lower wage rate, etc.) also increase the firm's optimal internal and external equity financing. An important exogenous factor which positively influences the rate of return on equity is a lower profit tax rate. When we introduced a dividend tax the optimality conditions (8: 18) became more complex. Then we found, not unexpectedly, that a higher dividend tax rate discriminates against external in favor of internal equity financing.

(b) *The discount rate as an increasing function of the leverage ratio*

Given a fluctuating rate of return on total capital over time an increased degree or leverage may raise the variability of the rate of return on equity and of the market value of the shares which, in turn, may increase the financial risk for the owners of the firm. Therefore, we assumed the discount rate to be an increasing function of the leverage ratio (h). Given our assumptions of how the discount rate is affected by the pay-out ratio (u) and leverage ratio (h) we have

$$k = k(u, h), \tag{8: 19}$$

where $\partial k/\partial u < 0$, $\partial k^2/\partial u^2 > 0$, $\partial k/\partial h > 0$ and $\partial^2 k/\partial h^2 < 0$.

Then, it can be shown that an optimal borrowing policy which maximizes the capital value P_t requires

$$(\partial r_E/\partial h)/r_E = (\partial k/\partial h)/k. \tag{8: 20}$$

According to the optimality condition (8: 20) the firm will choose a value of h implying maximization of the ratio of the rate of return on equity (r_E) and the discount rate (k). Because the discount rate increases with an increase in the leverage ratio ($\partial k/\partial h > 0$) if follows also from (8: 20) that P_t is maximized at a lower leverage ratio than that which maximizes the rate of return on equity.

Another important consequence of the assumption $\partial k/\partial h > 0$ was that the optimal borrowing decision of the firm depends on its dividend decision. Increased internal financing (decreased pay-out ratio) causes a change in the ratio $(\partial k/\partial h)/k$ at every given h which induces the firm to change its borrowing. This relationship between internal and external financing, furthermore, altered some results regarding the effects of outside changes. For example, a reduction in the profit tax rate—which decreases the optimal pay-out ratio—makes the firm reduce (rise) its optimal leverage ratio depending on whether the lowered pay-out ratio positively or negatively affects the $(\partial k/\partial h)/k$-function.

8.2. Further issue

8.2.1. The objectives of firms

A central assumption for us has been that the firm is owner-controlled and that it seeks to maximize the market value of its shares. However, there are other alternatives. According to the behaviorists, the firm is controlled by its management and management sees the firm's growth rate as the most important objective. In addition, it has been claimed that maximization of the market value of shares is hardly a meaningful objective considering the difficulties of predicting the future (Cyert [1969] and Baumol & Stewart [1971]). Furthermore, in some firms the employees rather than management or owners are the ones that exercise control. These firms may be expected to maximize current wages or the present value of wages per employee (see Vanek [1970] and Atkinson [1973]).

In the last section of chapter 7 we briefly discussed these questions and came to the conclusion that the management-controlled firm may be expected to retain a greater share of its profits than the owner-controlled one. If instead the firm switches from maximizing share value to maximization of wage per employee, we also concluded that its growth will be affected negatively. Furthermore, the wage maximizing firm was found to reduce its demand for labor in response to an externally caused increase in the product price or an autonomous increase in productivity if it can freely vary labor input. Thus in economies with this type of worker-controlled firms there seems to be no incentive for inducing firms with high productivity to attract resources from firms with low productivity. It would then be difficult to affect employment through traditional stabilization policy since, for example, measures which increase aggregate demand cannot be expected to induce firms to employ more labor.

However, it is not self-evident that worker ownership should necessary imply the maximization of wages per employee. It seems unlikely that a completely collectivized management of firms can exist in which all employees take part in economic decisions. In the same way as in a capitalist system, it ought to be necessary to delegate decision making to an elected group of managers. This group may be expected to run the firm primarily with the intention of fulfilling their own objectives, which would mean that the behavior of larger worker-controlled firms would not differ significantly from that of management-controlled capitalist firms (Atkinson [1973]).

It would be of interest to test empirically the theoretically derived behavioral differences that follow from different objectives. Unfortunately, existing theories do not give any precise quantitative statements about the behavior of the firm that would allow one to discriminate between them when the different objectives imply the same direction of change in the endogenous variables in response to an exogenous change. Therefore, econometric models should be formulated so that each specific objective can be identified by the signs of the regression coefficients. There are only a few empirical experiments concerning motivations of firms and they all confine themselves to examining management and shareholders' objectives. These studies suggest that firms mainly attempt to satisfy the interests of management, but that the interest of shareholders can be one important restriction that affects its decisions (see, for example Grabowski & Mueller [1972]).

8.2.2. Unbalanced growth

Balanced and steady-state growth, which was another central assumption in our analysis, is hardly a good description of how firms grow over a short period of time. For one thing, cyclical variations in product demand cause deviations from the long- run rate of growth. For another, certain events may involve significant irregularity in the growth rate. A case in point is expansion through acquisition of other firms or parts of other firms. Such phenomena should lead to discontinuous and non-steady-state growth. Of course it would be desirable to take account of various irregularities in the growth process where successive changes occur in the firms' behavior over time. But this requires very complex models with time lags between the variables where the lag-structure itself depends on the dynamic adjustment process.

In order to see more clearly all the consequences which follow from a completely general formulation in which account is taken of changing growth conditions, it may be useful to introduce the generalizations successively. In section 7.3 the first step was taken in this direction when we allowed for different rates of steady-state growth of the prices of the product, labor and real capital. We showed that if, for example, the rate of growth of input prices is increased or if the rate of growth of the product price is reduced, the firm must devote more resources to raising the rate of increase of total productivity; otherwise a permanent decline in the firm's profitability will occur. Then the problem arises of finding an optimal balance of resources between productivity raising activities and other activities of the firm. But this optimization problem only seems capable of being handled by a model which also permits different rates of growth for the monetary variables.

It should be pointed out that an analysis based on the assumption of balanced expansion with constant relations between all variables seems to be more valid in describing the long run behavior of firms than every other analysis which treats dynamic disequilibrium situations. This is the case, for example, in dynamic input–output systems with fixed coefficients and in dynamic systems which are based on neoclassical production functions in which the net return of the system is plowed back into the capital accumulation. Given different capital stocks in the initial period, a very long planning period and a certain maximization objective at the end of this period, in the absence of external disturbances, these systems will display growth paths which converge to a balanced steady-state growth (Dorfman, Samuelson & Solow [1958]).

If there were no growth costs—i.e., if the input factors which the firm uses were perfectly variable—the static optimal behavior at every point of time would also be dynamically optimal (see for example Söderström [1974]). When an exogenously caused change occurs, an instantaneous adjustment of the firm's endogenous variables to new optimal relations takes place. These relations hold until the next external disturbance. Only if there are no growth costs and no successive external disturbances are the assumptions of a comparative dynamic analysis satisfied. This is the situation which is implicitly assumed in the dynamic firm models of the steady-state type where the given initial conditions determine the optimal growth paths for all future time.

8.2.3. Some macroeconomic implications

In this study the individual firm has been the sole object of analysis. The firm's behavior has been studied under the assumption that the behavior of all other firms is given. This limits the generality of the analysis. For example, it is clear that firms in different markets affect each other through changes in their product supply and demand for input factors and financial capital. This interaction between firms may imply that their aggregate behavior departs from that which would characterize them individually.

Consider the effects of growth costs. These consist in part of costs of marketing and developing of new products. Given limited size of product markets measures taken by one firm in order to increase its product demand will reduce the demand for the products of other firms. Hence increased growth by one firm occurs at the expense of the growth of other firms. For this reason the aggregated macro function of growth costs may be expected to increase at a more rapid rate with higher rates of growth than the typical growth cost function of individual firms. Similarly a limited supply of financial capital can cause the interest rate on borrowed capital to increase at a faster rate when all firms attempt to expand their debt finance at the same time.

However, there are also factors operating in the opposite direction. The resources which are devoted to research and development generate knowledge from which other firms as well as the rest of society can benefit. This positive externality from devoting resources to, e.g., stimulating product demand may make the aggregate rate of return higher than that for the individual firm tending to reduce growth costs associated with growth for society as a whole.

Another interesting macroeconomic implication concerns the extent to which the flows of financial capital to different firms tend to bring about a reallocation of capital resources, which is efficient from the viewpoint of the whole business sector. In our cross-sectional data for individual firms there exists a clear positive relationship between the retention ratio and the profitability on total assets. Assuming that the more profitable firms are more efficient, this would suggest that the internally generated financial flows contribute to increasing total efficiency. On the other hand, it may be noted that we found a negative relationship between the leverage ratio and profitability, while there was no correlation between the new-issue ratio and profitability for most firms.

An important factor which affects the conditions on which firms obtain financial capital is the level of aggregate stock prices. If these prices increase it will be less expensive for firms to secure funds for investments through new issues. Whether differences in stock prices for different firms can contribute to a more efficient resource allocation in the business sector is of course dependent on the degree to which stock prices accurately reflect differences in firms' expected profitability. Stock-market prices also ought to affect resource allocation in other ways. If the price of a firm's shares declines due to incompetent management, this would seem to increase the likelihood that it will be taken over by outsiders who find it advantageous to manage the firm themselves. This situation would seem not infrequently to be a cause of mergers.

In addition, changes in share values affect the total income and wealth of households through realized or unrealized capital gains or losses. In this way total savings of households are affected. A model in which the change in the total value of shares is an argument in both the aggregate savings function of households and in the aggregate investment function of firms have been presented by Moore [1975]. He shows that capital gains or losses may operate as a stabilizing factor in establishing the equality between total planned saving and total planned investment. If, for example, total saving ex ante is greater than investment, share prices will rise. This, in turn, stimulates households' consumption with the consequence that the deflationary pressure within the whole economy is reduced.

Once the analysis is expanded to include households, the question arises as to how households and firms influence each other through supply of and demand for labor and goods, respectively. A full-fledged allocation model for a growing national economy in which these issues are analyzed has been developed by Brems [1973]. He assumes two industrial sectors each of which produces one good with a given production function. He also assumes a household sector with a given utility function which is the same for all individuals.

Every individual chooses that combination of the two goods which will maximize his utility subject to his budget constraint. The firms are assumed to demand the quantity of labor and to decide on the investment program which maximizes the present worth of all of their future profits. Given the conditions for equilibrium in the goods and factor markets, Brems is able to derive an optimal intertemporal allocation for the two industries and the household sector of labor, capital and goods. His optimal solution also gives the total money income, wage bill and profit bill.

Variable list

1. Variables

Monetary variables

Non-ratio variables

O = sales

F = value added (sales minus value of purchased inputs)

L = wages (direct plus indirect wage costs)

A = depreciation costs

R = interest costs

V' = surplus ($F-A-R$)

V = profit on total capital ($F-L-A$)

T_V = profit taxes

V_E = profit on equity capital ($V-R-T_V$)

K = total capital (total assets)

K_E = equity capital (share capital plus reserves, unallocated profit, and half of untaxed allocations and funds)

K_F = borrowed capital ($K-K_E$)

K_L = long-term debt

I_N = net investment (ΔK)

I_B = gross investment (I_N+A)

U = dividends to shareholders

S_N = net saving (V_E-U)

S_B = gross saving (S_N+A)

N = inflow of new-issue capital

ΔK_E = increase of equity capital ($S_N+N=\Delta K-\Delta K_F$)

P = capital value = present discounted value of all future dividends (see definition on p. 24).

P' = net capital value = present discounted value of all future net dividends (see definition on p. 96).

T_U = taxes on dividends.

Ratio variables

r_P = rate of return on working capital; the numerator is profit on total capital (V) minus financial revenues and the denominator is total capital (K) minus financial assets

r =rate of return on total capital (V/K)
r'_E =surplus divided by equity capital (V'/K_E)
r_E =rate of return on equity (V_E/K_E)
v =rate of growth of all monetary variables such as wages, value added, profit on total capital, etc.
i =rate of interest on borrowed capital (R/K_F)
d =dividend yield (U/P)
k =required rate of return of shareholders (discount rate)
z =price-earnings ratio (P/V_E)
y =earnings-price ratio (V_E/P)
ϱ =valuation ratio (P/K_E)
p_d =rate of product diversification (see definition on p. 38)
a_d =rate of dispersion of plant (see definition on p. 38)
m =share of long-term debt (K_L/K)
h =leverage ratio (K_F/K_E)
h_k =share of debt (K_F/K)
u =pay-out ratio (U/V_E)
n =new-issue share (N/K_E)
c =new-issue ratio (N/V_E)
u_N =net pay-out ratio ($u-c$)
t_u =rate of tax on dividends (T_u/U)
t_V =rate of profit tax [$T_V/(V-R)$]
a =rate of depreciation (A/K)
p =product price
p_1 =price of labor
p_2 =price of capital
v_p =rate of growth of the product price
v_{p1} =rate of growth of the price of labor
v_{p2} =rate of growth of the price of capital.

Combined monetary and real variables

k_I =capital intensity (total capital divided by number of employees)
V'_L =surplus per employee (V'/L)
V'_{LN} =present discounted value of all future paid-out surpluses (wages) per employee (see definition on p. 103)

Real variables

Non-ratio variables

$\hat{L}$ =quantity of labor
$\hat{K}$ =quantity of capital
$\hat{K}_E$ =quantity of equity capital

$\hat{K}_F$ = quantity of borrowed capital
$\hat{F}$ = volume of production
$\hat{T}$ = quantity of management services.

Ratio variables

$\hat{l}$ = labor intensity $(\hat{L}/\hat{K})$
$\hat{v}_L$ = rate of growth of $\hat{L}$
$\hat{v}_K$ = rate of growth of $\hat{K}$
$\hat{v}_l$ = rate of growth of $\hat{l}$
$\hat{v}_E$ = rate of growth of $\hat{K}_E$
$\hat{v}_f$ = rate of growth of $\hat{K}_F$
$\hat{v}_F$ = rate of growth of $\hat{F}$.

2. Coefficients

Function coefficients

ψ = total productivity term in the production function
γ = rate of increase of total productivity $(\partial\hat{F}/\partial t)/\hat{F}$
α = elasticity of production with respect to labor $(\partial\hat{F}/\partial\hat{L})/(\hat{F}/\hat{L})$
$(1-\alpha)$ = elasticity of production with respect to capital $(\partial\hat{F}/\partial\hat{K})/(\hat{F}/\hat{K})$
α_1 = elasticity of production with respect to management services $(\partial\hat{F}/\partial\hat{T})/(\hat{F}/\hat{T})$
π_1 = constant term in the demand function for management services
π_2 = elasticity term in the demand function for management services
λ_{11} = intercept term in the linear regression profitability function
λ_{12} = coefficient with respect to the rate of growth of the sales in the linear profitability function
τ_{11} = intercept term in the linear interest-rate function
τ_{12} = coefficient with respect to the leverage ratio in the linear interest-rate function
$\varkappa_{11}$ = constant term in the linear discount-rate function
$\varkappa_{12}$ = coefficient with respect to the pay-out ratio in the linear discount-rate function.

Regression coefficients

β_0 = intercept term in the linear regression equations
b_j = coefficient with respect to explanatory variable j in the linear regression equations
E_0 = intercept term in the linear-multiplicative regression equations
E_1 = constant term in the linear-multiplicative regression equations
e_j = elasticity with respect to explanatory variable j in the linear-multiplicative equations

σ_j = standard error of either b_j or e_j

R^2 = multiple coefficient of determination

F_R = F-ratio corrected for degrees of freedom, which tests the significance of the regression as a whole

$E(j)$ = mathematical expected value of variable j

ε = error term in the regression equations.

3. Other signs

$\check{}$ indicates that a variable is measured in real (not monetary) units

* indicates an optimum value of a variable, i.e., a value which according to our dynamic steady-state model is consistent with maximum capital value of the firm

$\breve{}$ denotes that the variable is exogenously determined and independent of the behavior of the firm

t indicates the time period for a variable

$'$ indicates that the statistical measure of a variable is corrected for various book-keeping dispositions

A, B, C and D are used to describe components in functions, identities, derivatives etc.

MC denotes marginal cost

MR denotes marginal revenue.

APPENDIX A

Some identities from chapter 2

In this appendix we derive:

1. the capital-value formula $P_0 = uV_{E0}/(k-v)$;
2. the identity for the rate of return on equity capital $r_E = (1-t_V)\{(1+h)r - ih\}$; and
3. the identities for profit on equity capital V_{Et}, dividends U_t, net saving S_{Nt}, etc.

1. The capital-value formula

Given (for period t):

U_t =dividends
v_t =rate of growth of U_t
k_t =discount rate
V_{Et}=profit on equity capital
u_t =share of profit on equity which is distributed as dividends, i.e. the pay-out ratio
K_{Et}=equity capital
P_t =discounted sum of dividends, i.e., the capital value

The firm pays dividends during an unlimited number of future periods beginning at $t=0$.

Proposition: Capital value P_0 is determined according to the relationship $P_0 = uV_{E0}/(k-v)$.

Derivation:

$$P_0 = \sum_{t=0}^{\infty} U_t \left\{\prod_{j=0}^{t} (1+k_j)^{-1}\right\} = U_0 \sum_{t=0}^{\infty} \left\{\prod_{j=0}^{t} (1+v_j)(1+k_j)^{-1}\right\}, \tag{A: 1}$$

where $v_0 = 0$ and $U_{t+1} = (1+v_t)U_t$.

(A: 1) is simplified if steady-state and balanced growth of the firm is assumed which means that $k_t = k_{t+j} = k$, $u_t = u_{t+j} = u$ and $v_t = v_{t+j} = v$, and if the growth of U_t takes place continuously. Then we obtain

$$P_0 = uV_{E0}\int_0^{\infty} e^{-kt+vt}dt = uV_{E0}\left\{\frac{e^{-(k-v)\infty} - e^{-(k-v)0}}{-k+v}\right\} = uV_{E0}/(k-v). \tag{A: 2}$$

2. The identity for the rate of return on equity capital

Given for period t:

V_t = profit on total capital
V_{Et} = profit on equity capital
R_t = interest costs
T_{vt} = profit taxes
K_{Et} = equity capital
K_t = total capital

and the identities $V_{Et} = V_t - R_t - T_{vt}$ and $K_t = K_{Et} + K_{Ft}$.

Proposition: The rate of return on equity capital after taxes is $r_E = (1 - t_V)\{(1+h)r - ih\}$.

Derivation: From the definitions of the variables t_V, h and i—see the variable list, p. 123—we have

$$T_{vt} = t_V(V_t - R_t);$$
$$R_t = ihK_{Et};$$
$$V_{Et} = V_t - ihK_{Et} - t_V(V_t - ihK_{Et}) = (1 - t_V)(V_t - ihK_{Et}).$$

Then it follows that

$$r_E = V_{Et}/K_{Et} = (1 - t_V)\left[\frac{V_t - ihK_{Et}}{K_{Et}}\right] = (1 - t_V)\left[\frac{r(1+h)K_{Et} - ihK_E}{K_{Et}}\right]$$
$$= (1 - t_V)[(1+h)r - ih].$$

3. Various financial identities

Given:

V_E = profit on equity capital[1]
U = dividends
S_N = net saving
S_B = gross saving
I_N = net investment
I_B = gross investment
ΔK_F = change of borrowing
(Note that we assume no outside quality financing ($N = 0$).)
From these definitions and those in the Variable list (p. 122) it now follows that:

$$V_E = r_E K_E = V - R - T_V = (p\hat{F} - p_1\hat{L} - p_2\hat{K} - ihK_E)(1 - t_V)$$
$$U = uV_E = ur_E K_E$$

[1] Note that the time index has been dropped.

$$A = aK = a(1+h)K_E$$
$$S_N = \Delta K_E = v_E K_E = (1-u)r_E K_E$$
$$S_B = \Delta K_E + A = v_E K_E + aK = [(1-u)r_E + a(1+h)]K_E$$
$$I_N = \Delta K = v_K K = v_E K_E + v_F K_F = [(1-u)r_E + (1-u)r_E h]K_E = (1-u)(1+h)r_E K_E$$
$$I_B = \Delta K + A = v_K K + aK = v_E K_E + v_F K_F + a(1+h)K_E = (1+h)[(1-u)r_E + a]K_E$$
$$\Delta K_F = \Delta K - \Delta K_E = v_K K - v_E K_E = I_N - S_N = I_B - S_B = h(1-u)r_E K_E$$

(Note that $v_K = v_E$ due to the assumption of equilibrium growth.)

APPENDIX B

Data, estimation methods and regression results for chapter 3

First, we describe the data of the Swedish Engineering Employers' Association which form the basis of the calculations in chapter 3. Then, we give a detailed description of the method of estimation for the relationship between profitability and growth. Finally, some regression results are presented and we show how capital-value isoquants are derived.

1. The data

a) Sample of firms

The profitability statistics of the Engineering Employers' Association (VS) began to be collected in 1963 and covered in that year all member firms with more than 500 employees, half of the firms with 150–500 employees and a third of those that had 50–150 employees. During 1964–66 the sample was successively expanded to cover in principle all member firms with more than 150 employees, while the lower size limit for firms in the sample increased from 50 to 75 employees. In 1967 the sample was again increased to include 75 % of the firms in the group with 75–150 employees. Thus the number of firms in the sample was approximately 100 in 1963, about 150 during 1964–66 and more than 200 during 1967–68.

However, the population of firms for which we have data is less than would appear from these figures. First, a number of firms have declined to supply information to the Association and/or supplied incorrect information. Second, certain firms in the Association have not given us at the Industrial Institute for Economic and Social Research permission to use the information supplied. This reduces the population for the years 1963–68 to 68, 86, 101, 110, 139 and 141 firms respectively.

Since we study (in chapter 3) an identical group of firms over the period 1963–68, the number of observations becomes still smaller. Of the firms which were in the population in 1963, 6 have in the following years been excluded from the data due to, among other reasons, mergers. All in all, therefore, we have only 62 firms in our sample. However, these 62 firms account for almost half of the employment and sales in the engineering industry (46 % and 47 %, respectively, in 1968).

The concept of the firm used in VS is the organizational-economic unit. That is, if several legal entities constitute an affiliated group (a parent company and subsidiaries) the whole group is included as one firm in VS though this applies only to affiliates located in Sweden. Thus the parent company and its Swedish affiliates are consolidated. Affiliates are defined (narrowly) as these firms of which 75 % or more is owned by the parent firm.

It should be noted that the primary data of the VS can be expected to be more reliable than that of other, official statistical sources. In VS firms have stated profit and capital information corrected for accelerated depreciation and appropriations to untaxed funds, etc. These corrections may be expected to give more reliable levels of profitability and also imply—most importantly for our purposes—that profitability has been calculated from uniformly defined magnitudes for all firms.

b) Principles underlying the measurement of profit and capital

b.1. *The valuation problem*

The fact that physical plant and working capital consist of various kinds of capital goods makes it necessary, when estimating profitability, to weight the different capital goods to obtain a homogeneous measure in which each unit of capital has the same productive capacity. In the VS-statistics capital goods are combined with price weights, i.e., a value measure is used. Current purchase prices are used and not the prices which a firm could be expected to receive if the capital goods were sold.

Even if capital were a completely homogeneous factor of production, an intertemporal valuation and combination problem would remain due to the fact that real capital goods are physically worn out, and their prices change over time. In order to make the volume of investments in different time periods comparable, the investments must be depreciated and revalued with a price index. In this context it would seem most proper to let depreciation express only the loss of productive capacity of the investments which is due to the use and wearing out of capital in production. If one also takes account of economic obsolescence which is due to technical progress, then older capital goods may be given weights, in the calculated capital measure, which are less than those corresponding to their actual productive capacity.

Similarly the most proper procedure would seem to be to revalue capital goods only according to those price increases which take place independently of technical progress. If one uses a price index which also includes price changes due to improvements of quality, older capital goods will be given price weights which are greater than those corresponding to their productive capacity.

b.2. *The measurement of profit*

When profit on total capital is calculated in VS the point of departure is the firm's officially reported net profit. To net profit are added the profit taxes, booked depreciations, interest costs, unallocated costs, extraordinary costs and increases of inventory reserves.

From net profit are subtracted normal depreciation on physical plants and equipment, allocated costs, extraordinary revenues and reductions of inventory reserves.[1]

Unallocated costs are defined as appropriations to pension funds (excluding the PRI fund) and other pension costs, and recorded research and development costs if any.

Allocated costs are defined as the same cost items, but correctly distributed over time.

Extraordinary costs are defined as allocations to untaxed investment funds, donations, and similar allocations which are not deductible from taxes, writing down of receivables in excess of actual losses and accounting losses due to disposal of shares.

Extraordinary revenues are defined as utilization of untaxed investment funds, recovered receivables, recorded profits due to disposal of shares, land, and plant and refunds from own pension funds and transfers from such funds to PRI funds.

Inventory reserve increase or decrease is defined as outgoing inventories at the lowest value at the end of the year according to the first-in-first-out principle minus incoming inventories at the beginning of the year according to the same valuation principle.

Normal depreciation has been calculated every year to constitute 3 % of the taxable value of buildings and other plant, 10 % of the replacement value of machines and other equipment and 20 % of the replacement value of vehicles.

b.3. *The measurement of capital*

Buildings and land have been taken up at taxable values. These are revalued, prior to deduction of normal depreciation, to actual annual values by using the building price index of the Central Bureau of Statistics (SCB). The taxable values are determined on the basis of the information which firms supply to tax authorities concerning the physical characteristics of the capital goods (volume, surface, area and weight) and estimated sales values and fire-insurance values.

The values of machines, other equipment and vehicles are obtained by revaluing the historical acquisition costs with the SCB price index for machines

[1] Total profit calculated in this way may be obtained alternatively by subtracting from net sales costs of manufacture, marketing and administration and normal depreciation. Financial revenues are then included in the definition of profit.

and vehicles, respectively. From these revalued values normal depreciation is then deducted for each category of capital from the year of acquisition to the given final year (the reporting year).

Financial assets (cash and bank accounts, bonds, claims on firms, secured claims, blocked accounts in the Bank of Sweden, etc.) have been included at the values stated in the firm's balance sheets. As a rule shares are given at nominal values which are often much lower than their actual market values. In addition to the real and financial capital assets mentioned, prepayments made for current plant construction (buildings, machines and equipment) including advances to promoters, good will values, patent rights, certain organizational costs, and other similar items, are included in total capital.

2. Errors of measurement of profitability in firms' annual reports

When one wants to measure profitability it is convenient to use information from the firms' official income statements and balance sheets. However, this information is liable to various kinds or errors.

a) Causes of errors

Current tax regulations in Sweden give firms the opportunity to depreciate their tangible capital at a faster rate than that which corresponds to the reduction in its productive capacity or its ability to generate profits. Thus, for example, machines and equipment may be depreciated annually by 20 % of their original acquisition value. The maximum permitted depreciation rate on buildings would also seem to allow depreciation greater than that corresponding to its actual depreciation. In addition, inventories may be greatly undervalued since they are allowed to be carried on the books at as low as 40 % of acquisition or replacement value.

It is likely that firms utilize to differing degrees these opportunities offered them by the tax law to record lower taxable profits than their actual profits. Among other things, the underestimation of recorded profits may be expected to vary positively with actual profitability. The following are some of the reasons for this. Large profits are not infrequently regarded by the general public as unjustified and a sign of monopolistic price setting. Large recorded profits can also stimulate demands from shareholders for increased dividends. On the other hand, low recorded profits can also create problems for management. The stockholders may see this as a sign of incompetent management and may therefore try to replace it.

Overdepreciation of plant and equipment may also be expected to vary positively with the rate of growth of the firm, since the increased base for depreciation which follows from increased new investment creates greater opportunities to increase depreciation for tax purposes in relation to actual profits.[1] Empirical investigations have also found a negative relation between the effective profits tax rate and the growth of firms (Södersten [1971]).

b) Estimates of the size of the errors

Below, we attempt to estimate the approximate order of magnitude of differences between reported and actual profits (after depreciation) and capital assets by comparing the uncorrected balance-sheet figures in "Svenska Aktiebolag" (AB) with the corrected figures in the statistics of the Engineering Employers' Association (VS).

Our calculations of the ratio of equity capital to sales for manufacturing firms during the period 1963–68 show that according to AB this ratio is slightly more than 35 % of its value according to VS. This would suggest that equity capital in the official reports has been understated at slightly more than 35 % of its actual value.

In addition, in VS profits taxes constitute about 35 % of profit on equity. Since the nominal rate of tax during the period was somewhat more than 50 %, this difference between the nominal and effective tax rate indicates that firms, in utilizing profit-adjusting measures, have been able to record a profit on equity which constitutes approximately 35/50 = 70 % of the actual profit. If the book value of equity is 35 % of the actual value (see above), and book profit is 70 % of the actual, then the actual rate of return on equity will be 50 % of the recorded rate.[2]

It has also been possible to make profitability comparisons directly for about half of the 62 engineering firms in our sample. Then we found that the rate of return on total capital is approximately 20 % lower in the VS data than in the AB data. In addition, the rate of return on equity from VS is approximately 60 % of that from AB. This comparison thus gives a somewhat lower figure for the degree of overestimation of actual profitability than the indirect calculation carried out above.

3. The measure of the firm's rate of growth

In chapter 3, we have measured the firm's *rate of growth* as the percentage change in its sales per year.

According to the theory of growth costs (see pp. 33 f.) it is really the growth of the volume of sales which is assumed to influence the firm's productivity

---

[1] Overdepreciation is also dependent on the rate of price increase of tangible capital. For a theoretical discussion of the relationships between depreciations, effective taxation, growth and the rate of inflation, see Bröms [1974].

[2] Note that the ratio of actual profitability to book profitability equals the ratio of book equity to actual equity (35 %) divided by the ratio of book profit to actual profit (70 %).

and profitability. The idea is that differences in growth rates between firms that are due to differences in exogenously changing prices of their products do not give rise to adjustment costs.[1] Thus instead of the growth rate of sales, the growth rate of deflated sales ought to be used.

The reason why we have not used such a measure of real growth is that it has not been possible to deflate sales satisfactorily for every individual firm. Most firms in our sample are highly diversified, while available price series are only for large aggregates of commodity groups and only reflect price changes for a few representative commodities within each aggregate.[2] Therefore, one cannot exclude the possibility that the errors in the regression estimates which would occur with price deflation would be at least as large as those which can occur when the growth measure has not been deflated at all.

4. Estimation of the influence of growth on profitability

In the following we describe the empirical determination of the influence of the firm's growth on its profitability on the basis of our sample of 62 engineering firms.

a) The problem

In order to simplify the presentation, we assume that the relationship between profitability and growth is linear and that the only explanatory variable is growth. However, these assumptions do not alter the principle behind the estimation procedure we shall describe. The profitability function to be estimated may be written

$$r = \lambda_{11} + \lambda_{12} v_0 + \varepsilon, \qquad \text{(B: 1)}$$

where r is total profitability, v_0 is the actual rate of growth of sales and ε is a random error term. The coefficients λ_{11} and λ_{12} are assumed to be equal for all firms. Due to the fact that an increase in profits makes it easier to finance more rapid growth by internally generated funds v_0 ought also to be a function of r. This relationship may be written generally as

$$v_0 = f(r). \qquad \text{(B: 2)}$$

Since r is an explanatory variable for v_0, v_0 will be correlated with the error term ε in (B: 1). Single equation estimation of (B: 1) with ordinary least squares

[1] On the other hand, endogenously caused price changes due to advertising, improvement of product quality, etc., ought to be allowed to affect the growth measure.

[2] The wholesale price index of the Central Bureau of Statistics for different industry subgroups covers at the highest level of disaggregation, fivedigit statistical classifications according to *Statistiska meddelanden*.

(OLS) will then yield coefficients which are distorted by simultaneity bias. In order to eliminate this bias, we apply an estimation procedure which is analogous to two-stage least squares.

b) The estimation procedure

We begin by calculating for each firm a growth variable which is purged of any direct influences from the firm's profitability r. This profitability-adjusted growth variable is defined as

$$v_0' = v_{0/E} + (1-u)(1-t_V)[\bar{r} + h(\bar{r} - i)] + n, \tag{B: 3}$$

where $v_{0/E} = v_0 - v_E$ is the relative change in the ratio of sales to equity capital, $\bar{r}$ is the arithmetic mean of total profitability for all firms, t_V is the rate of profit tax, u is the pay-out ratio, h is the leverage ratio, i is the interest rate and n is the new-issue ratio.

We then estimate with OLS a relationship with v_0 as the dependent variable, and v_0' as the explanatory variable. On the basis of the estimated coefficients $\hat{\lambda}_{21}$ and $\hat{\lambda}_{22}$ in this relationship, we obtain for each firm

$$\hat{v}_0 = \hat{\lambda}_{21} + \hat{\lambda}_{22} v_0', \tag{B: 4}$$

where $\hat{v}_0$ is the calculated rate of growth of sales corrected for the influence of profitability. Finally, using $\hat{v}_0$ as the explanatory variable a cross-sectional OLS-regression is run of the profitability relationship

$$r = \lambda_{11}' + \lambda_{12}' \hat{v}_0. \tag{B: 5}$$

It can be shown that consistent estimates of λ_{11}' and λ_{12}' are obtained if $\hat{v}_0'$ is not indirectly affected by r. An important condition for this is either that none of the explanatory variables for v_0' is influenced by r or that a change of r only leads to changes in the explanatory variables which according to (B: 3) do not systematically influence v_0'.

Twelve firms in our data have recorded a level of profit on equity which is clearly less than the sum of paid profit taxes and dividends. However, there is reason to believe that these firms cannot permanently pay profits taxes and dividends in excess of their profit on equity. We have, therefore, in the regressions for these firms assigned the term $(1-u)(1-t_V)$ a value of zero.

We have also carried out regressions of (B: 5) with these firms excluded. For the group of firms with positive rates of growth ($\hat{v}_0 > 0$) we then obtained coefficients of $\hat{v}_0$ which are still significantly negative at the 5 % level, and which differ by only five to ten hundredths from the coefficients in the corresponding regressions when those firms were included.

5. Regression estimates for the influence of the rate of growth on profitability

The following are results of the regressions in which the rate of return on working capital and the rate of return on total capital are explained by

1) the actual rate of growth of sales with a linear specification (table B: 1)
2) the calculated rate of growth of sales with a linear specification (table B: 2)
3) the calculated rate of growth of sales with a linear specification for five different groups of firms ordered according to values of the growth variable (table B: 3) and
4) the calculated rate of growth of sales and the rate of product diversification, the rate of plant dispersion, size and capital intensity for two different growth classes. Group 1 includes firms with negative growth rates and group 2 firms with positive growth rates (tables B: 4–B: 6 refer to linear specifications and tables B: 7–B: 9 to logarithmic specifications).

The regressions with the calculated rate of growth of sales has been done with the two-stage estimation procedure described above (see p. 134).

Table B: 1. *Regressions showing the impact of the actual growth rate on the rate of return on working capital and on total capital*

All firms. Linear specifications. Ordinary least squares

	B	*b*	σ	*e*	R^2
Rate of return on working capital	0.0399	0.3232***	0.0826	0.2604	0.2032
Rate of return on total capital	0.0382	0.2376***	0.0549	0.2127	0.2376

Note: *B* is the intercept term, *b* is the regression coefficient, σ is the standard error of the regression coefficient, *e* is the elasticity calculated at the means of the variables, and R^2 is the coefficient of multiple determination. Regression coefficients which are significant at the 10 %, 5 % and 1 % levels are indicated by *, ** and ***, respectively.

Table B: 2. *Regressions showing the impact of the calculated growth rate on the rate of return on working capital and on total capital*

All firms. Linear specifications. Two-stage least squares

	B	*b*	σ	*e*	R^2
Rate of return on working capital	0.0600	−0.1430	0.1215	−0.1119	0.0226
Rate of return on total capital	0.0515	−0.0692	0.0827	−0.0601	0.0116

Note: See note to table B: 1.

Table B: 3. *Regressions showing the impact of the growth rate on the rate of return on working capital and on total capital*

Five groups of firms with different growth rates. Linear specifications. Two-stage least squares

		Group 1	Group 2	Group 3	Group 4	Group 5
Rate of return on working capital	b	0.7785**	−1.3855	−1.0200	−0.8980	−0.5945*
	σ	0.3246	1.5310	2.3896	1.3513	0.3422
	e	0.5183	−0.5959	−0.9364	−1.2117	−2.3010
	$\bar{v}$	−0.0477	0.0263	0.0538	0.0682	0.1132
Rate of return on total capital	b	0.5104**	−0.3015	−0.1116	−0.8037	−0.3388
	σ	0.1960	1.0649	0.6891	1.5659	0.2441
	e	0.4307	−0.1279	−0.1221	−1.1851	−1.2566
	$\bar{v}$	−0.0457	0.0233	0.0521	0.0694	0.1128
Number of firms		12	13	12	12	13

Note: $\bar{v}$ is the mean value of the growth variable in each growth group. Concerning other symbols see the note to table B: 1.

Table B: 4. *Regressions showing the impact of the growth rate on the rate of return on working capital*

Firms with negative growth rates. Linear specifications. Two-stage least squares

	Rate of growth of sales	Rate of product diversification	Rate of plant dispersion	Size	Capital intensity	B / R^2 / F_R
b	0.7785**					0.1072
σ	0.3246					0.3652
e	0.5183					5.752
b	0.8508**	−0.2196				0.1200
σ	0.3654	0.4271				0.3833
e	0.5610	−0.1724				2.797
b	0.8508**	−0.2196	0.0			0.1200
σ	0.3876	0.4530	0.0			0.3833
e	0.5610	−0.1724	0.0			1.657
b	0.3699	0.3537	0.0	0.0303**		0.0176
σ	0.3525	0.4143	0.0	0.0119		0.6810
e	0.2442	0.2777	0.0	1.0144		3.735
b	0.3818	0.3536	0.0	0.0278**	0.0002	0.0083
σ	0.3802	0.4444	0.0	0.0154	0.0007	0.6854
e	0.2521	0.2776	0.0	0.9297	0.2612	2.614

Note: See the note to table B: 1.

Table B: 5. *Regressions showing the impact of the growth rate on the rate of return on working capital*

Firms with positive growth rates. Linear specifications. Two-stage least squares

	Rate of growth of sales	Rate of product diversification	Rate of plant dispersion	Size	Capital intensity	B R^2 F_R
b	−0.4920**					0.0818
σ	0.1869					0.1262
e	−0.6467					6.930
b	−0.4075**	−0.0406				0.0808
σ	0.2040	0.0393				0.1455
e	−0.5355	−0.0899				4.002
b	−0.4054*	−0.0474	0.0059			0.0805
σ	0.2062	0.0485	0.0241			0.1466
e	−0.5328	−0.1049	0.0171			2.634
b	−0.4282**	−0.0359	0.0018	0.0029*		0.0742
σ	0.2006	0.0475	0.0235	0.0015		0.2127
e	−0.5628	−0.0795	0.0051	0.1447		3.039
b	−0.3937*	−0.0406	0.0031	0.0036**	−0.0002	0.0750
σ	0.2012	0.0473	0.0234	0.0016	0.0001	0.2402
e	−0.5174	−0.0900	0.0091	0.1777	−0.2879	2.781

Note: See the note to table B: 1.

Table B: 6. *Regressions showing the impact of the growth rate on the rate of return on total capital*

Firms with positive growth rates. Linear specifications. Two-stage least squares

	Rate of growth of sales	Rate of product diversification	Rate of plant dispersion	Size	Capital intensity	B R^2 F_R
b	−0.3868***					0.0823
σ	0.1312					0.1534
e	−0.5243					8.696
b	−0.3034**	−0.0400				0.0712
σ	0.1415	0.0273				0.1904
e	−0.4192	−0.0936				5.0526
b	−0.3026**	−0.0428	0.0024			0.0711
σ	0.1432	0.0337	0.0168			0.1907
e	−0.4181	−0.1001	0.0074			3.614
b	−0.3205**	−0.0338	−0.0008	0.0023**		0.0661
σ	0.1376	0.0326	0.0162	0.0010		0.2708
e	−0.4428	−0.0791	−0.0025	0.1202		4.179
b	−0.3046**	−0.0359	−0.0002	0.0026**	−0.0001	0.0711
σ	0.1394	0.0328	0.0162	0.0011	0.0001	0.2823
e	−0.4209	−0.0841	−0.0006	0.1363	−0.1331	3.461

Note: See the note to table B: 1.

Table B: 7. *Regressions showing the impact of the growth rate on the rate of return on working capital*

Firms with negative growth rates. Logarithmic specifications. Two-stage least squares

	Rate of growth of sales	Rate of product diversification	Rate of plant dispersion	Size	Capital intensity	B / R^2 / F_R
e	0.6482**					0.0984
σ	0.2702					0.3652
						5.753
e	0.6990**	−0.1890				0.1087
σ	0.3037	0.4214				0.3791
						2.747
e	0.6990**	−0.1890	0.0			0.1087
σ	0.3221	0.4468	0.0			0.3791
						1.628
e	0.2309	0.5060	0.0	0.0595**[a]		0.1821
σ	0.2815	0.3995	0.0	0.0204		0.7200
						4.497
e	0.2543	0.5612	0.0	0.0507*[a]	0.0445[a]	−0.0239
σ	0.2792	0.3985	0.0	0.0218	0.0414	0.7651
						3.909

[a] These elasticities are not comparable with those in table B: 4, since the value of all variables except size and capital intensity have been increased by one for the regressions with the logarithmic functional form. *Note:* See the note to table B: 1.

Table B: 8. *Regressions showing the impact of the growth rate on the rate of return on working capital*

Firms with positive growth rates. Logarithmic specifications. Two-stage least squares

	Rate of growth of sales	Rate of product diversification	Rate of plant dispersion	Size	Capital intensity	B / R^2 / F_R
e	−0.4382**					0.0745
σ	0.1864					0.1032
						5.526
e	−0.3309	−0.0671				0.0741
σ	0.2019	0.0506				0.1356
						3.686
e	−0.3346	−0.0802	0.0190			0.0735
σ	0.2035	0.0565	0.0351			0.1411
						2.518
e	−0.3790*	−0.0673	0.0084	0.0038[a]		0.0784
σ	0.2093	0.0582	0.0369	0.0040		0.1575
						2.102
e	−0.3797*	−0.0636	0.0068	0.0083[a]	−0.0217[a]	0.1320
σ	0.2083	0.0580	0.0368	0.0055	0.0183	0.1837
						1.981

[a] These elasticites are not comparable with those in table B: 5 since the value of all variables, except size and capital intensity, have been increased by one for the regressions with the logarithmic functional form. *Note:* See the note to table B: 1.

Table B: 9. *Regressions showing the impact of the growth rate on the rate of return on total capital*

Firms with positive growth rates. Logarithmic specifications. Two-stage least squares

	Rate of growth of sales	Rate of product diversification	Rate of plant dispersion	Size	Capital intensity	B R^2 F_R
e	−0.4023***					0.0705
σ	0.1342					0.1577
						8.986
e	−0.3008**	−0.0564				0.0694
σ	0.1469	0.0356				0.2003
						5.887
e	−0.3035**	−0.0642	0.0114			0.0691
σ	0.1482	0.0396	0.0243			0.2041
						3.933
e	−0.3710**	−0.0467	−0.0016	0.0047*[a]		0.0758
σ	0.1506	0.0402	0.0250	0.0028		0.2520
						3.790
e	−0.3706**	−0.0446	−0.0025	0.0073*[a]	−0.0127[a]	0.1325
σ	0.1506	0.0402	0.0250	0.0038	0.0124	0.2690
						3.245

[a] These elasticites are not comparable with those in table B: 6 since the value of all variables, except size and capital intensity, have been increased by one for the regressions with the logarithmic functional form.
Note: See the note to table B: 1.

6. Derivation of capital-value isoquants

Below we derive capital-value isoquants which show optimal combinations of profitability (r) and rate of growth (v) for various given capital values.

Assumptions: Assumptions 1)–3) in chapter 3, p. 45, and the model equations (2: 10)–(2: 17) give us the simplified financial system

$$v = (1-u)r \qquad \text{(B: 6)}$$

$$k = \varkappa_1(1/u) + \varkappa_2 \qquad \text{(B: 7)}$$

$$\varrho = P/K_E = ur/(k-v). \qquad \text{(B: 8)}$$

We recall here: v and r are the rate of growth of dividends and the rate of return on total capital, respectively, u is the pay-out ratio, k is the discount rate, P is the capital value and K_E is equity capital.

Derivation:

(B: 6) and (B: 8) give

$$\varrho(k-v) = (r-v), \qquad \text{(B: 9)}$$

(B: 6), (B: 7) and (B: 9) give

$$\varrho[\varkappa_2+\varkappa_1 r/(r-v)-v]=r-v. \tag{B: 10}$$

(B: 10) is first multiplied by $(r-v)$ and then by $(\varrho-1)$. Then we collect the terms in v^2, v, vr, r and r^2 and obtain

$$(\varrho-1)^2 v^2-\varkappa_2\varrho(\varrho-1)v-2(\varrho-1)\frac{(\varrho-2)}{2}vr+(\varkappa_1+\varkappa_2)\varrho(\varrho-1)r-(\varrho-1)r^2=0. \tag{B: 11}$$

After completing the square in (B: 11) we get

$$\left[(\varrho-1)v-\frac{2}{\varrho-2}r-\frac{\varkappa_2\varrho}{2}\right]^2=\frac{\varrho^2}{4}r^2-2\frac{\varrho}{2}r\left[\varkappa_1(\varrho-1)+\frac{\varkappa_2}{2}\varrho\right]+\tfrac{1}{4}\varkappa_2^2\varrho^2. \tag{B: 12}$$

In addition, after completing the square in the right-hand side of (B: 12), we obtain

$$\left[(\varrho-1)v-\frac{\varrho-2}{2}r-\tfrac{1}{2}\varkappa_2\varrho\right]^2-\left[\frac{\varrho}{2}r-\varkappa_1(\varrho-1)-\frac{\varkappa_2}{2}\right]^2$$
$$=-\varkappa_1^2(\varrho-1)^2-\varkappa_1\varkappa_2\varrho(\varrho-1). \tag{B: 13}$$

Using the conjugate rule and dividing by $(\varrho-1)$, gives

$$[r-v-\varkappa_1]\{r+(\varrho-1)v-[\varkappa_1(\varrho-1)+\varkappa_2\varrho]\}=\varkappa_1[\varkappa_1(\varrho-1)+\varkappa_2\varrho]. \tag{B: 14}$$

Since equity capital (K_E) has been assumed to be predetermined, to each valuation ratio (ϱ) corresponds one capital value (P). Thus (B: 14) states for given values of P the capital-value isoquants expressed as combinations of r and v.

If the discount rate is assumed to be independent of the pay-out ratio, i.e., if $\varkappa_1=0$—(B: 14) is simplified to $(r-v)[r+(\varrho-1)v-\varkappa_2\varrho]=0$, or

$$r+(\varrho-1)v-\varkappa_2\varrho=0. \tag{B: 14$'$}$$

The capital-value isoquants are then straight lines. It is also clear from (B: 14)′ that these isoquants are positively sloped for $\varrho<1$ and negatively sloped for $\varrho>1$. Note that capital value P in the former case is less than equity capital K_E, while in the latter case the contrary is true.

APPENDIX C

Data, estimation procedures, regression results, etc., for chapter 4

1. Statistics from Swedish Corporations and the Financial Journal

In chapter 3 the profitability statistics of the Swedish Engineering Employers' Association (VS) were used. An important advantage of these statistics is that their measures of capital and profit have been corrected for book-keeping inclinations such as overdepreciation of durable assets, writing down of inventories, etc. However, VS contains no information on various types of debt, e.g., long-term and short-term debt. Nor is there in VS any information on the market value of the shares of firms. Since these variables are of central importance for the analysis, in chapter 4, of the factors determining the interest rate on borrowed capital (interest rate) and the discount rate, it was necessary to turn to other statistical sources. We have used the publications *Svenska Aktiebolag* (Swedish Corporations) and Finanstidningen (The Financial Journal).[1] In the following we denote these two sources of statistics as FS.

FS contains firms listed on the Stockholm Stock Exchange (the A-list). Of these only industrial firms are included in our sample. Banks, shipping firms, insurance companies and financial investment firms have been excluded, since these firms differ sharply in many respects from industrial firms, e.g., as concerns their liquidity, debt composition, dividend policy, etc. Our data cover the period 1963–70. Due to mergers and changes in their operations, some firms which were reported in FS in 1963 had been deleted from FS in 1970. This has further restricted our final sample, which consists of only fifty-six industrial firms.

The concept of a firm in FS is the organizational decision unit which includes the parent firm and its subsidiaries both in Sweden and abroad. As a rule all firms which are at least 50 % owned by the parent firm are counted as subsidiaries. Note that this definition differs from that which is used in VS, which counts only the Swedish part of the group, i.e., the parent firm plus

[1] In 1968 the name of this magazine was changed to Affärsvärlden–Finanstidningen.

Swedish subsidiaries. In addition, VS counts as subsidiaries only firms which are at least 75 % owned by the parent firm.

For a smaller number of stockmarket-listed industrial firms there is in FS information concerning the income statement of only the parent firm. For these firms we have had to use profit and interest-cost data applying to the parent-firm unit. In cases in which variables have been calculated on the basis of data from both the income statement and the balance sheet, e.g., the rate of profit and the interest rate, the information for balance sheet items has also been obtained from the balance sheet of the parent firm. In most firms for which income statements are given only for the parent company, the parent firm is without doubt the clearly dominating part of the group.

A number of items in the balance sheets of the firms have been difficult to classify into different capital categories. We have allocated half of the following items to equity and half to long-term debt: reserves for bankruptcy risk, specially allocated funds, untaxed reserves, fire damage reserves and reserves against receivables. In addition, we assigned to long-term debt minority interests and appropriations to pension funds, while tax reserves, unpaid taxes, prepayments on orders and acceptances are assigned to short-term debt. These items are relatively small and constitute on the average one to two per cent of total assets. Finally, it may be noted that 50 % of appropriations to investment funds have been counted as equity.

2. Leverage ratio, risk of bankruptcy, risk aversion and interest rate

Below we derive under some simplifying assumptions a relationship between lenders' required rate of return (the interest rate) and the leverage ratio.

Assume that if the firm goes bankrupt, lenders receive no interest income and lose a certain share (x) of their capital invested in the firm. Their loss will then amount to xhK_E, where h is the leverage ratio and K_E is the firm's equity capital. If, on the other hand, no bankruptcy occurs, the borrowed capital is paid back in full and the lenders also receive interest income ihK_E, where i is the interest rate. Lenders' expected net income from lending is thus $[-\mu xh K_E+(1-\mu)ihK_E]$, where μ is the probability of bankruptcy. It is clear from this expression that the dispersion of this net income increases as h increases.

In addition, it is assumed that lenders' income exclusive of net revenues from lending, (y) is a non-stochastic variable and that lenders have no time preference. The lenders' expected utility of y plus the net income from lending may be written

$$E(M)=\mu M(y-xhK_E)+(1-\mu)M(y+ihK_E). \qquad \text{(C: 1)}$$

It is now assumed that lenders choose an optimal leverage ratio (h) so that their expected utility according to (C: 1) is maximized. For given values of x and i, this maximization gives the first-order condition (see the similar presentation of Mossin [1973] chapter 3):

$$\frac{\partial E(M)}{\partial h} = -\mu \frac{\partial M(y - xhK_E)}{\partial(y - xhK_E)} xK_E + M(y - xhK_E)\frac{\partial \mu}{\partial h} + (1-\mu)\frac{\partial M(y + ihK_E)}{\partial(y + ihK_E)} iK_E$$

$$- M(y + ihK_E)\frac{\partial \mu}{\partial h}. \qquad \text{(C: 1)}'$$

(C: 1)′ is the desired relationship.

Our next objective is to show, on the basis of this relationship, how the optimal h varies with changing values of i. To do this we must specify certain properties of the lenders' utility function which have to do with the extent to which the lenders do or do not display risk aversion.

Case 1. Lenders are risk-averse, i.e., $\partial M/\partial y > 0$ and $\partial^2 M/\partial y^2 < 0$.

If μ were not influenced by h—i.e., $\partial\mu/\partial h = \partial^2\mu/\partial h^2 = 0$—then we would have $\partial^2 E(M)/\partial h^2 < 0$ since $\partial^2 M/\partial y^2 < 0$. From (C: 1)′ we obtain a determinate optimal h, which increases when i is given higher values. If lenders are to be induced to increase their lending to the firm, the firm must consequently raise the interest rate (i). The increased dispersion of net lending revenues due to an increased h can thus be expected by itself to lead to a higher required interest rate. Should also the risk of bankruptcy (μ) be a positive function of the leverage ratio (h), there would be another reason for a higher interest rate when h is raised. Hence a positive relationship between the interest rate and the leverage ratio may exist due to both an increased dispersion of the net revenues from lending and an increased risk of bankruptcy.

Case 2. Lenders are risk-neutral, i.e., $\partial M/\partial y > 0$ and $\partial^2 M/\partial y^2 = 0$.

If the probability of bankruptcy (μ) is independent of the leverage ratio, i.e., $\partial\mu/\partial h = \partial^2\mu/\partial h^2 = 0$, then we have $\partial^2 E(M)/\partial h^2 = 0$ and (C: 1)′ gives no determinate optimal leverage ratio (h). If on the other hand μ is a linear increasing function of h—i.e., $\partial\mu/\partial h > 0$ and $\partial^2\mu/\partial h^2 = 0$—then $\partial^2 E(M)/\partial h^2 < 0$ according to (C: 1)′ so that the higher the interest rate, the higher the chosen h will be. In this case, the relationship between the interest rate and the leverage ratio will be positive only because of the increased probability of bankruptcy due to increased indebtedness of the firm.

3. Estimation of the influence of the leverage ratio on the interest rate

In the following we describe how we estimated the influence of the leverage ratio on the interest rate in our sample of fifty-six industrial firms quoted on the Stockholm Stock Exchange in order to obtain regression coefficients which are not biased by the fact that the interest rate also affects the leverage ratio.

a) The problem

In order to simplify the presentation, we assume that all relationships between the variables are linear and that the leverage ratio is the only explanatory variable for the interest rate. These assumptions do not alter the basic idea behind the estimation procedure that we shall describe here. The interest- rate function, which will be estimated cross-sectionally, may thus be written

$$i = \tau_{11} + \tau_{12} h + \varepsilon_i, \qquad \text{(C: 2)}$$

where i is the interest rate, h is the leverage ratio, ε_i is a random error term which contains the unexplained variation in the interest rate and τ_{11} and τ_{12} are constants assumed equal for all firms.

According to the analysis in chapter 5, the firm's optimal leverage ratio is determined by the rate of return on total capital and by the marginal borrowing cost. This implies that both total profitability and the interest rate may be explanatory variables for the leverage ratio.[1] In addition, the risk which is associated with the real activities of the firm may be expected to vary systematically with its size (see p. 49), so that size should be an important explanatory variable for the leverage ratio.

We interpret the above as implying that there exists a leverage ratio relationship of the form:

$$h = \theta_{21} + \theta_{22} i + \theta_{23} r + \theta_{24} s. \qquad \text{(C: 3)}$$

Due to this relationship, the error term (ε_i) in the interest-rate function (C: 2) will be correlated with the explanatory variable (h), since $\theta_{22} \neq 0$. Direct estimation of (C: 2) with ordinary least squares (OLS) cannot then give unbiased estimates. Therefore we use a two-stage least squares procedure instead.

b) The estimation procedure

The first stage

The following relationship is estimated with OLS on the basis of our data:

$$h = \theta_{31} + \theta_{32} r + \theta_{33} s + \varepsilon_h. \qquad \text{(C: 4)}$$

[1] Even if the model used there were not an adequate description of how the firm's debt decisions are made—e.g., due to these decisions not being made with the objective of maximizing capital value—total profitability and the interest rate still ought to influence the leverage ratio. The reason is that these two variables determine the inflow to the firm of financial capital through its own saving, as borrowing at the same time ought to be influenced by savings.

Using the estimated coefficients in (C: 4) we then receive a calculated leverage ratio ($\hat{h}$) for each firm according to the formula

$$\hat{h} = \hat{\theta}_{31} + \hat{\theta}_{32} r + \hat{\theta}_{33} s, \tag{C: 5}$$

where

$$h = \hat{h} + \hat{\varepsilon}_h. \tag{C: 5)'$$

The second stage

With $\hat{h}$ as an explanatory variable an OLS-regression is performed for the borrowing-rate function

$$i = \tau_{11} + \tau_{12} \hat{h} + \varepsilon_i', \tag{C: 6}$$

where

$$\varepsilon_i' = \tau_{12} \hat{\varepsilon}_h + \varepsilon_i. \tag{C: 6)'$$

In order to get consistent estimates of τ_{11} and τ_{12} it is necessary that the explanatory variable ($\hat{h}$) and the error term (ε_i') be independent of each other. This means that neither r nor s may be influenced by i.

It seems unlikely that the interest rate should affect firm sizes. On the other hand, one cannot exclude the possibility of a certain indirect influence from the interest rate to total profitability (r), since the interest rate influences the leverage ratio—see above—while the leverage ratio can in turn affect total profitability. However, this indirect influence from the interest rate to total profitability ought to be of a minor order of magnitude.

That estimation of (C: 6) with OLS subject to the assumptions mentioned above gives consistent estimates may be shown as follows.

c) Proof of consistency

Estimation of (C: 6) with OLS gives:

$$\hat{\tau}_{12} = \frac{\sum(\hat{h} - \bar{\hat{h}})(i - \bar{i})}{\sum(\hat{h} - \bar{\hat{h}})^2} = \frac{\sum(\hat{h} - \bar{\hat{h}})[\tau_{12}(h - \bar{h}) + (\varepsilon_i - \bar{\varepsilon}_i)]}{\sum(\hat{h} - \bar{\hat{h}})^2}$$

$$= \frac{\sum(\hat{h} - \bar{\hat{h}})[(\tau_{12}\{\hat{h} - \bar{\hat{h}}) + (\hat{\varepsilon}_h - \bar{\hat{\varepsilon}}_h)\} + (\varepsilon_i - \bar{\varepsilon}_i)]}{\sum(\hat{h} - \bar{\hat{h}})^2}$$

$$= \tau_{12} + \tau_{12} \frac{\sum(\hat{h} - \bar{\hat{h}})(\hat{\varepsilon}_h - \bar{\hat{\varepsilon}}_h)}{\sum(\hat{h} - \bar{\hat{h}})^2} + \frac{\sum(\hat{h} - \bar{\hat{h}})(\varepsilon_i - \bar{\varepsilon}_i)}{\sum(\hat{h} - \bar{\hat{h}})^2}. \tag{C: 6)''$$

The second term on the right hand side is equal to zero, since $\hat{h}$ and $\hat{\varepsilon}_i$ are the estimate and residual, respectively, in a least-squares regression and are thus uncorrelated. The third term is not exactly equal to zero, and neither is its expected value, but its probability limit is zero. Thus from (C: 6)″ it follows that

$$p \lim_{n\to\infty} (\hat{\tau}_{12}) = \tau_{12}.$$

4. Conditions for a time-invariant discount rate

Consider a firm which grows continuously and pays dividends to its owners. The rate at which the owners discount dividends in each future time period is assumed to depend on both the expected variability of dividends over time and the reaction of the owners to changes in this variability. On the basis of highly simplified assumptions concerning these relations, we derive in this section, first, the expected variance of dividends with respect to any future time period $t=n$ given the dividends in the initial time period $t=0$. Then, we derive on the basis of this variance the function for the owners' risk aversion which makes their discount rate equal for every future time period.

a) The relative variability of dividends

Assume that the firm's dividends grow at a constant expected rate (v) and that they therefore develop over time as a Markov process or random walk. Dividends during period t (U_t) are thus equal to dividends during the preceding period (U_{t-1}) multiplied by a growth factor $(1+v)$ and a random term $\exp(\varepsilon_{t-1})$, i.e. $U_t=(1+v)\,U_{t-1}e^{\varepsilon_{t-1}}$. ε_t is assumed to have an expected value equal to zero in each period, i.e., $E(\varepsilon_t)=0$. In addition all ε_t are assumed to have a constant variance in each period, i.e., $E(\varepsilon_t^2)=\sigma^2$ and a constant covariance between any two periods which is smaller than σ^2, i.e., $E(\varepsilon_t\varepsilon_{t-j})=\varrho\sigma^2$ for $j\neq 0$, where $0\leqslant\varrho\leqslant 1$. The given dividends in the initial period $t=0$ are $U(0)=U_0$. We then obtain

$$U_n = U_0(1+v)^n \prod_{t=0}^{n-1} \exp(\varepsilon_t) \quad \text{or} \tag{C: 7}$$

$$\log U_n = \log U_0 + n \log(1+v) + \sum_{t=0}^{n-1} \varepsilon_t$$

$$E(U_n) = U_0(1+v)^n, \tag{C: 7)$'$}$$

where $E(U_n)$ is the expected value of U_n.

$$\operatorname{Var}(\log U_n) = \sum_{t=0}^{n-1} E(\varepsilon_t^2) + 2\sum_{t=0}^{n-1}\sum_{j=0}^{n-1} E(\varepsilon_t\,\varepsilon_{t-j}) = n\sigma^2 + 2\binom{n}{2}\varrho\sigma^2 = [n + n(n-1)\,\varrho]\,\sigma^2. \tag{C: 8}$$

b) The discount rate for period *n*

Assume that the owners of the firm are risk averse. This means that the utility they derive from $E(U_n)$ declines as the relative variance of $E(U_n)$, i.e., var $(\log U_n)=\hat{\sigma}_n^2$ increases. $\hat{\sigma}_n^2$ may be regarded as a measure of the risk they associate with $E(U_n)$.

Let us first express the owners' present value of $E(U_n)$ discounted back to $t=0$ in terms of certainty equivalents. Imagine $E(U_n)$ being discounted with a riskless time-invariant rate (k_0) which is determined by only the time preference of the owners. Then the present value of $E(U_n)$ can be written (see Robichek and Myers [1965]):

$$U_n^N = E(U_n)f(\hat{\sigma}_n^2)/(1+k_0)^n, \tag{C: 9}$$

where $f(\hat{\sigma}_n^2)$ summarizes the effect of risk with $E(U_n)$ given the risk aversion of the owners. The certainty equivalent is $E(U_n)f(\hat{\sigma}_n^2)$, which states the price the owners are willing to pay for $E(U_n)$ which in the absence of risk gives the same worth for them as does $E(U_n)$ when risk exists.

Let us then express in the usual way the owners' present value of $E(U_n)$ given a discount rate factor $(1+k_n)^n=\prod_{t=1}^{n}(1+k_t)$ which reflects both their time preference and financial risk:

$$U_n^N = E(U_n)/(1+k_n)^n. \tag{C: 10}$$

(C: 9) and (C: 10) give

$$\log(1+k_n) = \log(1+k_0) - \{\log f(\hat{\sigma}_n^2)\}/n. \tag{C: 11}$$

One can imagine two extreme cases concerning the degree of covariance over time in the random terms of dividends: (1) the random terms are completely independent of each other ($\varrho=0$), and (2) they are perfectly correlated ($\varrho=1$).

Case 1: $\varrho=0$

$$\log(1+k_n) = \log(1+k_0) - \{\log f[n\sigma^2]\}/n. \tag{C: 12}$$

Case 2: $\varrho=1$

$$\log(1+k_n) = \log(1+k_0) - \{\log f[n\sigma^2+n(n-1)\sigma^2]\}/n. \tag{C: 12)'$$

In order that dividends in every future period be discounted with the same rate—i.e., in order that $\partial k_n/\partial n=0$ holds—it is necessary that the risk-aversion function $f(\hat{\sigma}^2)$ of the owners declines exponentially with increasing n. This in turn implies that $f(n\sigma^2)$ and $f[n\sigma^2+n(n-1)\sigma^2]$ will decline exponentially with time according to (C: 12) and (C: 12)′ respectively.

5. Estimation of the influence of the pay-out ratio on the discount rate

In the following, we describe how we have estimated the influence of the pay-out ratio on the discount rate in our sample of 56 industrial firms quoted by the Stockholm Stock Exchange in order to obtain regression coefficients which are not biased by the feed-back effect of the discount rate on the pay-out ratio.

a) The problem

In order to simplify the presentation, it is assumed that all variable relationships are linear and that the pay-out ratio is the only explanatory variable for the discount rate. Thus the discount-rate function to be estimated may be written

$$k = \varkappa_{11} + \varkappa_{12} u + \varepsilon_k, \tag{C: 13}$$

where k is the discount rate, u is the pay-out ratio, and ε_k is the random error term. $\varkappa_{11}$ and $\varkappa_{12}$ are coefficients which are assumed to be the same for all firms.

According to the analysis in chapter 5, the firm's optimal pay-out ratio is influenced by the rate of return on equity and by the discount rate. In addition, firm size may be expected to influence the optimal pay-out ratio, since firms of different sizes have a different inclination to finance their operations through retained earnings due to differences in the degree of owner-management and in opportunities of securing financial capital through share issues (Marris [1964]).

We interpret these considerations as implying the existence of a pay-out ratio relationship of the form

$$u = \eta_{21} + \eta_{22} k + \eta_{23} r_E + \eta_{24} s + \varepsilon_u, \tag{C: 14}$$

where r_E is the rate of return on equity, and s is the size of the firm (measured by sales). Due to (C: 14), the error term (ε_k) in (C: 13) will be correlated with the explanatory variable (u), since η_{22} ought to be non-zero. Regression of (C: 13) with ordinary least squares (OLS) will then not produce consistent coefficients. This is the reason why we use two-stage least squares (TSLS).

b) The estimation procedure

In the first stage of estimation, the following relationship is estimated cross-sectionally with OLS:

$$u = \eta_{31} + \eta_{32} r_E + \eta_{33} s + \varepsilon_u'. \tag{C: 15}$$

On the basis of the estimated coefficients in (C: 15), we then calculate for each firm a corrected pay-out ratio (u) according to

$$\hat{u} = \hat{\eta}_{31} + \hat{\eta}_{32} r_E + \hat{\eta}_{33} s. \tag{C: 16}$$

In the second stage of estimation $\hat{u}$ is substituted for u in (C: 13) and this function is OLS-estimated cross-sectionally.

$$k = \varkappa'_{11} + \varkappa'_{12}\hat{u} + \varepsilon'_k. \qquad \text{(C: 17)}$$

According to (C: 13), (C: 15) (C: 16), and (C: 17), $\varepsilon'_k = \varkappa'_{12}\hat{\varepsilon}'_u + \varepsilon_k$. In order to obtain consistent estimates of (C: 17), it is necessary that $E(\hat{u}\varepsilon'_k) = 0$, or that $E[(\varkappa'_{12}\hat{\varepsilon}'_u + \varepsilon_k)\hat{u}] = 0$. This requires in turn that the discount rate (k) does not influence the explanatory variables (r_E and s) in equation (C: 16). It is hardly likely that k influences s but k might influence r_E through its impact on the pay-out ratio. However, this indirect effect of k on r_E would appear to be insignificant.

6. Regression results

This section presents regression estimates that indicate the influence of the leverage ratio on the interest rate (table C: 1) and the influence of the pay-out ratio on the discount rate (table C: 2). The estimates in these tables are for two separate groups of twenty-eight firms, each, in which firms have been ranked according to increasing value of the leverage ratio and the pay-out ratio, respectively. (The estimates in these tables are discussed in chapter 4, pp. 51 f. and 60 f.)

Table C: 1. *Regressions for the interest rate as a function of the leverage ratio*

Two groups. Linear specifications

Equation	Group	B_0	b	σ	R^2
1	1	0.0114	0.0101***	0.0033	0.2715
(OLS)	2	0.0277	0.0015*	0.0008	0.1224
2	1	0.0141	0.0127*	0.0068	0.0981
(TSLS)	2	0.0234	0.0034	0.0048	0.0290

All firms in group 1 have lower leverage ratios than those in group 2.
Note: Explanations of symbols are given in table 3, p. 52.

Table C: 2. *Regression estimates for the discount rate as a function of the pay-out ratio*

Two groups. Linear specifications

Equation	Group	B_0	b	σ	R^2
1	1	0.1904	−0.1358***	0.0270	0.4925
(OLS)	2	0.0966	−0.0221**	0.0109	0.1359
2	1	0.1515	−0.0781*	0.0438	0.1093
(TSLS)	2	0.1460	−0.0719**	0.0328	0.2767

All firms in group 1 have lower pay-out ratios than those in group 2.
Note: Explanations of symbols are given in table 3, p. 52.

APPENDIX D

Derivatives and optimality conditions for chapter 5

1. The partial derivatives $\partial^2 P/\partial \hat{l}\,\partial u = \partial^2 P/\partial h\,\partial u = 0$

Given: The equation system (2: 5)–(2: 17) in chapter 2, p. 25 under the assumption of no growth costs. This assumption implies that the rate of growth of real capital ($\hat{v}_K$) drops out as an explanatory variable in the production function (2: 8). In addition the product price (p), wage rate (p_1), real capital price (p_2), the rate of depreciation (a) and the rate of profit tax (t_V) are assumed exogenously given. For definitions of the other variables in the equation system, see pp. 122–4.

Statement: The pay-out ratio (u) will not influence the partial derivatives of the firm's capital value (P_t) with respect to its decision variables labor-intensity ($\hat{l}$) and leverage ratio (h), i.e., $\partial^2 P/\partial \hat{l}\,\partial u = \partial^2 P/\partial h\,\partial u = 0$.

Proof: Partial differentiation of the first-order conditions (5: 1) and (5: 2) in chapter 5 with respect to u gives

$$\frac{\partial^2 P}{\partial \hat{l}\,\partial u} = (k-v)^{-2} u r_E K_{Et} \left\{ \frac{\partial^2 r_E}{\partial \hat{l}\,\partial u}\left[\left(\frac{k-v}{r_E}\right) + (1-u)\right] + \left(\frac{\partial r_E}{\partial \hat{l}}\right)\frac{\partial}{\partial u}\left[\left(\frac{k-v}{r_E}\right) + (1-u)\right]\right\}$$

$$= \frac{u r_E K_{Et}}{(k-v)^2}\,\frac{\partial^2 r_E}{\partial \hat{l}\,\partial u}\,\frac{k}{r_E} \qquad \text{(D: 1)}$$

$$\frac{\partial^2 P}{\partial h\,\partial u} = (k-v)^{-2} u r_E K_{Et} \left\{ \frac{\partial^2 r_E}{\partial h\,\partial u}\left[\left(\frac{k-v}{r_E}\right) + (1-u)\right] + \left(\frac{\partial r_E}{\partial h}\right)\frac{\partial}{\partial u}\left[\left(\frac{k-v}{r_E}\right) + (1-u)\right]\right\}$$

$$= \frac{u r_E K_{Et}}{(k-v)^2}\,\frac{\partial^2 r_E}{\partial h\,\partial u}\,\frac{k}{r_E}. \qquad \text{(D: 2)}$$

Note, in this differentiation we use the fact that $\partial r_E/\partial \hat{l} = 0$, $\partial r_E/\partial h = 0$ from (5: 1)′ and (5: 2)′ as well as the identity $[(k-v)/r_E + (1-u)] = k/r_E$.

We must also determine the derivatives $\partial^2 r_E/\partial \hat{l}\,\partial u$ and $\partial^2 r_E/\partial h\,\partial u$. To do so we use, given $t_V = 0$, the profit identity $V_{Et} = r_E K_{Et} = p\hat{F}_t - p_1\hat{L}_t - p_2 a\hat{K}_t - ihK_{Et}$. After partial differentiation we obtain

$$\frac{\partial r_E}{\partial \hat{l}} = [p(\partial \hat{F}/\partial \hat{L})(\partial \hat{L}/\partial \hat{l}) - p_1(\partial \hat{L}/\partial \hat{l})]/K_{Et}$$

$$\frac{\partial^2 r_E}{\partial \hat{l}\,\partial u} = [p(\partial^2 \hat{F}/\partial \hat{L}\partial u)(\partial \hat{L}/\partial \hat{l})]/K_{Et}. \tag{D: 3}$$

Note that equity capital (K_{Et}) is assumed to be given, $\partial \hat{L}/\partial \hat{l} = \hat{K}_t$ is independent of u and the prices (p and p_1) are exogenously given.

$$\frac{\partial r_E}{\partial h} = [p(\partial \hat{F}/\partial \hat{K})(\partial \hat{K}/\partial h) - \{p_2 a\,\partial \hat{K}/\partial h + (i + h\,\partial i/\partial h)\,K_{Et}\}]/K_{Et}$$

$$\frac{\partial^2 r_E}{\partial h\,\partial u} = [p(\partial^2 \hat{F}/\partial \hat{K}\,\partial u)(\partial \hat{K}/\partial h) - \partial\{p_2 a\,\partial \hat{K}/\partial h + (i + h\,\partial i/\partial h)\,K_{Et}\}/\partial u]/K_{Et}. \tag{D: 4}$$

Since, in the absence of growth costs, the marginal productivities of factors of production ($\partial \hat{F}/\partial \hat{L}$ and $\partial \hat{F}/\partial \hat{K}$) are not influenced by the growth of the firm (see above), they are not affected by the pay-out ratio (u) either, so that $\partial^2 \hat{F}/\partial \hat{L}\partial u = \partial^2 \hat{F}/\partial \hat{K}\,\partial u = 0$. From the identity $p_2 \hat{K}_t = (1+h)K_{Et}$ it follows that $\partial \hat{K}/\partial h = K_{Et}/p_2$ and $\partial^2 \hat{K}/\partial h\,\partial u = 0$ since p_2 and K_{Et} are given. Furthermore, we have $\partial i/\partial u = 0$ and $\partial^2 i/\partial h\,\partial u = 0$ according to the system (2: 5)–(2: 17). Thus we obtain

$$\partial^2 r_E/\partial \hat{l}\,\partial u = \partial^2 r_E/\partial h\,\partial u = 0. \tag{D: 5}$$

When $k \neq v$, it finally follows from (D: 1), (D: 2) and (D: 5) that

$$\frac{\partial^2 P}{\partial \hat{l}\,\partial u} = \frac{\partial^2 P}{\partial h\,\partial u} = 0.$$

2. The second-order condition for a maximum capital value

Given: The same assumptions as in section 1 above, p. 151.
Statement: The first-order conditions (5: 1), (5: 2) and (5: 3) in chapter 5 are sufficient to maximize capital value (P_t). On pp. 66 f. it was shown that this is the case if $\partial^2 P/\partial \hat{l}^2 < 0$, $\partial^2 P/\partial h^2 < 0$, $\partial^2 P/\partial u^2 < 0$ and $\{(\partial^2 P/\partial \hat{l}^2)(\partial^2 P/\partial h^2) - (\partial^2 P/\partial \hat{l}\partial h)(\partial^2 P/\partial h\partial \hat{l})\} > 0$.

Proof: We will first show that $\partial^2 P/\partial \hat{l}^2 < 0$, $\partial^2 P/\partial h^2 < 0$ and $\partial^2 P/\partial u^2 < 0$ (point a). Then we show that $\{(\partial^2 P/\partial \hat{l}^2)(\partial^2 P/\partial h^2) - (\partial^2 P/\partial \hat{l}\partial h)(\partial^2 P/\partial h\partial \hat{l})\} > 0$ (point b).

a) When P_t in equation (2: 17) is differentiated with respect to $\hat{l}$, h and u respectively, we obtain

$$\frac{\partial^2 P}{\partial \hat{l}^2} = \frac{u r_E K_{Et}}{(k-v)^2}\,\frac{k}{r_E}\,\frac{\partial^2 r_E}{\partial \hat{l}^2} \tag{D: 6}$$

$$\frac{\partial^2 P}{\partial h^2}=\frac{ur_E K_{Et}}{(k-v)^2}\frac{k}{r_E}\frac{\partial^2 r_E}{\partial h^2} \tag{D: 7}$$

$$\frac{\partial^2 P}{\partial u^2}=u\frac{r_E K_{Et}}{(k-v)^2}\left[-\frac{\partial^2 k}{\partial u^2}\right]. \tag{D: 8}$$

For these differentiations we use the optimality conditions (5: 1) and (5: 2) implying $\partial r_E/\partial \hat{l}=0$, $\partial r_E/\partial h=0$ and the identity $[(k-v)/r_E+(1-u)]=k/r_E$. In addition we use the identity $v=(1-u)r_E$, which in the absence of growth costs gives $\partial v/\partial u=-r_E$ and $\partial^2 v/\partial u^2=0$. Furthermore, from chapter 5 we have $\partial k/\partial u<0$ and $\partial^2 k/\partial u^2>0$. Since we have $k>v$, $u>0$, $r_E>0$ and $K_{Et}>0$, it now follows immediately from (D: 8) that $\partial^2 P/\partial u^2<0$.

When $t_V=0$ we have from the profitability identity

$$r_E=V_{Et}/K_{Et}=(p\hat{F}_t-p_1\hat{L}_t-p_2\hat{K}_t-ihK_{Et})(1/K_{Et})$$

we obtain

$$\frac{\partial^2 r_E}{\partial \hat{l}^2}=\frac{\partial^2 V_{Et}}{\partial \hat{l}^2}\left(\frac{1}{K_{Et}}\right)=p\frac{\partial^2 \hat{F}}{\partial \hat{L}^2}\left(\frac{\partial \hat{L}}{\partial \hat{l}}\right)^2\left(\frac{1}{K_{Et}}\right) \tag{D: 9}$$

$$\frac{\partial^2 r_E}{\partial h^2}=\frac{\partial^2 V_{Et}}{\partial h^2}\left(\frac{1}{K_{Et}}\right)=\left[p\frac{\partial^2 \hat{F}}{\partial \hat{K}^2}\left(\frac{\partial \hat{K}}{\partial h}\right)^2+A\right]\frac{1}{K_{Et}}, \tag{D: 10}$$

where A is equal to $K_{Et}[-2(\partial i/\partial h)-h(\partial^2 i/\partial h^2)]$.

According to chapter 4, the borrowing rate (i) is a logarithmically increasing function of the leverage ratio (h) so that A is negative. The partial derivatives $\partial^2\hat{F}/\partial\hat{L}^2$ and $\partial^2\hat{F}/\partial\hat{K}^2$ are both assumed to be negative. Since u, r_E, K_{Et}, $(k-v)$, h and $(1-u)$ are all positive, it follows from (D: 6), (D: 7), (D: 9) and (D: 10) that $\partial^2 P/\partial\hat{l}^2$ and $\partial^2 P/\partial h^2$ are both negative. Q.E.D.

b) P_t in equation (2: 17) is differentiated partially with respect to $\hat{l}$ and h and with respect to h and $\hat{l}$.

$$\frac{\partial^2 P}{\partial \hat{l}\,\partial h}=\frac{ur_E K_{Et}}{(k-v)^2}\frac{k}{r_E}\frac{\partial^2 r_E}{\partial \hat{l}\,\partial h} \tag{D: 11}$$

$$\frac{\partial^2 P}{\partial h\,\partial \hat{l}}=\frac{ur_E K_{Et}}{(k-v)^2}\frac{k}{r_E}\frac{\partial^2 r_E}{\partial h\,\partial \hat{l}}. \tag{D: 12}$$

Then the profit identity $r_E=V_{Et}/K_{Et}=(p\hat{F}_t-p_1\hat{L}_t-p_2 a\hat{K}_t-ihK_{Et})(1/K_{Et})$ is differentiated with respect to $\hat{l}$ and h, and with respect to h and $\hat{l}$. (Note that K_{Et} is given.) We then obtain:

$$\frac{\partial^2 r_E}{\partial \hat{l}\,\partial h}=p\frac{\partial^2 \hat{F}}{\partial \hat{L}\,\partial \hat{K}}\left(\frac{\partial \hat{L}}{\partial \hat{l}}\right)\left(\frac{\partial \hat{K}}{\partial h}\right)\left(\frac{1}{K_{Et}}\right) \tag{D: 13}$$

$$\frac{\partial^2 r_E}{\partial h\,\partial \hat{l}}=p\frac{\partial^2 \hat{F}}{\partial \hat{K}\,\partial \hat{L}}\left(\frac{\partial \hat{K}}{\partial h}\right)\left(\frac{\partial \hat{L}}{\partial \hat{l}}\right)\left(\frac{1}{K_{Et}}\right). \tag{D: 14}$$

(D: 6)–(D: 14) gives

$$D_{33}=\frac{\partial^2 P}{\partial \hat{l}^2}\frac{\partial^2 P}{\partial h^2}-\frac{\partial^2 P}{\partial \hat{l}\partial h}\frac{\partial^2 P}{\partial h\partial \hat{l}}=\left[\frac{ur_E K_{Et} k}{(k-v)^2 r_E}\right]^2\left[\frac{\partial^2 r_E}{\partial \hat{l}^2}\frac{\partial^2 r_E}{\partial h^2}-\frac{\partial^2 r_E}{\partial \hat{l}\partial h}\frac{\partial^2 r_E}{\partial h\partial \hat{l}}\right] \tag{D: 15}$$

or

$$D_{33}=CB\left\{\frac{\partial^2 \hat{F}}{\partial \hat{L}^2}\frac{\partial^2 \hat{F}}{\partial \hat{K}^2}+\frac{A}{p}\left(\frac{\partial h}{\partial \hat{K}}\right)^2\left(\frac{\partial^2 \hat{F}}{\partial \hat{L}^2}\right)-\frac{\partial^2 \hat{F}}{\partial \hat{L}\partial \hat{K}}\frac{\partial^2 \hat{F}}{\partial \hat{K}\partial \hat{L}}\right\}, \tag{D: 16}$$

where

$$C=\left[\frac{ur_E K_{Et}}{(k-v)^2}\left(\frac{k}{r_E}\right)\right]^2 \quad \text{and} \quad B=\left(\frac{p}{K_{Et}}\right)^2\left(\frac{\partial \hat{L}}{\partial \hat{l}}\right)^2\left(\frac{\partial \hat{K}}{\partial h}\right)^2.$$

We have assumed that the production function has the following properties:

$\partial \hat{F}/\partial \hat{L} > 0$

$\partial^2 \hat{F}/\partial \hat{L}^2 < 0$

$\partial \hat{F}/\partial \hat{K} > 0$

$\partial^2 \hat{F}/\partial \hat{K}^2 < 0$

$(\partial \hat{F}/\partial \hat{L})(\hat{L}_t/\hat{F}_t)+(\partial \hat{F}/\partial \hat{K})(\hat{K}_t/\hat{F}_t)=1.$

Such a function may be written in the form $F_t=\psi \hat{L}_t^{\alpha}\hat{K}_t^{1-\alpha}$. From this function is obtained:

$$\partial^2 \hat{F}/\partial \hat{L}^2=\alpha(\alpha-1)\frac{\hat{F}_t}{\hat{L}_t^2}$$

$$\partial^2 \hat{F}/\partial \hat{K}^2=\alpha(\alpha-1)\frac{\hat{F}_t}{\hat{K}_t^2}$$

$$-\partial^2 \hat{F}/\partial \hat{L}\partial \hat{K}=\alpha(\alpha-1)\frac{\hat{F}_t}{\hat{L}_t\hat{K}_t}$$

$$-\partial^2 \hat{F}/\partial \hat{K}\partial \hat{L}=\alpha(\alpha-1)\frac{\hat{F}_t}{\hat{L}_t\hat{K}_t}$$

Thus we have $\partial^2 \hat{F}/\partial \hat{L}^2\cdot\partial^2 \hat{F}/\partial \hat{K}^2-\partial^2 \hat{F}/\partial \hat{L}\partial \hat{K}\cdot\partial^2 \hat{F}/\partial \hat{K}\partial \hat{L}=[\alpha(1-\alpha)]^2.$

$$\left\{\left(\frac{\hat{F}_t}{\hat{L}_t\hat{K}_t}\right)^2-\left(\frac{\hat{F}_t}{\hat{L}_t\hat{K}_t}\right)^2\right\}=0. \tag{D: 17}$$

From (D: 16) and (D: 17) it then follows that D_{33} is positive, since $(\partial^2 \hat{F}/\partial \hat{L}^2)<0$ and $A=K_{Et}[-2(\partial i/\partial h)-h\partial^2 i/\partial h^2]<0$.

Observe, $A<0$ if the interest rate is a positive function of the leverage ratio (h). If, for example, the interest rate were independent of the leverage ratio ($\partial i/\partial h=\partial^2 i/\partial h^2=0$), A would equal zero, and no determinate optimum solution would exist under our assumptions of exogenously given prices and constant returns to scale.

3. Conditions for maximum rate of return on equity

Below is shown that maximization of the rate of return on equity (r_E) with respect to the labor intensity ($\hat{l}$) and leverage ratio (h) gives the first-order marginal conditions $p\partial\hat{F}/\partial\hat{L}=p_1$ and $p\partial\hat{F}/\partial\hat{K}=p_2(a+i+\hat{K}_{Ft}\partial i/\partial\hat{K})$.

Given: The same assumptions as in section 1, p. 151, plus the identity

$$r_E=\frac{V_{Et}}{K_{Et}}=\frac{1-t_V}{K_{Et}}[p\hat{F}_t-p_1\hat{L}_t-p_2 a\hat{K}_t-ihK_{Et}], \text{ where } K_{Et} \text{ is given.}$$

Definitions of the variables are given in section 2.2 in the main text.

Derivation: We differentiate r_E partially with respect to $\hat{l}$ and h.

$$\frac{\partial r_E}{\partial\hat{l}}=(1-t_V)\left[p\frac{\partial\hat{F}}{\partial\hat{L}}\frac{\partial\hat{L}}{\partial\hat{l}}-p_1\frac{\partial\hat{L}}{\partial\hat{l}}\right]\frac{1}{K_{Et}} \tag{D: 18}$$

$$\frac{\partial r_E}{\partial h}=(1-t_V)\left[p\frac{\partial\hat{F}}{\partial\hat{K}}\frac{\partial\hat{K}}{\partial h}-p_2 a\frac{\partial\hat{K}}{\partial h}-\left(i+h\frac{\partial i}{\partial h}\right)K_{Et}\right]\frac{1}{K_{Et}}. \tag{D: 19}$$

A maximum for r_E is obtained when $\partial r_E/\partial\hat{l}=\partial r_E/\partial h=0$.

$$\therefore\begin{cases} p\dfrac{\partial\hat{F}}{\partial\hat{L}}\dfrac{\partial\hat{L}}{\partial\hat{l}}-p_1\dfrac{\partial\hat{L}}{\partial\hat{l}}=0 & \text{(D: 20)}\\[2ex] p\dfrac{\partial\hat{F}}{\partial\hat{K}}\dfrac{\partial\hat{K}}{\partial h}-p_2 a\dfrac{\partial\hat{K}}{\partial h}-p_2\left(i+h\dfrac{\partial i}{\partial h}\right)\dfrac{\partial\hat{K}}{\partial h}=0. & \text{(D: 21)}\end{cases}$$

Note that $p_2\hat{K}_t=(1+h)K_{Et}$ gives $K_{Et}=p_2(\partial\hat{K}/\partial h)$.

Equations (D: 20) and (D: 21) may be written alternatively:

$$p\frac{\partial\hat{F}}{\partial\hat{L}}-p_1=0 \tag{D: 22}$$

$$p\frac{\partial\hat{F}}{\partial\hat{K}}-p_2\left(a+i+\hat{K}_{Ft}\frac{\partial i}{\partial\hat{K}}\right)=0, \tag{D: 23}$$

since $\partial i/\partial h=(\partial i/\partial\hat{K})(\partial\hat{K}/\partial h)=(\partial i/\partial\hat{K})K_{Et}/p_2$ and $h=p_2\hat{K}_{Ft}/K_{Et}$.

4. The optimum condition $r=i+h\,\partial i/\partial h$

Given: The linear homogeneous production function $\hat{F}_t=\hat{F}(\hat{L}_t, \hat{K}_t)$ and the first-order conditions $p\partial\hat{F}/\partial\hat{L}=p_1$ and $p\partial\hat{F}/\partial\hat{K}=p_2(a+i+\hat{K}_{Ft}\partial i/\partial\hat{K})$.

Statement: At the optimum point the rate of return on total capital (r) equals the marginal cost of borrowed capital ($i+h\partial i/\partial h$).

Derivation: Since the production function is linear homogeneous and since we have $\partial i/\partial\hat{K}=(\partial i/\partial h)(p_2/K_{Et})$ and $\hat{K}_{Ft}=h(K_{Et}/p_2)$—see section 3 above—

the first-order conditions may alternatively be written:

$$p\alpha\frac{\hat{F}_t}{\hat{L}_t}=p_1 \tag{D: 24}$$

$$p(1-\alpha)\frac{\hat{F}_t}{\hat{K}_t}=p_2(a+i+h\,\partial i/\partial h), \tag{D: 25}$$

where

$$\alpha=\frac{\partial\hat{F}}{\partial\hat{L}}\frac{\hat{L}_t}{\hat{F}_t} \quad \text{and} \quad (1-\alpha)=\frac{\partial\hat{F}}{\partial\hat{K}}\frac{\hat{K}_t}{\hat{F}_t}.$$

Substitution of (D: 24) and (D: 25) into the identity for the rate of return on total capital

$$r=\frac{p\hat{F}_t}{p_2\hat{K}_t}-\frac{p_1\hat{L}_t}{p_2\hat{K}_t}-a$$

yields

$$r=\frac{a+i+h\,\partial i/\partial h}{1-\alpha}-\frac{\alpha(a+i+h\,\partial i/\partial h)}{1-\alpha}-a=a+i+h\,\partial i/\partial h-a=i+h\,\partial i/\partial h. \tag{D: 26}$$

Q.E.D.

5. The inequality $k>y$

Here it is shown that if $r_E>k$ holds, then $k>y=V_{Et}/P_t$.

Given: The earning-price ratio $y=V_{Et}/P_t=(k-v)/u$ according to (2: 13) and (2: 17), and $v=(1-u)r_E$ according to (2: 14) and (2: 15)—see chapter 2.

Proof: If $r_E>k$ holds, the given identities imply $k-(1-u)k>(k-v)=uy$, i.e., $uk>uy$ or $k>y$ for $0<u<1$. Q.E.D.

6. Maximization of capital value with respect to the labor intensity ($\hat{l}$) and leverage ratio (h) when growth costs exist

Below are derived the first-order conditions for maximum capital value under the assumption that the rate of growth of real capital influences the firm's volume of production negatively, i.e., $\partial\hat{F}/\partial\hat{v}_K<0$.

Given: The equation system (2: 5)–(2: 17) in chapter 2. The production function is written $\hat{F}_t=\psi\hat{L}_t^{\alpha}\hat{K}_t^{(1-\alpha)}\cdot f(\hat{v}_K)$. For definitions of variables, see the Variable list, pp. 122 ff.

Derivation: When the capital-value relationship $P_t = ur_E K_{Et}/(k-v)$ is differentiated partially with respect to $\hat{l}$ and h, we obtain:

$$\frac{\partial P}{\partial \hat{l}} = \frac{ur_E K_{Et}}{(k-v)^2}\left\{\frac{\partial r_E}{\partial \hat{l}}\left[\frac{k-v}{r_E} + (1-u)\right]\right\}, \tag{D: 27}$$

where

$$\frac{\partial r_E}{\partial \hat{l}} = \frac{1-t_V}{K_{Et}}\left\{p\frac{\partial \hat{F}}{\partial \hat{L}}\frac{\partial \hat{L}}{\partial \hat{l}} - p_1\frac{\partial \hat{L}}{\partial \hat{l}}\right\} \tag{D: 28}$$

$$\frac{\partial \hat{F}}{\partial \hat{L}} = \frac{\partial \hat{F}}{\partial \hat{L}_{\hat{v}_K=\text{konst}}} + \frac{\partial \hat{F}}{\partial \hat{v}_K}\frac{\partial \hat{v}_K}{\partial \hat{L}} \tag{D: 29}$$

$$\frac{\partial \hat{F}}{\partial \hat{L}_{\hat{v}_K=\text{konst}}} = \alpha\psi \hat{L}_t^{\alpha-1}\hat{K}_t^{1-\alpha}\cdot f(\hat{v}_K) \tag{D: 30}$$

$$\frac{\partial P}{\partial h} = \frac{ur_E K_{Et}}{(k-v)^2}\left\{\frac{\partial r_E}{\partial h}\left[\frac{k-v}{r_E} + (1-u)\right]\right\}, \tag{D: 31}$$

where

$$\frac{\partial r_E}{\partial h} = \frac{1-t_V}{K_{Et}}\left\{p\frac{\partial \hat{F}}{\partial \hat{K}}\frac{\partial \hat{K}}{\partial h} - ap_2\frac{\partial \hat{K}}{\partial h} - (i + h\,\partial i/\partial h)\,K_{Et}\right\} \tag{D: 32}$$

$$\frac{\partial \hat{F}}{\partial \hat{K}} = \frac{\partial \hat{F}}{\partial \hat{K}_{\hat{v}_K=\text{konst}}} + \frac{\partial \hat{F}}{\partial \hat{v}_K}\frac{\partial \hat{v}_K}{\partial \hat{K}} \tag{D: 33}$$

$$\frac{\partial \hat{F}}{\partial \hat{K}_{\hat{v}_K=\text{konst}}} = (1-\alpha)\,\psi \hat{L}_t^{\alpha}\hat{K}_t^{-\alpha}\cdot f(\hat{v}_K). \tag{D: 34}$$

Assuming that an inner optimum solution exists, maximum capital value is obtained by setting the partial derivatives $\partial P/\partial \hat{l}$ and $\partial P/\partial h$ equal to zero. According to (D: 27) and (D: 31), $\partial P/\partial \hat{l}$ is zero when $\partial r_E/\partial \hat{l} = 0$ and $\partial P/\partial h$ is zero when $\partial r_E/\partial h = 0$.

Since $v = \hat{v}_K = (1-u)r_E$, it follows from $\partial r_E/\partial \hat{l} = \partial r_E/\partial h = 0$ that we have

$$\partial \hat{v}_K/\partial \hat{l} = (\partial \hat{v}_K/\partial \hat{L})(\partial \hat{L}/\partial \hat{l}) = 0 \quad \text{and } \partial \hat{v}_K/\partial h = (\partial \hat{v}_K/\partial \hat{K})(\partial \hat{K}/\partial h) = 0,$$

so that the second terms on the right hand sides of (D: 29) and (D: 33) are zero. (D: 28)–(D: 30) and (D: 32)–(D: 34) then give:

$$p\alpha\psi \hat{L}_t^{\alpha-1}\hat{K}_t^{1-\alpha}f(\hat{v}_K) - p_1 = 0 \tag{D: 35}$$

$$p(1-\alpha)\,\psi \hat{L}_t^{\alpha}\hat{K}_t^{-\alpha}f(\hat{v}_K) - p_2(a + i + h\,\partial i/\partial h) = 0.\text{[1]} \tag{D: 36}$$

After division by p_2, substitution of $p\alpha\psi \hat{L}_t^{\alpha-1}\hat{K}_t^{(1-\alpha)}f(\hat{v}_K) = p_1$ and $\hat{F}_t =$

[1] Note that $K_{Et} = p_2\partial \hat{K}/\partial h$.

$\psi \hat{L}_t^{\alpha} \hat{K}_t^{(1-\alpha)} f(\hat{v}_K)$ in (D: 36) gives:

$$i + h\,\partial i/\partial h = \frac{p(1-\alpha)\,\psi \hat{L}_t^{\alpha} \hat{K}_t^{1-\alpha} f(\hat{v}_K)}{p_2 \hat{K}_t} - a = \frac{p\psi \hat{L}_t^{\alpha} \hat{K}_t^{1-\alpha} f(\hat{v}_K)}{p_2 \hat{K}_t}$$

$$-\frac{p\alpha\psi \hat{L}_t^{\alpha} \hat{K}_t^{1-\alpha} f(\hat{v}_K)}{p_2 \hat{K}_t} - a = \frac{p\hat{F}_t}{p_2 \hat{K}_t} - \frac{p_1 \hat{L}_t}{p_2 \hat{K}_t} - a = r. \qquad \text{(D: 37)}$$

(D: 35) and (D: 37) are the optimum conditions (5: 17) and (5: 18) given in chapter 5, p. 74.

7. Maximization of capital value with respect to the pay-out ratio (u) when growth costs exist

Here we derive the first-order condition for maximization of capital value with respect to the pay-out ratio when the rate of growth of real capital is assumed to influence the firm's volume of production negatively due to growth costs. In chapter 5 we have shown that this means that the rate of return on equity is influenced positively by the pay-out ratio ($\partial r_E/\partial u > 0$).

Given: The capital-value relationship $P_t = ur_E K_{Et}/(k-v)$ and the identities and functions (2: 5)–(2: 16) in chapter 2.

Derivation: When P_t is differentiated partially with respect to the pay-out ratio (u) we obtain:

$$\frac{\partial P}{\partial u} = \frac{r_E K_{Et}}{(k-v)^2}\left\{\left(\frac{\partial r_E}{\partial u}\frac{u}{r_E} + 1\right)(k-v) + u\left(\frac{\partial v}{\partial u} - \frac{\partial k}{\partial u}\right)\right\}$$

$$= \frac{r_E K_{Et}}{(k-v)^2}\left\{\frac{\partial r_E}{\partial u}\frac{u}{r_E}k + k - u(1-u)\frac{\partial r_E}{\partial u} - (1-u)r_E + u(1-u)\frac{\partial r_E}{\partial u} - ur_E - u\frac{\partial k}{\partial u}\right\}$$

$$= \frac{r_E K_{Et}}{(k-v)^2}\left\{\left(\frac{\partial r_E}{\partial u}\frac{u}{r_E} + 1\right)k - r_E - u\frac{\partial k}{\partial u}\right\}, \qquad \text{(D: 38)}$$

where $v = (1-u)r_E$. A maximum is obtained for P_t when $\partial P/\partial u = 0$, which gives:

$$k\left(\frac{\partial r_E}{\partial u}\frac{u}{r_E} + 1\right) - u\frac{\partial k}{\partial u} = r_E. \qquad \text{(D: 39)}$$

(D: 39) is the optimum condition (5: 19) given in chapter 5, p. 74.

APPENDIX E

Variable definitions, partial derivatives, simulation curves, etc., for chapter 6

1. Correction of the rate of return and discount rate for excess depreciation and capital revaluation

The values of the rate of return and of the discount rate which are used for the empirical tests in chapter 6 are based on information from firms' annual reports. However, plant, equipment and inventories are probably depreciated in the annual reports at a faster rate than that which corresponds to the true economic depreciation of these kinds of capital due to liberal tax provisions. In addition firms may be expected to revalue their capital assets in their balance sheets due to an increase of prices for capital goods.

In this appendix we will calculate the values of the rate of return which would have obtained had there been no excess depreciation (point a) and values of the discount rate which would have obtained if there had been no revaluation of capital due to price increases (point b). Then the same tests are performed for the inequality and marginal conditions as in chapter 6 on the basis of these corrected variable values (point c).

a) The profitability variables

According to calculations carried out in appendix B, p. 133, the rate of return on total capital should be approximately 20 per cent lower and the rate of return on equity approximately 40 per cent lower if there had been no excess depreciation. The reported (uncorrected) rates of return on total and equity capital are 0.0758 and 0.1356, respectively.[1] Correction for excess depreciation should thus give values of these two profitability variables equal to $r' = 0.0758 \cdot 0.80 = 0.0606$ and $r'_E = 0.1356 \cdot 0.60 = 0.0814$, respectively.

On the other hand we have seen no reason to correct the profitability variables for revaluations of capital assets. The upward adjustments of the reported

[1] These figures are averages of annual values for 1963–70 for the fifty-six stockmarket-listed industrial firms which constitute our statistical sample in chapter 6.

values of capital assets in the balance sheets are clearly done to avoid the value of existing real capital being understated due to increases in the price of capital goods. If the revaluations correspond to actual increases in the price of capital goods, the relations between values of investments in different years would be same as those obtaining if there had been no price increases.

b) The discount rate

The average value of the pay-out ratio (u) according to the annual reports is 0.76, and the average value of the new-issue share (n) is 0.012. In Appendix B the undervaluation of equity was estimated to be about 60 per cent. The corrected average new-issue share is thus $0.40 \cdot 0.012 = 0.0048$. Moreover, according to point a) above, the corrected rate of return on equity is $r'_E = 0.0814$. The rate of growth of equity which is then obtained, and which is a function only of u, r'_E and n', is $v'_E = 0.0243$.[1]

According to the firm's balance sheets, the average rate of growth of equity (v_E) is 0.0764. The difference between v_E and v'_E, which is 0.0521, ought to show how much lower the rate of growth of equity would have been if there had been neither excess depreciation nor revaluation of capital assets. In balanced growth, with no trend in the relation between dividends and the value of equity, the corresponding difference for the rate of growth of dividends will be the same, i.e., $v_u - v'_u = 0.0521$. The book value of the discount rate is 0.0906, while the corresponding value after correction for overdepreciation and revaluation would consequently be $k' = 0.0906 - 0.0521 = 0.0385$.

c) Test results

Below we present test results on the basis of the corrected variable values r', r'_E and k' for the same inequalities and marginal conditions as in the main text, p. 83. We assume that the interest rate (i) is not influenced by excess depreciation or revaluation.

c.1. *The inequality conditions*

The average values of 0–1 observations for the inequalities (equal to unity if the firm satisfies the inequality and equal to zero otherwise) for our 56 firms are:

1) $r' > i$ equal to 0.89
2) $r'_E > r'$ equal to 0.75
3) $r'_E > r' > i$ equal to 0.70
4) $k' > y'$ equal to 0.73
5) $r'_E > k'$ equal to 0.80
6) $r'_E > k' > y'$ equal to 0.52.

[1] $v'_E = (1-u) r'_E + n' = 0.24 \cdot 0.0814 + 0.0048 = 0.0243$.

Assuming that the 0–1 observations are determined randomly, the mathematical expectation and the standard deviation will be 0.5 and 0.0671, respectively, for the single inequalities and 0.167 and 0.0500, respectively for the double inequalities (see p. 85). For the former inequalities the probability is 1/100 that the mean of this theoretically given distribution will exceed the critical value of 0.66.[1] The corresponding critical value for the double inequalities is 0.29.[1]

c.2. *The marginal conditions*

The mean differences which have been calculated for the marginal conditions are:[2]

$$\bar{d}_1' = (r'-i) - h\cdot b_{ih} = 0.0323 - 0.0102 = 0.0221$$

$$\bar{d}_2' = (r'-i) - (i - E_{i0})e_{ih} = 0.0323 - 0.0133 = 0.0190$$

$$\bar{d}_3' = (r_E' - k') + u\cdot b_{ku} = 0.0429 - 0.0637 = -0.0208$$

$$\bar{d}_4' = (r_E' - k') + (k' - E_{k0})e_{ku} = 0.0429 - 0.0264 = 0.0165.$$

The standard errors of the $\bar{d}_i'$ have been calculated to be $\bar{\sigma}_1' = 0.0044$, $\bar{\sigma}_2' = 0.0042$, $\bar{\sigma}_3' = 0.0092$ and $\bar{\sigma}_4' = 0.0066$. The normalized differences are then calculated to be:

$$\hat{d}_1' = \bar{d}_1'/\bar{\sigma}_1' = 5.0227$$

$$\hat{d}_2' = \bar{d}_2'/\bar{\sigma}_2' = 4.5238$$

$$\hat{d}_3' = \bar{d}_3'/\bar{\sigma}_3' = -2.2261$$

$$\hat{d}_4' = \bar{d}_4'/\bar{\sigma}_4' = 2.5000.$$

2. Exogenous values of interest rate, discount rate and profitability

First we define the exogenous values of the interest rate, the discount rate and the rate of return on total capital which were used for the regressions in chapter 6, pp. 88 f. Then, we describe how the exogenous values are calculated. Finally, the justifications for the calculations are discussed.

---

[1] These critical values are computed as follows: $0.500 + 2.33 \cdot 0.0671 \approx 0.66$ and $0.1670 + 2.33 \times 0.0500 \approx 0.29$.

[2] The mean values in our sample of firms for h, i and u are 1.7268, 0.0283 and 0.7638, respectively. In addition we have $b_{ih} = 0.0059$, $e_{ih} = 0.4689$, $E_{i0} = 0.0000$ and $E_{k0} = -0.0050$, $b_{ku} = -0.0834$, $e_{ku} = -0.6062$. (See the two-stage estimated coefficients in tables 3–6 in chapter 4.)

a) The definitions

We assume linear functions for the interest rate and the discount rate and assume for the present that the leverage ratio is the only explanatory variable in the former function and that only the pay-out ratio is an explanatory variable in the latter function. We thus have:

$$i = \tau_{11} + \tau_{12} \cdot h + \varepsilon_i \tag{E: 1}$$

$$k = \varkappa_{11} + \varkappa_{12} \cdot u + \varepsilon_k, \tag{E: 2}$$

where i is the interest rate, h is the leverage ratio, k is the discount rate, u is the pay-out ratio, τ_{11}, τ_{12}, $\varkappa_{11}$ and $\varkappa_{12}$ are coefficients and ε_i and ε_k are random error terms.

The exogenous value of the interest rate is defined as that part of it which is not determined by h. If there are no other explanatory variables for the interest rate, its exogenous value will be $\check{i} = i - \tau_{12} h$. In an analogous way the exogenous value of the discount rate is defined as $\check{k} = k - \varkappa_{12} u$.

The exogenous value of total profitability cannot immediately be identified with a specific equation in our model, however, it is obtained by solving the firm's production function and the identity for the rate of return on total capital. If growth costs exist (see for example p. 74) these equations may be written:

$$\hat{F} = \psi \hat{L}^{\alpha} \hat{K}^{1-\alpha} f(\hat{v}_K) \tag{E: 3}$$

$$r = \frac{p\hat{F}}{p_2 \hat{K}} - \frac{p_1 \hat{L}}{p_2 \hat{K}} - a, \tag{E: 4}$$

where $\hat{F}$ is the volume of production, $\hat{L}$ is the labor input, $\hat{K}$ is the input of real capital, $\hat{v}_K$ is the rate of growth of $\hat{K}$, p is the price of $\hat{F}$, p_1 is the price of $\hat{L}$, p_2 is the price of $\hat{K}$ and a is the rate of depreciation of $\hat{K}$. Solving (E: 3) and (E: 4) gives:

$$r = B_1 + B_2 \hat{v}_K, \tag{E: 5}$$

where

$$B_1 = \frac{p\psi \hat{l}^{\alpha} f(0)}{p_2} - \frac{p_1 \hat{l}}{p_2} - a$$

$$B_2 \hat{v} = \frac{p}{p_2} \psi \hat{l}^{\alpha} [f(\hat{v}_K) - f(0)], \quad \hat{l} = \hat{L}/\hat{K} \quad \text{and} \quad f(0) = 1.$$

If it is assumed that the labor intensity ($\hat{l}$) varies insignificantly between firms, then B_1 and B_2 may be regarded as constants for every individual firm. In the model it has been assumed that the prices p, p_1 and p_2 are exogenously given. The exogenous value of total profitability is then obtained according to equation (E: 5) as $\check{r} = r - B_2 \hat{v}_K$.

b) The calculations

For the calculations we use the coefficients in the linear regressions for total profitability, the interest rate and the discount rate estimated in chapters 3 and 4 using two-stage least squares. Assuming that these coefficients (b_{ih}, b_{ku} and $b_{r\hat{v}}$) are identical for all firms, the parts of i, k, and r which for a given firm j are explained by h_j, u_j and $\hat{v}_j$, respectively, equal $b_{ih}h_j$, $b_{ku}u_j$ and $b_{rv}\hat{v}_j$, respectively. The calculated exogenous values of the rate variables for the jth firm are now obtained in accordance with the definitions under point a) above as the following differences:

$$\check{i}_j = i_j - b_{ij}\cdot h_j$$

$$\check{k}_j = k_j - b_{ku}\cdot u_j$$

$$\check{r}_j = r_j - b_{r\hat{v}}\hat{v}_j.$$

The values used for the regression coefficients are $b_{ih} = 0.0059$, $b_{ku} = -0.0834$, and $b_{r\hat{v}} = -0.3868$. They are obtained from tables 1, 3 and 5.

c) The justifications

The fact that h, u and $\hat{v}$ are explanatory variables for i, k and r, respectively is the reason why we do not allow h and u to be functions directly of i, k and r in the regressions of chapter 6, but instead use $\check{i}$, $\check{k}$ and $\check{r}$. Since we have calculated $\check{i}$, $\check{k}$ and $\check{r}$ on the basis of the two-stage estimated coefficients b_{ik}, b_{ku} and $b_{r\hat{v}}$, these exogenous rate variables may be expected to be capable of reflecting the exogenously caused variations between firms in the interest rate, the discount rate and the rate of return on total profitability.

The reason why we use coefficients from the linear functions and not from the linear-multiplicative functions is that in the latter the partial influence of each explanatory variable is dependent on the values of the other explanatory variables. Thus unlike the linear relationships, it is then impossible to separate out the effect on the dependent variable of each particular explanatory variable.

3. Simulation results

In figures E: 1–E: 3 simulation curves are presented for the optimal values of the endogenous variables of the model, that have been discussed in chapter 6, pp. 90–2.

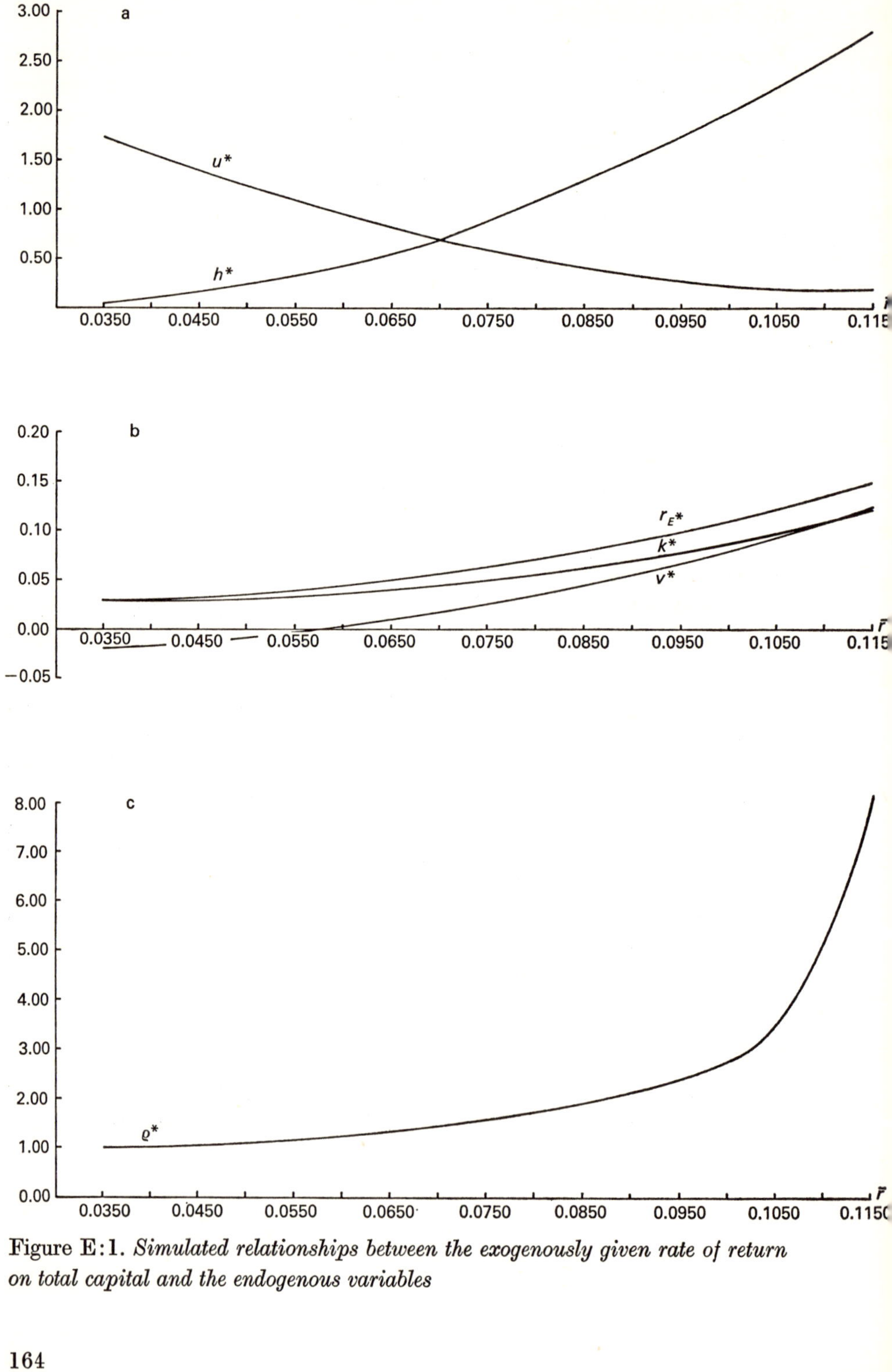

Figure E:1. *Simulated relationships between the exogenously given rate of return on total capital and the endogenous variables*

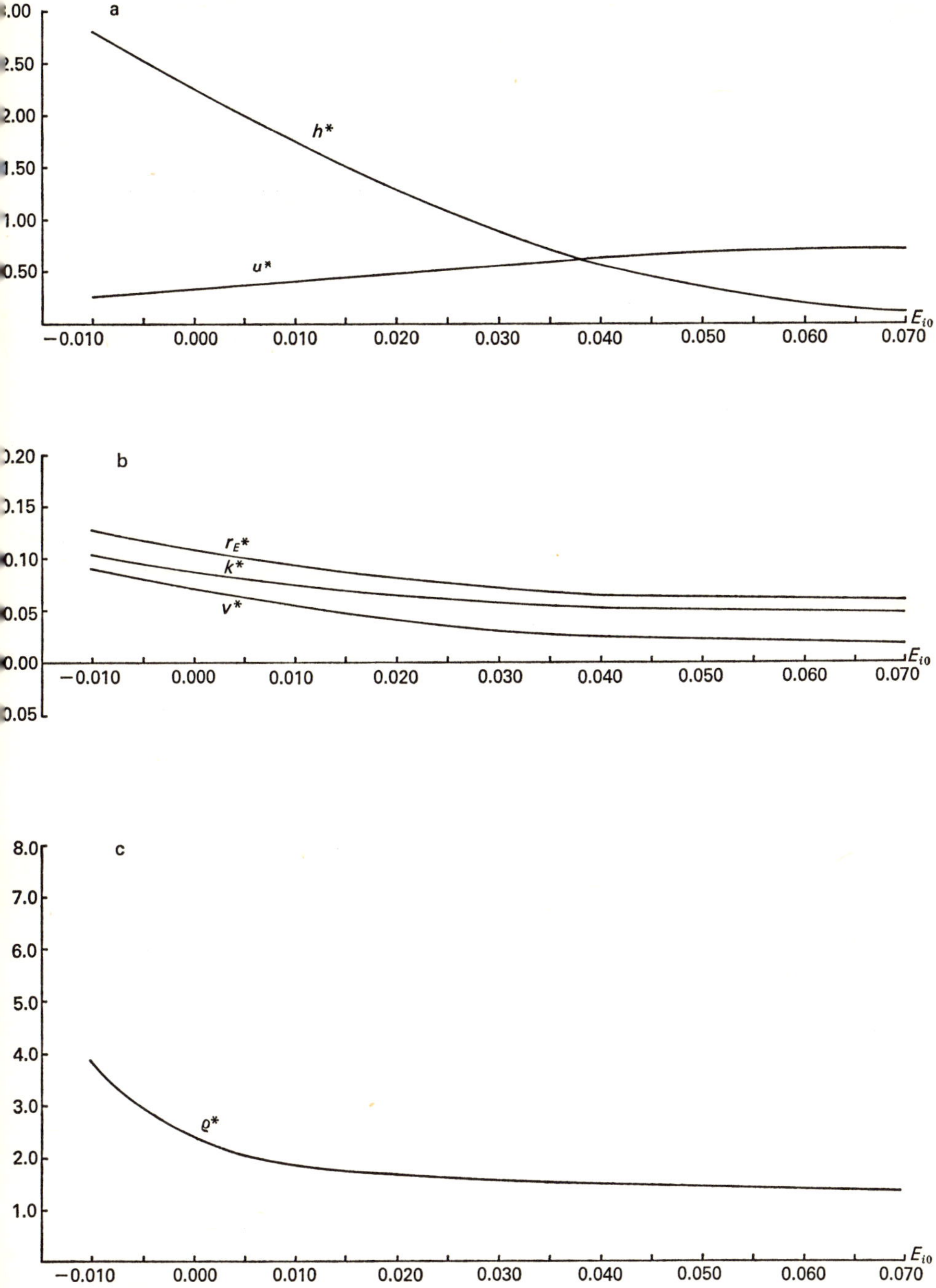

Figure E:2. *Simulated relationships between the exogenously given interest rate and the endogenous variables*

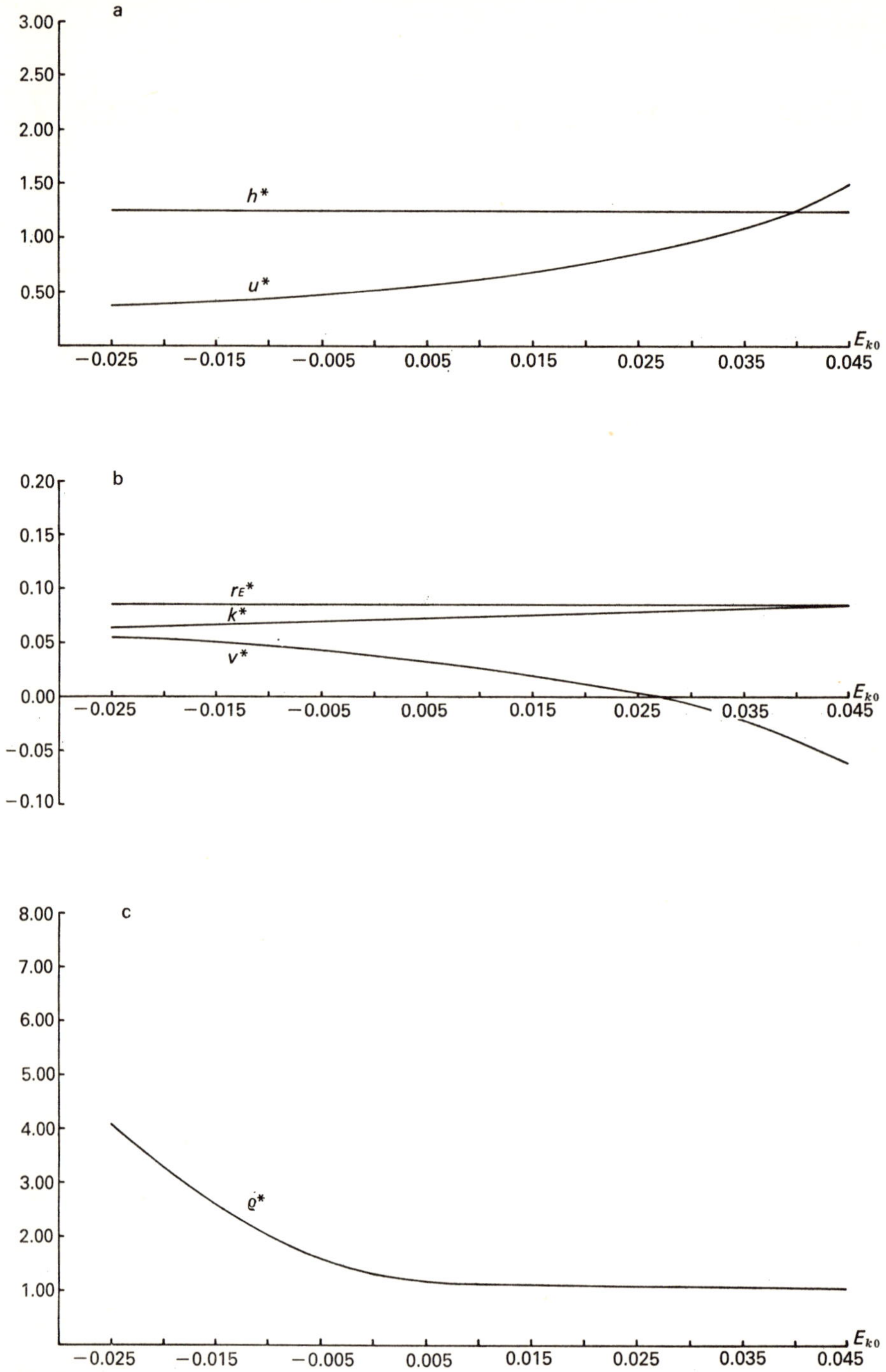

Figure E:3. *Simulated relationships between the exogenously given discount rate and the endogenous variables*

Optimum conditions for chapter 7

1. The first-order conditions for maximum net capital value with respect to the pay-out ratio and the new-issue ratio when dividends are taxed

Given: The following equations:[1]

$$U_t = (1-t_u)ur_E K_{Et}$$
$$N_t = cr_E K_{Et}$$
$$U_t - N_t = [(1-t_u)u - c]r_E K_{Et}$$
$$v = (1-u+c)r_E$$
$$k = k(u, c)$$
$$P'_t = [(1-t_u)u - c]r_E K_E/(k-v).$$

According to assumptions in chapter 7, pp. 96 f. we have:

$$\partial k/\partial u < 0 \quad \partial^2 k/\partial u^2 > 0 \quad \partial^2 k/\partial u \partial c < 0$$

$$\partial k/\partial c > 0 \quad \partial^2 k/\partial c^2 > 0 \quad \partial^2 k/\partial c \partial u < 0.$$

The assumption of no growth costs implies $\partial v/\partial u = -r_E$ and $\partial v/\partial c = r_E$.

Derivation. Net capital value (P'_t) is differentiated partially with respect to the decision variables (u and c), and the partial derivatives are set equal to zero. (In order to simplify the presentation the dividend tax term $(1-t_u)$ is replaced by m.)

$$\frac{\partial P'}{\partial u} = B\left\{m(k-v) - (mu-c)\left(\frac{\partial k}{\partial u} - \frac{\partial v}{\partial u}\right)\right\} = B\left\{-mr_E + mur_E - mcr_E - mur_E + cr_E\right.$$
$$\left. + mk - (mu-c)\frac{\partial k}{\partial u}\right\} = -B\left\{[m(1+c)r_E - cr_E] - \left[mk - (mu-c)\frac{\partial k}{\partial u}\right]\right\} = 0 \qquad \text{(F: 1)}$$

$$\frac{\partial P'}{\partial c} = B\left\{-k + v - (um-c)\left(\frac{\partial k}{\partial c} - \frac{\partial v}{\partial c}\right)\right\} = B\left\{r_E - ur_E + cr_E + mur_E - cr_E - k\right.$$
$$\left. - (um-c)\frac{\partial k}{\partial c}\right\} = B\left\{[(1-u)r_E + mur_E] - \left[k + (mu-c)\frac{\partial k}{\partial c}\right]\right\} = 0, \qquad \text{(F: 2)}$$

[1] The definitions of the variables in these equations are given in the Variable list, pp. 122 f.

where

$B = r_E K_{Et}/(k-v)^2.$

From (F: 1) and (F: 2) we define the net marginal cost of a reduction of u as

$$NMC_u = \left\{c\frac{\partial k}{\partial u} + cr_E + m\left[k - u\frac{\partial k}{\partial u} - (1+c)\,r_E\right]\right\},$$

and the net marginal cost of an increase of c as

$$NMC_c = \left\{k - c\frac{\partial k}{\partial c} - (1-u)\,r_E + m\left(u\frac{\partial k}{\partial c} - ur_E\right)\right\}.$$

Note that

$$m\left(u\frac{\partial k}{\partial c} - ur_E\right) < 0,$$

$$m\left[k - u\frac{\partial k}{\partial u} - (1+c)\,r_E\right] < 0, \quad \text{and}$$

$$\left(u\frac{\partial k}{\partial c} - ur_E\right) < \left[k - u\frac{\partial k}{\partial u} - (1+c)\,r_E\right].$$

Two conclusions follow from this.

1) An increase of t_u (a reduction of m) shifts the NMC_u and NMC_c functions upward. It then follows, from the signs of the derivatives of the function $k(u, c)$ given above, that the optimal net pay-out ratio $(u-c)$ must increase in order to restore the condition $NMC_u = NMC_c = 0$.

2) The reduction of m shifts the NMC_c function upward more than the NMC_u function, which ought to imply that c is more strongly influenced than u.

In addition it follows directly from (F: 1) and (F: 2) that:

3) When m equals unity:

$$\frac{\partial P'}{\partial u} = -B\left\{r_E - \left[k - (u-c)\frac{\partial k}{\partial u}\right]\right\} = 0.$$

$$\frac{\partial P'}{\partial c} = B\left\{r_E - \left[k + (u-c)\frac{\partial k}{\partial c}\right]\right\} = 0.$$

These simplified first-order expressions thus become the same as (7: 3) and (7: 4) in chapter 7.

4) When c is zero:

Changes in m (i.e., changes in the rate of tax on dividends) then do not influence the firm's optimal pay-out ratio.

2. The first-order conditions for a maximum value of all future paid-out profits (wages) per employee with respect to the leverage ratio and the pay-out ratio

In chapter 7, pp. 103 f., we defined the following identities:[1]

$$V'_{LN} = uV'_L/(k-v') \tag{F: 3}$$

$$V'_L = V'/\hat{L} \tag{F: 4}$$

$$V' = p\hat{F} - p_2 a\hat{K} - ihK_E \tag{F: 5}$$

$$v' = (1-u)V'/K_E, \tag{F: 6}$$

where V'_{LN} is the present value of all future wages, V'_L is profit per employee, V' is profit, v' is rate of growth of all monetary variables of the firm and u is the share of profit which is paid out in wages.

From the equation system (2: 5)–(2: 17) we also have:[2]

$$\hat{F} = \hat{F}(\hat{L}, \hat{K}) \tag{F: 7}$$

$$i = i(h) \tag{F: 8}$$

$$k = k(u). \tag{F: 9}$$

These equations are the firm's production function, interest-rate function, and discount-rate function, respectively, where

$$\partial\hat{F}/\partial\hat{L} > 0 \quad \partial^2\hat{F}/\partial\hat{L}^2 < 0$$

$$\partial\hat{F}/\partial\hat{K} > 0 \quad \partial^2\hat{F}/\partial\hat{K}^2 < 0$$

$$\partial i/\partial h > 0 \quad \partial^2 i/\partial h^2 < 0$$

$$\partial k/\partial u < 0 \quad \partial^2 k/\partial u^2 > 0.$$

In addition we use the identity

$$p_2\hat{K} = (1+h)K_E. \tag{F: 10}$$

Equity capital (K_E) is exogenously given, as are the product price (p), the capital price (p_2), and the rate of capital depreciation (a). According to earlier assumptions, the production function is also linearly homogeneous. Since the firm's rate of growth has been assumed not to influence its volume of production, different values of the pay-out ratio (u) will not influence gross profits in the same period either, i.e., $\partial V'/\partial u = 0$. (See the Variable list, pp. 122–4, for definitions of variables not defined here.)

---

[1] In order to simplify the formulas the time index is dropped from the non-ratio variables. All such variables refer to the same time period.

[2] The assumption of no growth costs implies that the growth rate ($\hat{v}_K$) drops out of the production function.

a) Maximization with respect to the leverage ratio (h)

Partial differentiation of (F: 3) with respect to h gives, taking into consideration (F: 4) and the fact that $\hat{L}$ and u are held constant,

$$\frac{\partial V'_{LN}}{\partial h}=\left\{\frac{1}{\hat{L}}\frac{(k-v')\,u\,\partial V'/\partial h+uV'\,\partial v'/\partial h}{(k-v')^2}\right\}. \tag{F: 11}$$

From (F: 6) follows

$$\partial v'/\partial h=[(1-u)/K_E]\partial V'/\partial h. \tag{F: 12}$$

Substitution of (F: 12) in (F: 11) gives

$$\frac{\partial V'_{LN}}{\partial h}=\frac{u}{\hat{L}(k-v')^2}\left\{(k-v')+V'\frac{(1-u)}{K_E}\right\}\frac{\partial V'}{\partial h}. \tag{F: 13}$$

From (F: 5) and (F: 8) is obtained

$$\frac{\partial V'}{\partial h}=p\frac{\partial \hat{F}}{\partial h}-p_2 a\frac{\partial \hat{K}}{\partial h}-(i+h\,\partial i/\partial h)\,K_E. \tag{F: 14}$$

Also from (F: 7) and (F: 10) is obtained

$$\frac{\partial \hat{F}}{\partial h}=\frac{\partial \hat{F}}{\partial \hat{K}}\frac{\partial \hat{K}}{\partial h} \tag{F: 15}$$

$$\frac{\partial \hat{K}}{\partial h}=\frac{K_E}{p_2}. \tag{F: 16}$$

Substitution of (F: 15) and (F: 16) in (F: 14) gives

$$\frac{\partial V'}{\partial h}=\left\{p\frac{\partial \hat{F}}{\partial \hat{K}}-p_2(a+i+h\,\partial i/\partial h)\right\}\frac{K_E}{p_2}. \tag{F: 17}$$

According to (F: 13) and (F: 17), V'_{LN} is maximized when $\partial V'/\partial h=0$ or when

$$p\frac{\partial \hat{F}}{\partial \hat{K}}=p_2(a+i+h\,\partial i/\partial h). \tag{F: 18}$$

b) Maximization with respect to the pay-out ratio (u)

Partial differentiation of (F: 3) with respect to u gives, taking into account (F: 4) and that $\partial V'/\partial u=0$:

$$\frac{\partial V'_{LN}}{\partial u}=\frac{1}{\hat{L}}\left\{\frac{(k-v')\,V'-uV'(\partial k/\partial u-\partial v'/\partial u)}{(k-v')^2}\right\}. \tag{F: 19}$$

From (F: 6) is obtained

$$\frac{\partial v'}{\partial u}=-\frac{V'}{K_E}. \tag{F: 20}$$

Substitution of (F: 20) in (F: 19) gives

$$\frac{\partial V'_{LN}}{\partial u} = \frac{V'}{\hat{L}(k-v')^2}\left\{(k-v') - u\frac{\partial k}{\partial u} - u\frac{V'}{K_E}\right\}. \qquad \text{(F: 21)}$$

Substitution of (F: 6) in (F: 21) gives

$$\frac{\partial V'_{LN}}{\partial u} = \frac{V'}{\hat{L}(k-v')^2}\left\{k - u\frac{\partial k}{\partial u} - \frac{V'}{K_E}\right\}. \qquad \text{(F: 22)}$$

V'_{LN} is maximized when $\partial V'_{LN}/\partial u = 0$; from (F: 22) we then obtain

$$k - u\frac{\partial k}{\partial u} = \frac{V'}{K_E}. \qquad \text{(F: 23)}$$

3. First-order conditions for a maximization of the present value of all future paid-out profits per employee with respect to labor intensity

Given: The same equations and assumptions as in section 2 above. In addition note the definition

$$\hat{l} = \hat{L}/\hat{K}. \qquad \text{(F: 24)}$$

From the assumption of constant returns to scale in production it follows that

$$\hat{F} = \hat{L}\partial\hat{F}/\partial\hat{L} + \hat{K}\partial\hat{F}/\partial\hat{K}. \qquad \text{(F: 25)}$$

The other two decision variables of the firm, the leverage ratio (h), and the pay-out ratio (u), are held constant in maximizing the present value of its future paid-out profits V'_{LN}. Partial differentiation of (F: 3) gives

$$\frac{\partial V'_{LN}}{\partial \hat{l}} = u\left\{\frac{(k-v')\partial V'_L/\partial\hat{l} + V'_L\partial v'/\partial\hat{l}}{(k-v')^2}\right\}. \qquad \text{(F: 26)}$$

From (F: 4) and (F: 6) follows

$$\frac{\partial v'}{\partial \hat{l}} = \frac{1-u}{K_E}\left(\frac{\partial V'}{\partial \hat{l}}\right) = \frac{1-u}{K_E}\left(V'_L\frac{\partial\hat{L}}{\partial\hat{l}} + \hat{L}\frac{\partial V'_L}{\partial\hat{l}}\right). \qquad \text{(F: 27)}$$

Substitution of (F: 27) in (F: 26) gives

$$\frac{\partial V'_{LN}}{\partial \hat{l}} = \frac{u}{(k-v')^2}\left\{\left[(k-v') + V'_L\frac{1-u}{K_E}\hat{L}\right]\frac{\partial V'_L}{\partial\hat{l}} + \frac{(1-u)}{K_E}(V'_L)^2\frac{\partial\hat{L}}{\partial\hat{l}}\right\}. \qquad \text{(F: 28)}$$

From (F: 4), (F: 5) and (F: 10) follows

$$\frac{\partial V'_L}{\partial \hat{l}} = \frac{1}{\hat{L}^2}\left\{\hat{L}\frac{\partial V'}{\partial\hat{l}} - V'\frac{\partial\hat{L}}{\partial\hat{l}}\right\} = \frac{1}{\hat{L}^2}\left\{\hat{L}\frac{\partial V'}{\partial\hat{l}} - \left[p\hat{F} - p_2\left(a\hat{K} + \frac{ih}{1+h}\hat{K}\right)\right]\frac{\partial\hat{L}}{\partial\hat{l}}\right\}. \qquad \text{(F: 29)}$$

In addition, from (F: 6), (F: 7) and (F: 24) follows

$$\frac{\partial V'}{\partial \hat{l}} = p\frac{\partial\hat{F}}{\partial\hat{L}}\frac{\partial\hat{L}}{\partial\hat{l}}. \qquad \text{(F: 30)}$$

Substitution of (F: 30) in (F: 29) gives

$$\frac{\partial V_L'}{\partial \hat{l}} = \frac{1}{\hat{L}^2}\left\{\left(\hat{L}p\frac{\partial \hat{F}}{\partial \hat{L}} - p\hat{F}\right) + p_2\left(a\hat{K} + \frac{ih}{i+h}\hat{K}\right)\right\}\frac{\partial \hat{L}}{\partial \hat{l}}. \qquad \text{(F: 31)}$$

Taking into account (F: 25), we obtain

$$\frac{\partial V_L'}{\partial \hat{l}} = \frac{\hat{K}}{\hat{L}^2}\frac{\partial \hat{L}}{\partial \hat{l}}\left\{-p\frac{\partial \hat{F}}{\partial \hat{K}} + p_2\left(a + \frac{ih}{i+h}\right)\right\}. \qquad \text{(F: 32)}$$

The first-order condition for maximization of V_{LN}', i.e. $\partial V_{LN}'/\partial \hat{l} = 0$, requires according to (F: 28) that $\partial V_L'/\partial \hat{l}$ be negative. From (F: 32) then follows $p\partial \hat{F}/\partial \hat{K} > p_2[a + ih/(1+h)]$, which is the condition for labor (7: 15) given in chapter 7.

Note the special case when u equals unity, i.e, when all profits are distributed. Then according to (F: 28) we have $\partial V_{LN}'/\partial \hat{l} = 0$ simultaneously with $\partial V_L'/\partial \hat{l} = 0$, i.e., a maximum for both V_{LN}' and V_L' is reached at the same value of labor intensity ($\hat{l}$). This means that the following equality condition holds instead:

$$p\partial \hat{F}/\partial \hat{K} = p_2[a + ih/(1+h)]. \qquad \text{(F: 33)}$$

We have shown (see p. 170) that V_{LN}' is maximized with respect to the leverage ratio (h) when

$$p\frac{\partial \hat{F}}{\partial \hat{K}} = p_2(a + i + h\partial i/\partial h). \qquad \text{(F: 34)}$$

From (F: 33) and (F: 34) we obtain

$$i + h\partial i/\partial h + h^2 \partial i/\partial h = 0. \qquad \text{(F: 35)}$$

Given the linear-multiplicative interest-rate function

$$i = E_{i0} + E_{i1}h^{e_{ih}}, \qquad \text{(F: 36)}$$

in our model, where the coefficients E_{i0}, E_{i1} and e_{ih} are all positive, there is clearly no positive value of h which satisfies (F: 35). Thus the simultaneous maximization of V_{LN}' with respect to $\hat{l}$ and h gives a negative level of indebtedness. It has been assumed, however, that h cannot take values lower than zero. If h is allowed to take the value of zero, (F: 33) is reduced to

$$p\frac{\partial \hat{F}}{\partial \hat{K}} = p_2 a, \qquad \text{(F: 37)}$$

which is the optimum condition for labor when the pay-out ratio (u) equals unity (7: 18), given on p. 105.

References

Alexander, S., 1949, The Effect of Size of Manufacturing Corporation on the Distribution of the Rate of Return. *Review of Economics and Statistics.*

Atkinson, A., 1973, Worker Management and the Modern Enterprise, *Quarterly Journal of Economics.* Vol. LXXXVII, August 1973.

Aukrust, O., and Bjerke, J., 1959, Real Capital and Economic Growth in Norway 1900–56. *Income and Wealth.* Series VIII.

Bain, J. S., 1956, *Barriers to New Competition.* Cambridge.

Baumol, W. J., 1959, *Business Behavior, Value and Growth.* New York.

Baumol, W. J., and Stewart, M., 1971, On the Behavioral Theory of the Firm in *The Corporate Economy: Growth, Competition and Innovative Potential* (eds R. Marris and A. Wood). London.

Baxter, N. P., 1967, Leverage, Risk of Ruin, and the Cost of Capital. *Journal of Finance,* September 1967.

Bennet, J. W., Graham, K. R., and Tran Van Hoa, 1969, The Determination of Yields on Corporate Shares: An Empirical Study. *Economic Record,* December 1969.

Bodenhorn, D., 1959, On the Problem of Capital Budgeting. *Journal of Finance,* Vol. XIV, December 1959.

Brems, H., 1973, *Labor, Capital and Growth.* London.

— 1976, Growth and Financing of Firms—A Review. *Scandinavian Journal of Economics.* Vol. 78, No. 1, 1976.

Brigham, E. F., and Gordon, M. J., 1968, Leverage, Dividend Policy and the Cost of Capital. *Journal of Finance,* March 1968.

Bröms, J., 1974, *Räntabilitet, skatter och förräntningsanspråk* (Profitability, Taxes, and Required Rates of Return). Mimeo, Sveriges Industriförbund, Stockholm.

Cyert, R., 1969, Uncertainty, Behavioral Rules and the Firm. *Economic Journal,* March 1969.

Dean, J., 1951, *Managerial Economics.* New York.

Dorfman, R., Samuelson, P., and Solow, R. M., 1958, *Linear Programming and Economic Analysis.* New York.

Douglas, P. H., 1948, Are There Laws of Production. *American Economic Review,* Vol. 38.

Downie, J., 1958, *The Competitive Process.* London.

Duesenberry, J. S., 1958, *Business Cycles and Economic Growth.* New York.

Eisner, R., 1960, A Distributed Lag Investment Function. *Econometrica,* Vol. 28, No. 1, 1960.

Eisner, R., and Strotz, R., 1963, Determinants of Business Investment Research Study Two in *Impacts of Monetary Policy,* prepared for the Commission on Money and Credit. Englewood Cliffs, New Jersey.

Galbraith, J. K., 1952, *American Capitalism.* London.

Gordon, M. J., 1960, Security and a Financial Theory of Investment. *Quarterly Journal of Economics,* August 1960.

— 1962, *The Investment, Financing, and Valuation of the Corporation.* Homewood, Ill.

— 1964, Security and Investment: Theory and Evidence. *Journal of Finance,* Vol. XIX, December 1964.

Gould, J. P., 1968, Adjustment Costs in the Theory of Investment of the Firm. *Review of Economic Studies,* Vol. XXXV, January 1968.

Grabowski, H. G., and Mueller, D. C., 1972, Managerial and Stockholder Welfare Models of Firm Expenditures. *Review of Economics and Statistics.* Vol. LIV, February 1972.

Hall, M. and Weiss, L., 1967, Firm Size and Profitability. *Review of Economics and Statistics.* Vol. XLIX, August 1967.

Hymer, S., and Pashigian, P., 1962, Firm Size and Rate of Growth. *Journal of Political Economy,* Vol. LXX, December 1962.

Jensen, O., and Johansson, S. E., 1969, *Företagets finansieringsproblem* (The Financing Problems of the Firm). Falköping.

Johnston, J., 1960, *Econometric Methods.* New York.

Jones, W. T., 1969, *Size, Growth and Profitability in the Mechanical Engineering Industry.* National Economic Developed Office, London.

Jorgenson, D. W., and Siebert, C. D., 1968, Optimal Capital Accumulation and Corporate Investment Behavior. *Journal of Political Economy,* Vol. 76, November 1968.

Kalecki, M., 1937, The Principle of Increasing Risk. *Economica,* Vol. 4, November 1937.

King, M. A., 1974, Taxation and the Cost of Capital. *Review of Economic Studies,* Vol. XLI, February 1974.

Kuh, E., 1960, Capital Theory and Capital Budgeting. *Metroeconomica,* Vol. XII, August–December 1960.

— 1963, *Capital Stock Growth: A Micro-economic Approach.* Amsterdam.

Laudadio, L., 1963, Size of Bank, Size of Borrower, and the Rate of Interest. *Journal of Finance,* Vol. XVIII, March 1963.

Lerner, E. M., and Carleton, W. T., 1964, The Integration of Capital Budgeting and Stock Valuation. *American Economic Review,* Vol. 54, September 1964.

— 1966, *A Theory of Financial Analysis.* New York.

Leverson, A. M., 1962, Interest Rates and Cost Differentials in Bank Lending to Small and Large Business. *Review of Economics and Statistics,* Vol. XLIV, May 1962.

Lintner, J., 1962, Dividends, Earnings, Leverage, Stock Prices, and the Supply of Capital to Corporations. *Review of Economics and Statistics,* Vol. XLIV, August 1962.

— 1963, The Cost of Capital and Optimal Financing of Corporate Growth. *Journal of Finance,* May 1963.

— 1964, Optimal Dividends and Corporate Growth under Uncertainty. *Quarterly Journal of Economics,* February 1964.

Lucas, R., 1967, Optimal Investment Policy and the Flexible Accelerator. *International Economic Review,* February 1967.

Lutz, V., and Lutz, F., 1951, *The Theory of the Investment of the Firm.* Princeton.

Marris, R. L., 1964, *The Economic Theory of 'Managerial' Capitalism.* London.

— 1966, Incomes Policy and the Rate of Return. *Journal of the Manchester Statistical Society.*

— 1971, An Introduction to Theories of Corporate Growth in *The Corporate*

Economy: Growth, Competition and Innovative Potential (eds R. Marris and A. Wood). London.

Meyer, J. R. and Glauber, R. R., 1964, *Investment Decisions, Economic Forecasting, and Public Policy.* Boston.

Miller, M. H., and Modigliani, F., 1961, Dividend Policy, Growth, and the Valuation of Shares. *Journal of Business,* Vol. XXXIV, Oct. 1961.

— 1966, Some Estimates of the Cost of Capital in the Electric Utility Industry, 1954–57. *American Economic Review,* Vol. 56, June 1966.

Modigliani, F., and Miller, M., 1958, The Cost of Capital, Corporation Finance, and the Theory of Investment. *American Economic Review,* Vol. 48, June 1958.

Moore, B. J., 1975, Equities, Capital Gains, and the Role of Finance in Accumulation. *American Economic Review,* Vol. LXV, December 1975.

Mossin, J., 1973, *Theory of Financial Markets.* Englewood Cliffs, New Jersey.

Muth, R., 1960, The Demand for Non-Farm Housing in *The Demand for Durable Goods* (ed. A. C. Harberger). Chicago.

Nabseth, L. et al, 1971, *Svensk industri under 70-talet med utblick mot 80-talet* (The Swedish Industry during the Seventies and the Outlook up to 1980). IUI. Stockholm.

Niitamo, O., 1958, The Development of Productivity in Finnish Industry 1925–52. *Productivity Measurement Review,* No. 15, 1958.

Penrose, E., 1959, *The Theory of the Growth of the Firm.* Oxford.

Robichek, A., and Myers, S., 1965, *Optimal Financing Decisions.* Palo Alto, Calif.

Rothchild, M., 1971, On the Cost of Adjustment. *Quarterly Journal of Economics,* Vol. LXXXV, November 1971.

Rydén, B., 1972, *Mergers in Swedish Industry.* Stockholm.

Singh, A., and Whittington, G., 1968, *Growth, Profitability and Valuation.* Cambridge.

Smith, V. L., 1966, *Investment and Production.* Cambridge.

Solomon, E., 1955, Measuring a Company's Cost of Capital. *Journal of Business,* XXVIII, October 1955.

Solow, R. M., 1960, Investment and Technical Progress in *Mathematical Methods in the Social Sciences* (eds K. Arrow, S. Karlin, and P. Suppes). Palo Alto, Calif.

— 1971, Some Implications of Alternative Criteria for the Firm in *The Corporate Economy: Growth, Competition and Innovative Potential* (eds R. Marris and A. Wood). London.

Statistiska Centralbyrån, 1968, *SOS: Industri* (Official Statistics: Industry). Stockholm.

Stekler, H. O., 1963, *Profitability and Size of Firm.* Berkeley.

— 1964, The Variability of Profitability with Size of Firm, 1947–58. *American Statistical Association Journal,* December 1964.

Stiglitz, J. E., 1973, Taxation, Corporate Financial Policy and the Cost of Capital. *Journal of Public Economics,* January 1974.

Svenska Aktiebolag (Swedish Corporations).

Sveriges Verkstadsförenings lönsamhetsstatistik (Swedish Engineering Employers' Association's Profitability Statistics).

Södersten, J., 1971, *Företagsbeskattning och resursfördelning i svensk finanspolitik i teori och praktik.* EFI. Stockholm.

Söderström, H. T., 1974, *Studies in the Microdynamics of Production and Productivity Change.* Mimeo, Institute for International Economic Studies, University of Stockholm.

Treadway, A. B., 1967, *Rational Entrepreneurial Behavior and the Dynamics of Investment.*

Turnovsky, S. J., 1970, Financial Structure and the Theory of Production. *Journal of Finance,* Vol. XXV, December 1970.

Walter, J. E., 1956, Dividend Policies and Common Stock Prices. *Journal of Finance,* Vol. XI, March, 1956.

— 1963, Dividend Policy: Its Influence on the Value of the Enterprise. *Journal of Finance,* Vol. XVIII, May 1963.

Walters, A. A., 1962, *Economies of Scale in the Aggregate Production Function.* Mimeo, University of Birmingham, Birmingham.

Vanek, J., 1970, *The General Theory of Labor-Managed Market Economies.* Ithaca.

Weiss, L. W., 1963, Average Concentration Ratios and Industrial Performance. *Journal of International Economics,* July 1963.

Weston, J. F., 1961, The Management of Corporate Capital: A Review Article. *Journal of Business,* Vol. XXXIV, April 1961.

— 1963, A Test of Cost of Capital Propositions. *Southern Economic Journal,* Vol. XXX, October 1963.

Vickers, D., 1968, *The Theory of the Firm: Production, Capital, and Finance.* New York.

— 1970, The Cost of Capital and the Structure of the Firm. *Journal of Finance,* Vol. XXV, March 1970.

Wippern, R. F., 1966, Financial Structure and the Value of the Firm. *Journal of Finance,* Vol. XXI, December 1966.

Åberg, Y., 1969, *Produktion och produktivitet i Sverige 1861–1965* (Production and Productivity in Sweden 1861–1965). IUI. Stockholm.